RAILS, MINES, AND PROGRESS: SEVEN AMERICAN PROMOTERS IN MEXICO, 1867-1911

Published under the direction of the American Historical Association from the income of the Albert J. Beveridge Memorial Fund.

For their zeal and beneficence in creating this fund the Association is indebted to many citizens of Indiana who desired to honor in this way the memory of a statesman and a historian.

Rails, Mines, and Progress: Seven American Promoters in Mexico, 1867-1911

BY DAVID M. PLETCHER

Hamline University

PUBLISHED FOR THE

American Historical Association

CORNELL UNIVERSITY PRESS

ITHACA, NEW YORK

CORNELL UNIVERSITY PRESS

First published 1958

The Library of Congress card information
will be found on page 321.

PRINTED IN THE UNITED STATES OF AMERICA BY THE
VAIL-BALLOU PRESS, INC., BINGHAMTON, NEW YORK

To My Father and Mother

Acknowledgments

LIKE many others of his former students I am indebted to Professor J. Fred Rippy, of the University of Chicago, the *doyen* of American writers on inter-American economic relations, for first directing my attention to the problem of United States investments in Latin America and for encouraging me to undertake the present study of American promoters in Mexico.

In preparing this manuscript for publication I have benefited especially from the careful criticism of Dr. and Mrs. Walter V. Scholes, who have sustained and restrained me at many points along the way. Others who have read portions of the manuscript and helped me with suggestions are Mrs. Shirley J. Bill, Alfred D. Chandler, Jr., T. R. Hay, William M. Lamers, Ralph Marsden, Hermann R. Muelder, Alfred W. Newcombe, Nuba M. Pletcher, and John L. Stipp.

I am indebted to Mr. Benjamin B. Richards and the staff of Knox College Library for obtaining a great number of books for me on interlibrary loan and for furnishing me a comfortable place to work for several years. Many other librarians have shown unfailing courtesy, both in helping me find material and in making it available for my use. In particular, I should like to acknowledge such assistance from the librarians of the Bancroft Library at the University of California, Berkeley, the British Museum, the Galesburg (Illinois) Public Library, the John Crerar Library, the Library of Congress, the Los Angeles Public Library, the National Archives, the Newberry Library, the New York Public Library, the Public Records Office, London, and the libraries of Harvard University, Stanford University

(Special Collections Division), the University of Chicago, the University of Kansas City, the University of Missouri, and the University of Texas. A number of persons and institutions have very kindly allowed me to use restricted material.

I should like to express my appreciation for permission to use copyrighted material, as follows:

To Appleton-Century-Crofts, Inc., for the passages in Chapter VII quoted from Ira B. Joralemon, *Romantic Copper: Its Lure and Its Lore.*

To Robert G. Caldwell for the passage in Chapter II quoted from his book *James A. Garfield, Party Chieftain.*

To Duke University Press for my article "The Building of the Mexican Railway" (*Hispanic American Historical Review*, XXX, 26–62).

To the *Journal of Economic History* for my article "The Fall of Silver in Mexico, 1870–1910, and Its Effect on American Investments" (*Journal of Economic History*, XVIII, 33–55).

To the Mississippi Valley Historical Association for my article "General William S. Rosecrans and the Mexican Transcontinental Railroad Project" (*Mississippi Valley Historical Review*, XXXVIII, 657–678), which is the basis of much of Chapter II.

To the *Pacific Historical Review* for my article "A Prospecting Expedition across Central Mexico, 1856–1857" (*Pacific Historical Review*, XXI, 21–41).

Last but by no means least, I am deeply indebted to the Institute of International Education for a senior research grant under the Fulbright Act, which made possible research for this book in London during 1953–1954, and to the Social Science Research Council for two half-time research grants in preceding years. I am also heartily grateful to the Committee on the Albert J. Beveridge Award, which selected this book for publication.

D. M. P.

St. Paul, Minnesota
July 1958

Contents

Maps

RAILS, MINES, AND PROGRESS:
SEVEN AMERICAN PROMOTERS
IN MEXICO, 1867-1911

Introduction

> Mexico, we claim, is one magnificent but undeveloped mine—
> our India in commercial importance—our Cuba and Brazil in
> tropical products—our complement in general characteristics,
> resources, supply, and demand—our Italy in climate and at-
> tractions—our Troy in antiquities and classic history—and our
> sister Republic, friend, and ally in international politics. It is
> all and more than Cortez dreamed. . . . It will, on the com-
> pletion of its isthmian highways between Oceans and Repub-
> lics . . . become "the bridge of commerce of the world."—
> A. D. ANDERSON, *Mexico from the Material Standpoint* (1884)

SOMETHING in the atmosphere of undeveloped lands drives
men to exaggeration. From Sir John Mandeville to Paul Bunyan
the unmeasured riches of Africa, Asia, and America yielded
their first bonanzas in the dozens of "tall stories" retailed to
delighted audiences, first in Europe and later on the east coast
of the United States. Early visitors to Latin America also in-
dulged their imaginations from time to time, and during the
colonial period the inflated reports of native wealth lured many
a European to sell his goods and go hounding off after El
Dorado. Even such a responsible observer as the distinguished

1

German scientist, Baron Alexander von Humboldt, could not suppress the overtones of enthusiasm in his scholarly study of Mexican resources, and in the early years of the nineteenth century his comprehensive volumes were translated, paraphrased, and quoted all over Europe.

As soon as Mexico became independent, hundreds of British investors, bewitched by reports of gold and silver, plunged their money into hastily organized mining companies and expected to make a fortune overnight. The Mexican mountains were full of silver, as Humboldt had said, but unexpected difficulties confronted the would-be miners, and the British shareholders, ill-prepared for a long haul, lost most of their investment. By mid-century nearly all the early mining companies had disappeared. Their memory had scarcely faded, however, when a new generation of promoters, American instead of British, appeared in Mexico to inspect silver mines and tropical plantations. During the last third of the nineteenth century more and more American periodicals, pamphlets, and government reports contained panegyrics about Mexico, "a land upon which nature has lavished her bounty . . . with all that can minister to human want or luxury" and containing "everything requisite to make a rich country . . . [except] a good government and an intelligent and energetic people."[1] In 1884 one pamphleteer pronounced Mexico a second India, Cuba, Brazil, Italy, and Troy all rolled into one.

At the time when they wrote, the moon-touched enthusiasm of these publicists was understandable. Between the end of the French intervention in 1867 and the overthrow of Porfirio Díaz in 1911 Mexico went through an unprecedentedly rapid economic development, in which the United States played a

[1] William S. Rosecrans, *The Memorial of Gen. W. S. Rosecrans: To the Honorable the Senate and the House of Representatives of the United States in Congress Assembled* [n.p., 1868?], p. 2; David Turner to Thomas H. Nelson, La Paz, Baja California, Sept. 25, 1869, U.S. Department of State, Despatches, Mexico, XXXVII, U.S. Bureau of Archives (hereafter cited as State Dept., Despatches, Mexico).

dominant part. During those years, for example, the annual commerce of the United States with Mexico increased from about $7,000,000 to $117,000,000. At the end of the period the United States had secured more of Mexico's trade than all the European nations together and was maintaining almost twice as many consulates in Mexico as the nearest European rival. What was perhaps more important, the total figure of American investments in Mexico rose from a few million dollars to about a billion dollars, and during the first decade of the present century Mexico received between one-fourth and two-fifths of all American direct investments sent abroad.[2] By 1911 Mexico was truly an economic satellite of the United States.

To what extent did the billion dollars of American capital really work for the best interests of Mexico? How adequate were the rewards which it earned for American investors? Americans and Mexicans disagree. Apologists for American industries, such as Isaac F. Marcosson, declare that this capital was "streaked with sweat and agony" and describe an "epic quality" in the Americans' "picturesque assault upon one of nature's sternest yet richest strongholds." [3] Mexicans see a different sort of agony dimly revealed in mines and on plantations and denounce *yanqui* exploitation. The arguments began in the last years of the Díaz regime, continued through the decade of civil war after 1910, and were finally focused upon the oil controversy of the 1920's and 1930's. This controversy alone brought out enough conflicting opinions on both sides of the border to fill a dozen volumes as large as this one.

The questions of Mexican benefits and American rewards are

[2] J. Fred Rippy, *The United States and Mexico* (rev. ed.; New York, 1931), p. 319; *The Mexican Year Book: A Financial and Commercial Handbook, Compiled from Official and Other Returns*, 1912 (Mexico, 1912), pp. 193–195; Cleona Lewis, *America's Stake in International Investments* (Washington, 1928), pp. 606, 612–614. See Appendix, Table 1, for an estimate of American investments in Mexico in 1911.

[3] Isaac F. Marcosson, "Our Financial Stake in Mexico," *Collier's*, LVII (July 1, 1916), 22.

indeed intricate, for both national pride and incomplete data blur the lines of argument. Those in search of answers must first study the writings and careers of the American promoters who carried capital and influence southward. From the writings of these men their intentions can be reconstructed: how they hoped to win profits in Mexico; what they expected to do for the country in return; what role they assigned to the Mexican government and people; and what aid, if any, they expected to receive from the United States government. From their careers it can then be determined how far they succeeded in carrying out their intentions and what obstacles they met.

Promotional work in nineteenth-century Mexico required many skills. The promoter needed discrimination to recognize Mexican needs and resources, considerable knowledge of political, economic, and social conditions in Mexico, and ability to get along with people. He had to be able to make allowances for the peculiar characteristics of the Mexican upper classes—their formal courtesy, which many Americans thought insincere, and the old-fashioned slowness with which they moved. Promotion in Mexico also required skill in organization and management. Operating from at least two headquarters, in Mexico and in some American financial center, the promoter had to seek out the best available subordinates to act for him while he was away. He needed enough literary ability to write a persuasive description of his project, emphasizing its strong points and hiding its flaws. Lastly, the promoter had to have almost unlimited optimism and energy, for he traveled a rocky, uphill road, and the goal often disappeared from view.

The dozens of men who promoted Mexican ventures between 1867 and 1911 displayed these qualities in varying degrees. The purpose of this book is to examine the careers of seven of these promoters, in order to determine what they intended to do, how they went about accomplishing their plans, and in some cases why they failed. This is not intended to be a comprehensive history of American economic activities in Mexico. It is primarily a study of the gap between aims and achievements of certain men during a period when Americans enjoyed unusual advantages; but from their experiences a few general conclusions may be drawn about American capital in Mexico.

Although availability of source materials has partly determined the choice of seven individuals to serve as case studies, they have been selected also with the idea of showing the widest possible variety of backgrounds and methods of action. In order to facilitate comparison the seven examples have been chosen from only two fields of promotion—railroads and mining—since these two fields accounted for about 85 per cent of American capital in 1911 and occupied pivotal positions in the Mexican economy. Oil promoters do not play a central role in this study, although after 1910 the oil industry became the most profitable and the most exciting of Mexican industries. During the Díaz period, in which this study is laid, Edward L. Doheny and other American oil promoters barely started their careers in Mexico, and their most controversial activities fall outside our time limits.

The seven promoters of this study represent a wide gamut of interests and origins: diplomacy, the army, business, politics, and social reform. These men disagreed on many subjects, but all of them saw chances for fame and fortune in Mexico, where, as one of them put it, the time had come for "the full and frank opening of the door for American enterprise." [4]

[4] Edward Lee Plumb to Hamilton Fish, New York, Aug. 15, 1873, Edward Lee Plumb Collection, Special Collections Division, Stanford University Libraries, Stanford, Calif. (hereafter cited as Plumb Collection).

I

Mexico and Díaz

NO one can properly understand the careers of American promoters in Mexico without some knowledge of the government and people with whom they had to deal. Like the United States, nineteenth-century Mexico was a republic, with a president, a congress, a supreme court, and (most of the time) a federal system which allotted considerable power to the individual state governments. Under the similarities of form, however, lay many profound differences. The vast majority of Mexicans were abysmally poor and ignorant. Not only land and large-scale business but also religious influence, political power, and even the Roman-Hispanic cultural heritage were largely the perquisites of the aristocracy, which prevented the Indians from advancing and then despised them for their backwardness.

Dominated by conservative aristocrats, the ramshackle economy of nineteenth-century Mexico had stalled along the road between medievalism and capitalism. Deprived of the necessary popular basis for democracy, the nation's republican government alternated between semianarchy and dictatorship during the first three decades of her independent history. In the 1850's Mexico produced her first significant progressive movement—usually called simply *la Reforma*—and for a time it seemed that she might take effective measures against poverty and ignorance. Other forces sidetracked the movement, however, and slowed it down, until, twenty years after its beginning, the country came under the rule of Porfirio Díaz, the most powerful dictator whom she had ever known. Díaz gave her peace, prosperity, and economic progress, but, as always, the greater part of the benefits went to the few. Ignorance and poverty remained the chief heritage of the many.

I

How did the dictatorship of Porfirio Díaz come into being? The soil in which it grew was plowed and cultivated by the liberal-democratic leaders of *la Reforma*. Deeply influenced by the Enlightenment, by utilitarianism, and by other European philosophies, these men laid out broad goals for Mexican development: popular sovereignty, equality before the law, universal education, and a modified form of capitalism in which absolute property rights would be subject to regulation for the public good. In 1855 the liberal reformers won their way to power and began to put their ideas into effect, passing laws for general education, non-Catholic immigration, religious toleration, and the secularization of Church lands.[1]

At this point the liberals struck bedrock—the opposition of the Roman Catholic Church, which, as the largest landholder in Mexico and the guardian of public morals, was naturally a bulwark of conservatism. For better or worse, the Reform soon acquired a predominantly anticlerical coloring which it never entirely lost in the public mind. Late in 1857 churchmen and other conservatives revolted against the reform government and plunged Mexico into a three-year civil war. Although divided between bickering moderates and radicals, the defenders of *la*

[1] Walter V. Scholes, *Mexican Politics during the Juárez Regime, 1855–1872* (University of Missouri Studies, vol. XXX; Columbia, Mo., 1957), chap. 1 and especially pp. 1–3.

Reforma soon found their proper leader in Benito Juárez, hitherto a figure of secondary importance in the movement.[2] Juárez assumed the presidency (recognized only by the liberals, of course), set up his capital in Veracruz, and gradually extinguished the rival conservative government. By 1861 the conservative armies were largely scattered, and Don Benito led his followers into Mexico City.

An exhausted Mexico needed peace and reconstruction, but a few proclerical leaders refused even then to accept defeat at the hands of the "godless" liberals. Beaten in the local theater of war, they called on foreign aid, and the soldiers of Napoleon III intervened to prolong the struggle for six years more in a fruitless effort to place Mexico under the imperial rule of the Archduke Maximilian of Austria. The French soon drove Juárez out of Mexico City again, but, migrating around the country according to the success of his armies, he held grimly and silently to his ideal of republican government and his executive powers. Without him republican government in Mexico would probably not have survived the French Intervention. Under his leadership it survived—in form, at least—but his reputation as Mexico's "indispensable man" greatly strengthened the element of personal rule in the government. Meanwhile, of course, the social and economic program of *la Reforma* had fallen by the wayside.

Instead of retiring in 1867 and leaving reconstruction to others, Don Benito directed Mexican affairs for five years longer, carefully dividing authority among his subordinates and dis-

[2] *Ibid., passim.* Another and even more detailed account of Juárez and his role in resisting the French Intervention is Ralph Roeder, *Juárez and His Mexico* (2 vols.; New York, 1947). When complete, the most comprehensive study of Mexico from 1867 to 1911 will be Daniel Cosío Villegas, *Historia moderna de México* (6 vols.; México, 1955–). Vols. I–III are subtitled *La República restaurada* and cover the years 1867–1876; and vols. IV–VI are subtitled *El Porfiriato* and cover the years 1876–1911. Vols. V and VI were not available in time for use in preparing the present monograph.

banding most of the Army. At his death, in 1872, two men led the ranks of would-be successors: Porfirio Díaz and Sebastián Lerdo de Tejada. Both agreed with the Juarist view of a powerful, centralized presidency, but in most other respects they were extremely unlike—Díaz was an Indian, a tough soldier, a man of action, and Lerdo a Creole (native-born white), a scholar, an orator, and a theorist. Both had helped to save Mexico from the French. General Díaz had a long and honorable military record, and he expected high rank in the restored government, but Juárez retired him on small pay. After an unsuccessful revolt in 1871, he subsided temporarily into the role of petty opposition chieftain. Lerdo preferred to gain power more peacefully. In Juárez' postwar cabinet he was chief justice of the supreme court and ex officio vice-president, so that when Juárez died, he was the legal successor. No one tried to challenge his right to the presidency.

During his four years as president of Mexico, Lerdo tried to expand the power of the central government, but he showed a surprising respect for civil liberty and allowed the opposition to denounce and caricature him at will.[3] He also reduced the power of the Church and cautiously developed public works as far as the feeble treasury would allow. For four years, however, his popularity steadily declined. Revolt followed revolt in outlying parts of Mexico, and banditry went almost unchecked. There were other undermining influences. Lerdo disappointed his followers by keeping the old Juárez cabinet in power. The Church conducted a "whispering campaign" against him. Would-be capitalists demanded more public works and prosperity. And always, in his native hills of Oaxaca, Díaz waited until, in January 1876, he thought he saw his chance and proclaimed revolt once again. The government forces proved more powerful

[3] Frank A. Knapp, Jr., *The Life of Sebastián Lerdo de Tejada, 1823–1889: A Study of Influence and Obscurity* (Austin, Texas, 1951), chap. ix *et passim*. See also Cosío Villegas, *Historia moderna de México*, vol. I, *passim*.

than the rebel had expected, and Lerdo survived long enough to carry through his re-election, but in October a large block of his supporters suddenly broke away, and in the resulting confusion Díaz counterattacked and carried the day. By the end of December he was president of Mexico.

Few believed that Don Porfirio would remain president long. Although not uneducated, as his opponents have insisted, he had no grasp of the serious economic problems which beset Mexico and made blunders which would have ruined anyone else. The United States refused to recognize his government for over a year, and the exiled Lerdo remained a focus of opposition until he died in 1889. Yet for two generations Díaz imposed his will on Mexico, evolving, as one critic put it, from revolutionary president successively into protector, consul, emperor, and finally grand mogul.[4]

He was shrewd enough to take only one step at a time. In his first term of office he contented himself with suppressing minor revolts, reducing banditry, and making a few modest public improvements. In 1880 he decided to observe the law prohibiting re-election (which he had earlier advocated as a propagandist measure against Lerdo) and retired in favor of General Manuel González, possibly because he thought that the loyal, unsophisticated soldier would be more likely than anyone else to hand back the presidency after four years. Events turned out even better than Díaz had planned, for after two years of relatively clear sailing, the González administration made a series of blunders. Attempts to subsidize immigration and a move to revise the coinage system ended in spectacular scandals, and although internal improvements advanced faster than ever before, the treasury was so nearly empty that the government had to suspend payment of officials' salaries. In 1884 the nation welcomed Don Porfirio back to the presidency with relief.[5]

[4] Wilfred H. Callcott, *Liberalism in Mexico, 1857–1929* (Stanford, Calif. 1931), p. 120, note.
[5] Many Mexican historians have dismissed the González administration

For two years after his return to power Díaz worked to force Congress into subservience. The dwindling number of old-line liberals who remained in active politics gradually chose to make peace with him and hope for the best. So also did a younger group of more conservative politicians who had come under the influence of Auguste Comte's positivism, then much in fashion among Mexican intellectuals. Believing in the great validity of scientific thought, they hoped to bring efficiency and progress to Mexico, and many were willing to sacrifice liberty temporarily to a strong president in order to gain their ends. Consequently an increasing number of old-line liberals and neo-conservatives reinforced the Díaz machine in Congress and over-rode opposition in stormy debates. After 1886 Congress usually contented itself with routine discussion of minor points in the government-sponsored legislation.[6]

Meanwhile supporters of the president introduced amendments to the Constitution, permitting him first one re-election and then (in 1890) an indefinite number. Thereafter his followers staged elections at regular intervals with scrupulous regard for form and for appearances abroad. In 1898 the dictator appeared for a moment to consider retirement and promised the candidacy for 1900 to his principal cabinet minister, José Y. Limantour, but when the election year arrived, the old instincts reasserted themselves.[7] Signs of Díaz' advancing age began to alarm the government party in 1901 and 1902, but when the younger

as a sinkhole of corruption and waste, but Carleton Beals argues that González has been treated too badly by those who wanted to use him as a foil for Díaz (Carleton Beals, *Porfirio Díaz, Dictator of Mexico* [Philadelphia, 1932], pp. 246, 262–263).

[6] This paragraph is based in considerable part on Herbert A. Crosman, "The Early Career of José Ives Limantour, 1854–1886," unpublished doctoral dissertation, Harvard University, 1950, pp. 202–222. Crosman also criticized the neoconservatives and Limantour for intensifying the already prevalent feeling of contempt for the backward Indian.

[7] José C. Valadés, *El porfirismo, Historia de un régimen: El crecimiento* (México, 1948), I, 39–42, 51–52, 53–60.

followers pleaded with him to designate a successor as vice-president, the suspicious old dictator chose Ramón Corral, an unpopular governor of the remote state of Sonora. Quite clearly he intended to hold the reins until he died.

After 1884 the Porfirian dictatorship rested on a solid foundation of ruthless terrorism. Few observers denied the crying need of Mexico for security measures. In 1878, for example, United States Minister John W. Foster reported that a company of soldiers had to escort every passenger train from Mexico City to Veracruz to protect it from bandits and that the owners of factories in the very suburbs of the capital dared not send out payroll money in ordinary streetcars without an armed guard.[8] Unfortunately, in attaining public security for Mexico, Díaz sacrificed the personal liberty of her citizens. When he ordered the wholesale arrest of bandits and sent them to the dank prison of San Juan de Ulua in Veracruz harbor to rot in underground cells, no one could be sure that the coffles of prisoners did not contain some of his political enemies along with the highway robbers. Worst of all, his officers shot down many under the notorious *ley fuga* (law of flight) and then reported that the dead men had tried to escape.

As terrorism increased, so did press censorship. By the 1890's fifteen out of twenty Mexico City newspapers were subsidized by officials or friends of the government, and the staff of the leading daily, *El imparcial,* was loaded with government officials.[9] In addition, Díaz maintained a well-lubricated political machine whose cogs and wheels extended into the smallest villages. Each local *jefe político* (political boss) was directly

[8] John W. Foster to Carlisle Mason, Mexico City, October 9, 1878, U.S· Department of State, *Papers Relating to the Foreign Relations of the United States* (Washington, 1862–), 1877–1878, p. 649 (hereafter cited as United States, *Foreign Relations*).

[9] Valadés, *El porfirismo: Crecimiento,* II, 79–80. For examples of press censorship see Beals, *Porfirio Díaz,* pp. 268–273; Ernest Gruening, *Mexico and Its Heritage* (New York, 1928), pp. 56–58.

responsible to the state organization, and the state governors made regular pilgrimages to Mexico City to report on their states and receive orders from the minister of *gobernación* (Home Office) in the cabinet. They also nominated congressmen subject to Díaz' approval, but these representatives were often natives of Mexico City. When Luis Pombo was made deputy for Colotlán, he wrote blandly, "Some day I hope to make the acquaintance of the *colotlanenses.*" Under these circumstances it was sometimes hard to awaken much enthusiasm during election campaigns, and on one occasion John W. Foster found a polling place to which not a single voter had come on election day. Needless to say, the official in charge submitted the expected poll list anyway.[10]

In such a government as this, American promoters soon discovered that personal contacts were all-important. John Hays Hammond, one of the best-known American mining engineers of his generation, related with pride how Díaz warned him against the grasping ways of petty Mexican officials and added, "If you have any trouble of this sort, come to me and I'll settle it." Thereafter, continued Hammond, he had only to make known that he planned a trip to Mexico City in order to bring the local *jefes* to terms.[11] Naturally not every promoter boasted personal acquaintance with Don Porfirio himself, but all of them knew at least a few cabinet officers, congressmen, or state governors who could serve as intermediaries in business negotiations.

Matías Romero was easily the foremost official Mexican supporter of American capital during the first half of the Díaz period. Scarcely out of law school, he joined the army of Juárez and was soon appointed Mexican minister to the United

[10] Valadés, *El porfirismo: Crecimiento*, I, 35; John W. Foster, *Diplomatic Memoirs* (Boston, 1909), I, 53–55.

[11] John Hays Hammond, *The Autobiography of John Hays Hammond* (New York, 1935), II, 508.

States. During most of the French Intervention he maintained
a vital line of communications between Juárez and the sympathetic Lincoln administration. After 1867 he alternated between the Mexican legation in Washington and the *hacienda*
(treasury) department, where he struggled with Mexico's mount-
ing debt. Admiring American material progress and initiative,
Romero threw himself into every sort of enterprise which
might bring these benefits to Mexico. He compiled thousands
of pages of government reports to put forward the best side
of Mexican economic history and wrote articles for all kinds
of magazines to answer every criticism of foreign investment
in Mexico.[12] His personal acquaintance with President Grant and
many other Americans often smoothed the way for promotional
projects in Mexico.

As Romero grew older, his place was gradually taken over
by José Y. Limantour, who became minister of *hacienda* in
1893 and was Díaz' principal economic adviser thereafter. The
scion of a wealthy French-Jewish family, Limantour had eagerly
absorbed the positivist teachings of the younger generation of
neoconservatives. He and his associates took the name *Científicos*
to indicate their desire for scientific, orderly development of
Mexican resources, and in time many of them entered Díaz'
cabinet. Like Romero, Limantour recognized Mexico's need for
foreign capital, but, unlike him, he proposed to regulate it in

---

[12] The best example of Romero's propaganda was a massive report
which he prepared in 1878 to answer John W. Foster's criticisms of
Mexico: México, *Exposición de la secretaría de hacienda de los Estados-
Unidos Mexicanos, de 15 de enero de 1879 sobre la condición actual de
México, y el aumento del comercio con los Estados-Unidos, rectificando
el informe dirigido por el Honorable John W. Foster, enviado extra-
ordinario y ministro plenipotenciario de los Estados-Unidos en México,
el 9 de octubre de 1878 al Sr. Carlile [sic] Mason, presidente de la asocia-
ción de manufactureros de la ciudad de Chicago en el estado de Illinois
de los Estados-Unidos de América* (México, 1879). The English edition,
published in New York in 1880, will henceforth be cited as Mexico, *Report on the Actual Condition of Mexico*.

the interest of the government and prevent any foreign group from gaining too much control over the Mexican economy.[13]

Although Limantour had a much clearer view of Mexican economic problems than Díaz, the aging dictator could not bring himself to promote his able financier to the presidency, and except for their influence on economic policy the *Científicos* did not materially affect the dictatorship itself, since Díaz carefully played off his principal generals against Limantour. During the last ten years of the Porfirian regime the Mexican government was largely a collection of mummies, kept in office out of caution, and critics sneered softly that the government offices were "Pyramids of Egypt joined to the Pyramids of Teotihuacán." [14] Everyone, Mexicans and foreigners alike, asked, "After Díaz, what?"

In 1910 and 1911 the question was answered. During the former year the dictator faced his final electoral campaign, prepared as before to go through the motions of democracy. Underestimating the amount of opposition sentiment, he announced that Mexico was at last ready for a free election, and several candidates took him at his word. After some maneuvering the opposition united behind Francisco I. Madero, a democratically minded member of a wealthy northern aristocratic family. As was to be expected, Madero lost the election by a wide margin, but to nearly everyone's surprise he resorted to military revolution. A few victories over the government troops released the pent-up hatred of thirty-five years against the dictator, and in May 1911, suffering agonies from an abscessed tooth and hardly knowing what he was doing, the senile Díaz signed his resignation and tottered off to exile in Europe.

[13] In addition to Crosman, "Early Career of Limantour," cited above, a detailed study of Limantour's policies, with special emphasis on the years after 1893, is Carlos Díaz Dufoo, *Les finances du Mexique, 1892–1911: Limantour, l'homme et l'œuvre*, trans. by Albert Dupont (Paris, 1926).

[14] James M. Callahan, *American Foreign Policy in Mexican Relations* (New York, 1932), p. 530.

II

What sort of people lived under the rule of Porfirio Díaz? In the nineteenth century there was no such thing as a typical Mexican, for the Conquest and Spanish colonial rule had dissected society with class and racial distinctions. The culture of Mexico was not a chemical compound but a poorly stirred mixture of native and European elements to which incoming Americans only added new ingredients. Basically there were three socioracial groups: whites, Indians, and *mestizos* (mixed-bloods). The whites, together with some *mestizos* and a few Indians, held all positions of influence and profit in the government, business, the Church, the army, and professions. The rest of the Indians and the lower-class *mestizos* formed the vast majority of the population and did most of the manual labor. At the beginning of the period many rural Indians still lived in the old tribal units, and all retained at least fragments of the ancient Indian cultures. Being almost entirely illiterate, however, they had not absorbed much of the white man's culture, and this ignorance placed them at a hopeless disadvantage in the society of Porfirian Mexico.[15]

American visitors came to know best the small minority of Mexicans living in the capital and other large cities. In 1900 Mexico City was a metropolis of perhaps 350,000, floating on a vast underground marsh (the remnant, after drainage, of a chain of Aztec lakes), which caused buildings to settle and buckle before they were even finished. In imitation of Paris, Maximilian had built parks and boulevards, and Díaz improved the southwestern district along the swank Paseo de la Reforma, which led out to his palace at Chapultepec. He also remodeled the façade of the Palacio Nacional after the Louvre and built

[15] The status of the Indian after 1867 is thoroughly surveyed in Cosío Villegas, *Historia moderna de México*, III, 149–325. Hereafter the term peon will be used collectively to indicate lower-class agrarian laborers of both Indian and *mestizo* descent.

most of the colossal, ostentatious Palacio de Bellas Artes. Unfortunately the underground marshes and an inadequate knowledge of sanitation often ruined the effect of his grandiose improvements. Indeed, as late as 1916 the mortality rate in Mexico City exceeded that in Cairo and Madras.[16]

Only the most insensitive visitor could have failed to recognize the abysmal gap between rich and poor in Mexico City. The elite formed a "town within a town" and lived a showy, parasitic life which largely ignored the rest of the country: ceremonial breakfasts (lasting all afternoon in some cases) off Sèvres china in some fashionable restaurant; a concert or a doleful, sentimental play at the theater; and endless, stereotyped balls which the sycophantic press reported in full detail. Nor were the morals of the rich any better than their taste. The spoils system pervaded society—gambling, for example, was forbidden in Mexico City, but no one could enforce the law because Manuel Romero Rubio, Díaz' father-in-law, had a virtual monopoly on gambling houses. President González made no effort to hide his love affairs; even his wife discussed them in public. Dueling became popular, apparently for the first time, and the rising suicide rate and the amount of libel in the press were also symptoms of bad moral health.[17]

In the same city, only a few blocks from the fashionable stores and restaurants, lived other Mexicans whom Hubert H. Bancroft called "a reproach to humanity . . . some of the poorest and most abject creatures on earth . . . thinly or but partially

[16] Valadés, *El porfirismo: Crecimiento*, II, 88 ff.; Alberto J. Pani, *La higiene en México* (México, 1916), pp. 17–18, as cited in Gruening, *Mexico and Its Heritage*, p. 533. From 1895 to 1911 the death rate for all Mexico hovered between 31 and 33 per thousand, as compared with about 17 or 18 (in 1900) for the United States (Cosío Villegas, *Historia moderna de México*, IV, 43).

[17] Excellent descriptions of Porfirian high society, from which these details are taken, are to be found in José C. Valadés, *El porfirismo, Historia de un régimen: El nacimiento (1876–1884)* (México, 1941), chap. iv, and Valadés, *El porfirismo: Crecimiento*, II, chap. viii. See also Cosío Villegas, *Historia moderna de México*, IV, pts. 3, 5.

clad. . . . The poorest live on whatever they can pick up in
the way of food, and at night huddle into huts or adobe apartments, or sleep on the ground or pavement." He added that not
even the Chinese would try to compete with them.[18] For the
social butterflies of the capital these wretches simply did not
exist. Understandably poor communications and press censorship
might have hidden from the aristocrats some of the worst
conditions in rural Mexico, but the crowded, stinking misery of
the poorer *barrios* (districts) of Mexico City lay beneath their
very noses. Misery bred drunkenness, prostitution, and crime,
but when the rate of arrests in the capital shot up, the governor
of the Federal District explained lamely that the efficiency of
the courts later freed many who had been wrongly arrested.[19]

Whatever the realities, life in the capital appeared so glamorous from a distance that every other city in Mexico did its
best to copy the European and American improvements. Outside these cities lay other areas of which tourists and even many
promoters gained only a partial, distorted knowledge: the
haciendas, ranchos, and villages of rural Mexico. According to
one estimate, an even distribution of Mexico's arable land in
1910 would have given each person two acres. Unfortunately
centuries of feudalism had produced chronic maldistribution,
and Díaz made matters worse by parceling out Church lands,
estates confiscated from rebels, and public lands of all description
to political favorites and foreign concessionaires. In the north
the granted lands were often too dry for anything but large-
scale grazing, but by 1910, even in the well-watered central
states, no more than 6 per cent of heads of families owned any
land at all.[20] The desire for land ranked high among the grievances which touched off the popular revolution against Díaz
in 1910 and 1911.

[18] San Francisco *Chronicle*, March 22, 1884.
[19] Valadés, *El porfirismo: Crecimiento*, II, 131–136.
[20] George McCutchen McBride, *The Land Systems of Mexico* (New
York, 1923), pp. 21, 155–156; Nathan L. Whetten, *Rural Mexico* (Chicago,
1948), chaps. iv, v; Cosío Villegas, *Historia moderna de México*, II, 61–79,
IV, 187–216.

During the Díaz period, therefore, the dominant power in rural Mexico was the wealthy *hacendado*, enjoying influence with the central government, serving it as local administrator of law and justice, and often living a part of each year in Mexico City. Like the serf of medieval Europe, the peon was bound to his plot of land and to his master by habit, custom, or debt. As John Bigelow remarked in the 1880's, a peon cost less to maintain than a farm horse in New England: for example, in Tabasco men worked twelve or fourteen hours a day for a monthly wage of five or eight pesos, a starvation diet, and infrequent medical attention.[21] To be sure, habit and the warm climate reduced the peon's needs to a bare minimum, but in the chronic inflation of the Díaz period the lag of wages behind rising prices sometimes wiped out his slender margin of existence. Unless he happened to live near a railroad or a mine which needed extra labor, the much-vaunted prosperity of Porfirian Mexico meant little to him.

III

Like Mexican society the nation's economy was a patchwork affair. Admirers of the dictator boasted that he had brought modern industry to Mexico and declared that "it is wholly to Díaz that her splendid prosperity is due." [22] In the last quarter of the nineteenth century, however, any neighbor of the expanding United States was certain to receive material improvements, and close examination of Mexican economic progress before 1890 shows a remarkable lack of planning and co-ordination, even by American standards of that day. It is true that Limantour often planned carefully and well, but even he was not omniscient, and frequently the ideal measure lay beyond his power.

The basic occupation of the majority of nineteenth-century Mexicans was agriculture. Held back by the reactionary system

[21] Valadés, *El porfirismo: Crecimiento*, I, 273; Callcott, *Liberalism in Mexico*, p. 189.
[22] William E. Carson, *Mexico: The Wonderland of the South* (New York, 1909), p. 206.

of land tenure, Mexican agriculture needed everything: more and better-trained farmers, irrigation, transportation to market, and capital for expansion.[23] Recognizing these needs, the Díaz regime tried to mobilize outside forces to modernize Mexican farming methods and set an example to *hacendado* and peon. The government imported European and American colonists, American capital and machinery, and foreign breeds of cattle and made feeble efforts toward education and the establishment of farm credit. Learning from more advanced agricultural systems was not a bad idea in itself, but some of the lessons were wretchedly taught, some of the fees exorbitant, and it was never intended that the fruits of learning should be evenly distributed.

From one point of view—that represented by export figures —Mexican agriculture developed substantially under Díaz. For the first time such crops as coffee, tobacco, henequen, and ixtle carried weight in the national commerce. The steady inflation of the Mexican currency, however, and the resulting favorable rate of exchange were partly responsible for the increased export of these products, and in the cases of henequen and ixtle the increases were obtained at the cost of a particularly vicious system of debt peonage in Yucatán. Meanwhile subsistence farming, the backbone of Mexican agriculture, fared much worse, and in 1910 a commission merchant interviewed by the Doheny Foundation estimated that although the normal annual demand for corn in Mexico was about 50,000,000 hectoliters (about 142,000,000 bushels) the normal production was only about 60,000,000 hectoliters.[24] But poor crops frequently wiped out this slender margin, and the nation was coming to rely on imports of this vital food from the United States.

[23] For a survey of Mexican agriculture about 1870 see Cosío Villegas, *Historia moderna de México*, II, 37–81.

[24] Doheny Research Foundation, "Mexico: An Impartial Study," typewritten manuscript in Los Angeles Public Library (n.d.), I, 176–190, II, 2–23.

Although agriculture fed and employed the majority of Don Porfirio's Mexicans, the industrial and financial structure of the country rested on mining and metallurgy. In 1867 wars and revolutions had all but ruined Mexican mining. Since new equipment was expensive and hard to install in the mountains and since Mexico lacked coal deposits to replace her dwindling forests, technology was still primitive and inefficient. In many a rich mineral district Indian labor painstakingly chipped out the richest ore, loaded it on mules, and took it over the hills to a crude stamping mill, leaving behind half the wealth of the deposit. State and Federal governments loaded excessive taxes on the shoulders of the few active miners. Many mines lay completely idle, for their owners were afraid to make money, lest they lose it in bandit raids, and perhaps their lives too.

For nearly twenty years after the French Intervention the Mexican government did practically nothing for the mining industry except compile dismal reports and halfhearted recommendations. Finally, on November 22, 1884, the outgoing González administration issued a liberal mining code which softened the traditional Spanish mining law, retaining requirements for the regular working of deposits and for periodic government inspection, but abandoning government ownership of nonmetallic deposits (including petroleum). Even in the case of metallic deposits the government's subsoil rights were not explicitly stated.[25] Subsequent laws made still more concessions, until an American remarked with some justice: "The mining laws of Mexico are far more advantageous to the operator than

[25] Marvin D. Bernstein, "The History and Economic Organization of the Mexican Mining Industry, 1890–1940," unpublished doctoral dissertation, University of Texas, 1951, I, 307–313, 339–342. The text of the 1884 law is found in Manuel Dublán and José María Lozano, eds., *Legislación mexicana o Colección legislativa completa de las disposiciones legislativas expedidas desde la independencia de la República* (50 vols.; México, 1876–1912), XV, 898–930. The title and editors vary in later volumes. A convenient survey of the depression in Mexican mining before 1876 is in Cosío Villegas, *Historia moderna de México*, II, 115–185.

our own laws. . . . The government protects you and requires nothing from you but the amount of your tax." [26]

The main purpose of the liberal mining laws was to attract new capital into the industry, especially from abroad, and in this the government succeeded brilliantly. In one year over two thousand titles to new mines were registered, and despite the steadily falling price of silver it was estimated that in 1889–1890 the total capital invested in mines rose from 400,000,000 pesos to 500,000,000 pesos.[27] In the long run this new capital, mainly American and British, lowered producing costs in Mexico by building convenient, efficient custom smelters, electrifying the richest mines, and introducing new machines and processes, such as the MacArthur-Forrest cyanide process for gold extraction.

The revived mining industry of the late nineteenth century differed from that of the colonial period in two ways. First of all, the Mexico of Juárez and Díaz was not a land of great bonanzas, for most miners looked for widespread, low-grade deposits similar to those in the Transvaal. These had to be worked on a large scale with modern methods if they were to be worked at all. Secondly, the new generation of miners in Mexico paid increased attention to ores of the base metals, especially copper, iron, lead, and zinc. The lack of convenient supplies of good coking coal retarded the development of Mexico's richest iron deposits in Durango, but William C. Greene's Cananea mines and others in northern Sonora and Lower California reflected the copper boom. Before 1900 almost

---

[26] *Modern Mexico*, Aug. 1897, p. 8.

[27] Louis de Launay, "Mines et industries minières," in E. Levasseur, ed., *Le Mexique au début du XXᵉ siècle* (Paris, n.d.), I, 269 ff.; U.S. Department of State, *Reports from the Consuls of the United States on the Commerce, Manufactures, etc., of Their Consular Districts*, no. 122 (Nov. 1890), pp. 541–542 (these reports were issued at one time or another by several different agencies of the U.S. government, under various titles; hereafter cited as United States, *Consular Reports*). See also Carlos Díaz Dufoo, *México y los capitales exteriores* (Paris, 1918), pp. 263–265.

everyone ignored the rich oil deposits along the Gulf coast in Tamaulipas and Veracruz, but after a decade of American and British exploration Mexico was producing about eleven million barrels of petroleum a year when Díaz fell.

At that time the mining and petroleum industries together accounted for perhaps one-fourth of all American capital invested in Mexico. An even larger proportion—probably more than 60 per cent, or about $644,000,000—was invested in Mexican railroads.[28] Mexico needed better communications of all kinds to unblock her trade lanes and bind the locally minded states into one nation. In the 1850's, for example, William P. Robertson reported that the main highway from Jalapa to Perote "in some parts was terrific, for though paved, the large blocks of stone were every where loosened, and lying about; while the great holes and ruts sent us jumping, every now and then, towards the roof of the coach."[29] Complaints like this from travelers were frequent. During the dry season freight traveled the main roads on crude wagons, except for one express route between Veracruz and Mexico City; in the back country cargoes were divided into three-hundred-pound lots and strapped on mules.

In the mid-nineteenth century Mexican and British capital concentrated on the construction of a single railroad from Veracruz, the principal port, to Mexico City. By 1867 various outfits had laid short stretches of track at both ends of the route, but much patriotic feeling had developed against the dominant British railroad company, which had aided the French Intervention. Eager for railroads, Juárez persuaded Congress to renew the British concession, and Lerdo inaugurated the completed railroad on January 1, 1873. Press and public, however, never forgot their grudge against *la compañía inglesa*, and their

[28] See Appendix, Table 1.
[29] William Parish Robertson, *A Visit to Mexico by the West India Islands, Yucatan, and United States, with Observations and Adventures on the Way* (London, 1853), I, 303.

accusations of bad management, bribery, and foreign penetration set the pace for antirailroad propaganda in Mexico.[30]

Between 1867 and 1873 the advance guard of American railroad promoters appeared in Mexico City to petition for concessions. The experiences of two of these men, General William S. Rosecrans and Edward Lee Plumb, will be described in later chapters. Anti-Americanism and the Panic of 1873 prevented much further railroad construction in Mexico before 1880. In the latter year, however, Díaz granted two important railroad concessions for lines between Mexico City and the Rio Grande —the Mexican Central to El Paso and the Mexican National to Laredo (see Map 1). Because of financial and engineering diffi-

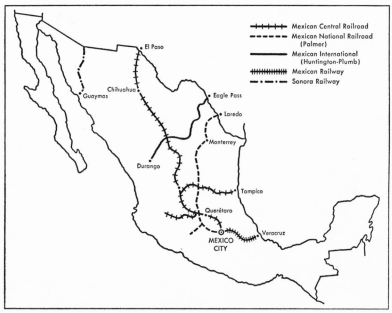

Map 1. Northern lines in operation about 1895

culties the promoting companies did not complete these lines until 1884 and 1888 respectively. These two concessions opened

[30] David M. Pletcher, "The Building of the Mexican Railway," *Hispanic American Historical Review*, XXX (Feb. 1950), 26–62. See also Cosío Villegas, *Historia moderna de México*, II, 608–670.

the floodgates of American capital, and thereafter the González administration granted "railroad concessions with subsidy to all who asked for them, without measure or prudence . . . without order or method." [31] Once back in office, Díaz exercised a little more care in granting concessions, especially after Limantour became minister of *hacienda* in 1893. At the end of the Díaz period Mexico possessed 24,717 kilometers of railroads.[32]

Other forms of communication developed more slowly. Public highways suffered neglect for a long time as a result of the railroad fever, but telegraphs spread across Mexico rapidly after 1870, and by 1911 several of the largest cities had small but growing telephone systems. As in the case of railroads, the Federal government subsidized steamship lines to the United States and Europe and gradually improved the principal harbors with breakwaters and other port works. Because of impending bankruptcy, however, the government could seldom do as much as it wished. The spirit was willing, but the treasury was weak.

Poor communications greatly hampered Mexico's foreign and internal trade during much of the Díaz period. If the importer with his goods survived the seasonal storms approaching the badly protected harbor of Veracruz and the deadly yellow fever of the Gulf coast, he still had to ship his cargo inland on wretched roads and pay so many tariff duties that even government officials lost track of them. Often the duties amounted to more than the original value of the goods. John W. Foster found that price rises of 500 or 600 per cent on goods shipped from the United States were not at all unusual.[33]

The absurd practice of protecting nonexistent industries and

---

[31] Pablo Macedo, *La evolución mercantil, Comunicaciones y obras públicas, La hacienda pública: Tres monografías que dan idea de una parte de la evolución económica de México* (México, 1905), p. 205.

[32] *Mexican Year Book*, 1912, p. 79.

[33] Foster to Mason, Mexico City, Oct. 9, 1878, United States, *Foreign Relations*, 1877–1878, pp. 641–647. For a discussion of Mexican protectionism and its defense see Cosío Villegas, *Historia moderna de México*, II, 98–114.

extracting virtually the entire governmental budget from foreign trade punished legitimate merchants and encouraged smugglers. Tariff schedules changed so often and their bases of computation were so varied and indirect that importing became an occult mystery, spiced by the knowledge that if a customs officer found an error in the invoice he could often levy a fine twice as large as the amount involved. This power was too much for the officials, who conspired with smugglers to rob the government of millions of pesos and made a mockery of import statistics.[34] The Federal government further complicated trade for many years by providing duty-free import of foreign goods into a strip of territory along the northern frontier (the *Zona Libre*) and by allowing states to collect *alcabalas* or internal tariffs at their borders if they wished. The Free Zone on the north became a smugglers' paradise, and the internal tariffs simply reinforced the natural isolation of rural communities.[35]

Beyond a doubt manufacturing was the weakest section of the nineteenth-century Mexican economy, and it accounted for only about 1 per cent of American direct investments in 1911. By 1867 the leading manufacturing industry, that of cotton textiles, had developed out of handicraft origins to a semicapitalist stage in which a few wealthy families operated factories much as if they were feudal haciendas.[36] They produced low-grade "shirtings" (*manta*), mainly worn by the peons, while the upper classes continued to import finer cotton cloth, woolens, and silks from England and France.

[34] *Mexican Financier*, April 19, 1884, p. 41, Aug. 23, 1884, p. 332; Mexico, *Report on the Actual Condition of Mexico*, pp. 320–322.

[35] Macedo, *La evolución mercantil*, pp. 108–110; *Bulletin of the Pan-American Union*, XXI (Sept. 1905), 791–796; Callahan, *American Foreign Policy in Mexican Relations*, pp. 342–345. For a survey of American-Mexican trade during the Díaz period see Jorge Espinosa de los Reyes, *Relaciones económicas entre México y Estados Unidos, 1870–1910* (México, 1951), pp. 50–67.

[36] *Mexican Financier*, June 21, 1884, p. 182; David A. Wells, *A Study of Mexico* (New York, 1887), pp. 136–137, 150–154; Cosío Villegas, *Historia moderna de México*, II, 82–98.

Similarly the manufacture of iron and steel products progressed more slowly than one would expect in a mining country such as Mexico. Enjoying the double advantage of a few nearby coal deposits and excellent railroad connections, the northern city of Monterrey increased its annual output to 20,000,000 pesos by 1900, but six years later an American visitor to the area reported that the steel mills were still embarrassed by the lack of skilled Mexican labor and the expense of hiring Americans.[37] He predicted that for the time being Mexico must confine herself to a limited production of low-grade metal products—a prediction which was certainly borne out by the long list of iron and steel imports in 1910 and 1911. The same might be said for other Mexican manufacturing industries of the Díaz period: that if they flourished, it was usually because they operated on a relatively small scale, meeting the local demands of the lower classes.

IV

Such was the Mexico of Porfirio Díaz—a mixture of culture and backwardness, of ostentation and misery, of abundant resources and haphazard exploitation. What did American tourists and promoters make of this kaleidoscope south of the Rio Grande? Relatively few Americans visited Mexico before 1880, partly because of the lack of direct, easy communications between the two countries and partly because the dictatorship of Porfirio Díaz had not yet proved its stability and its friendliness toward the United States. Between 1877 and 1880, as a matter of fact, the two countries were several times in danger of war over boundary raids.[38]

[37] Valadés, *El porfirismo: Crecimiento*, I, 323; U.S. Department of Commerce and Labor, Charles M. Pepper, *Report on Trade Conditions in Mexico* (59th Congress, 1st Session, Senate Document 246; Washington, 1906), pp. 13–14.

[38] Robert D. Gregg, *The Influence of Border Troubles on Relations between the United States and Mexico, 1867–1910* (The Johns Hopkins Studies in Historical and Political Science, Series LV, no. 3; Baltimore,

In 1880, however, American-Mexican relations changed for the better, as the Hayes administration withdrew its aggressive orders to American frontier troops, and Díaz showed his stability by engineering the peaceful election of Manuel González and his friendliness by granting concessions to the Mexican Central and Mexican National Railroads. The southward flow of capital increased at once, and a year or two later William H. Bishop described the Hotel Iturbide in Mexico City, once an imperial palace, as being crowded with "projectors." [39] Notables such as Jefferson Davis, Ulysses S. Grant, Charles A. Dana, and, later, William Jennings Bryan received gala official greetings in Mexico City, and after the opening of the international railroads ordinary tourists, salesmen, and visitors of all kinds followed them. As early as 1884 it was observed that the capital contained more Americans than at any other time since the departure of the United States troops in 1848.[40]

Most of the visitors returned home to praise the hospitable Mexicans, and articles, books, and consular reports on Mexico poured from the presses. One writer, for example, found the crops in Oaxaca "simply marvelous," the coffee "equal to the best known in any country," and the whole state better supplied than any other with "the natural elements making it a specially promising field for railway enterprise." [41] At the other side of Mexico, an American consul pronounced Sonora "a vast and virgin field to American capital," and when the Southern Pacific began to build an extension into Sinaloa, a journalist jauntily predicted: "Mountainous Tepic . . . and aristocratic, languor-loving Jalisco . . . are about to be swung upon the railway chain

---

1937); Daniel Cosío Villegas, *Estados Unidos contra Porfirio Díaz* (México, 1956).

[39] William Henry Bishop, *Old Mexico and Her Lost Provinces* (New York, 1883), pp. 54–61.

[40] *Mexican Financier*, April 26, 1884, p. 52.

[41] Robert B. Gorsuch, *The Mexican Southern Railway, to Be Constructed under a Charter from the Mexican Government, through the States of Vera Cruz and Oaxaca* (New York, 1881), pp. 3–7.

that Uncle Sam swings from his belt. . . . Soon the striped serapes that dazzle the morning sun will give way before Stein-Levy's ready-made overcoats." [42] Another writer predicted of the Pacific coast that "with marvelous fecundity its millions of acres will bring forth new wealth for the world's coffers, new employment for the world's people." [43]

To these visitors Mexico seemed not only rich but secure. As early as 1874, during the rule of Sebastián Lerdo de Tejada, the promoter Edward Lee Plumb assured Secretary of State Hamilton Fish that Mexico had worked out her problems of political reconstruction and that, having demolished "the massive walls" of clerical monarchism, "it has erected a new republican structure into which it has moved." [44] The revolution of 1876 and the border crisis of 1877–1880 dispelled hope for a time, but after 1880 peaceful elections and the rush of public works reassured the American public that a new age was really at hand. "There has been nothing like it in the history of the world," declared the *Mexican Financier* in 1885. "The feudal and spiritual lords have been shorn of their excessive powers; . . . a stable and just government has been founded." [45] Five years later the *Financier* gazed with alarm at populism and anarchism in the United States and offered Mexico as "a refuge for those honest though perhaps misguided persons who, having acquired property, hold to the old-fashioned idea that it is really theirs. . . . Mexico, in the most turbulent period of its history, was never so permeated with revolutionary ideas as is the United States today." [46]

Most Americans gave Díaz the credit for this apparent sta-

---

[42] United States, *Consular Reports*, no. 185 (Feb. 1896), pp. 251–252; Charles S. Aiken, "The Land of Tomorrow," *Sunset Magazine*, XXII (June 1909), 509–510.

[43] Arthur W. North, "On the Road to Guadalajara," *ibid.*, XVII (Oct. 1906), 342.

[44] Edward Lee Plumb to Hamilton Fish, New York, Aug. 14, 1875, Plumb Collection.

[45] *Mexican Financier*, March 14, 1885, p. 381.

[46] *Ibid.*, March 8, 1890, p. 580.

bility. When he resumed office in 1884, a New York correspondent welcomed him back as "a sagacious and patriotic statesman" working for the progress of his country. The dictator's sycophants and admirers called him "one of the most heroic figures—perhaps the most Olympian figure—of modern history," "a modern Cromwell," and "a Moses" who led his people "to the portals of peace and prosperity." Even Theodore Roosevelt burst out that Díaz was "the greatest statesman now living." [47]

Occasionally a sour note or two marred the hymns of praise. During the border crisis of the 1870's, for example, Minister John W. Foster sent to a group of industrialists a long letter, later reprinted as a pamphlet, in which he warned them that Mexico was not yet safe for American investments. Transportation was highly unreliable, he said, trade slow, smuggling everywhere prevalent, the government nearly bankrupt, and life and property insecure. Foster admitted that Mexico enjoyed abundant resources, but until the nation could control her finances, revolutions, and anti-Americanism he advised his correspondents not to risk more than a few salesmen and cases of samples. [48] Even the events of 1880 did not silence the critics. "The Mexicans, like all the Latin race, are inveterate gamblers," warned John Bigelow in 1882, "and of all the aleatory devices for improving their fortunes there is none to which they are more addicted than the game of revolution." Both he and David A. Wells agreed that the builders of the new railroads had exaggerated beyond all reason their expectations of profits. [49]

[47] *Ibid.*, Oct. 11, 1884, p. 21; Frederick Palmer in Chicago *Tribune*, Feb. 22, 1909; Alfred H. Lewis, "The Maligners of Mexico," *Cosmopolitan Magazine*, XLVIII (March 1910), 432c; Dillon Wallace, *Beyond the Mexican Sierras* (Chicago, 1910), pp. xiii–xix; James Creelman, *Díaz, Master of Mexico* (New York, 1916), p. 6.

[48] Foster to Mason, Mexico City, Oct. 9, 1878, United States, *Foreign Relations*, 1877–1878, pp. 636–654. Three years later, Foster's successor sent home a very similar description of Mexican conditions (Philip H. Morgan to James G. Blaine, Mexico City, Aug. 13, 1881, no. 254, confidential, State Dept., Despatches, Mexico, LXXIII).

[49] John Bigelow, "The Railway Invasion of Mexico," *Harper's Magazine*, LXV (1882), 747–748; see also New York *Times*, Jan. 27, 1886.

Toward the end of the century doubts grew less frequent, but in the last years of the Díaz period they reappeared, as evidence of oppression and lower-class discontent escaped the dictator's censorship. The strike of 1906 in William C. Greene's Cananea mines aroused criticism of Americans in Mexico. Soon after this John K. Turner published "Barbarous Mexico," a series of sensational magazine articles later gathered into a book, in which he described debt peonage in southern Mexico, the enslavement of the Yaqui Indians, and a secret alliance between the Mexican government and American business interests.[50] In 1910 the New York *Times* accused American officials of helping Mexican consuls to arrest and silence immigrants who published anti-Díaz progaganda in San Antonio and Los Angeles.[51]

These warnings grated harshly on the ears of promoters and financiers, for, as one sarcastic journalist wrote, Americans had invested about $800,000,000 in Mexico, and "the continuance of large profits on this capital requires the maintenance of the existing regime and the absolute cessation of agitation and criticism." [52] Consequently financial and other magazines tried to drown out the critics with pontifical statements that Díaz had brought Mexico to a plateau of permanent peace and prosperity. In 1910, with revolution imminent, a Chicago corporation lawyer declared solemnly that when Don Porfirio died there would be "no destructive revolution, no tearing down of the great works of Díaz, no looting of the public treasury. . . . The revolutionists of Mexico have passed away and in their stead has come a generation of peace-loving, prosperous citizens." [53] Next year, after the revolution had actually begun, another publicist wrote soothingly of "a family quarrel . . . purely local and

[50] John Kenneth Turner, *Barbarous Mexico* (Chicago, 1910), *passim.* For an account of Turner and reactions to his work see Cosío Villegas, *Historia moderna de México,* IV, 260–265.

[51] "How We Pull Díaz's Chestnuts Out of the Fire," New York *Times,* Aug. 7, 1910, Magazine Section, p. 3.

[52] W. J. Ghent, "Mexico Judged by Its Friends," *Independent,* LXVIII (Jan. 20, 1910), 136.

[53] Theodore K. Long in *World Today,* XVIII (1910), 638.

entirely political" and warned Americans that they would make "the mistake of their lives" if they withdrew from Mexico now.[54]

Events after 1911 rudely shook the dreamers awake. Díaz the infallible gave way to Madero the idealist, less friendly to foreign capital. Revolt and violence shattered the *pax porfiriana,* then engulfed and destroyed the unhappy Madero, and plunged Mexico into a new civil war as bitter as that of the 1850's. When the storm descended on them, Americans in Mexico reacted in different ways. Some fled to safety, leaving their mines to be flooded and their railroads uprooted by the rival armies. Others remained, hoping to save enough of their property to resume operations when the fighting shifted elsewhere.[55] Some appealed to the American government to intervene and save them. Others made whatever deals were necessary with local *jefes* and generals. When peace came in the 1920's a new spirit was in the air, the product of the voluminous antiforeign propaganda which had helped to supply an ideology for the confused fighters. Foreign development of Mexican resources was still possible, but the Americans now had to deal with Mexican labor as an active force and with a government which would not or dared not cooperate as smoothly as in the past. The happy days of Don Porfirio were gone forever.

Why were most Americans unprepared for the violence of the decade after 1910? Few realized the intensity of the social pressure building up against Díaz or heeded the evidence that they were living in a fool's paradise, benefiting from a lucky combination of political and economic circumstances which could not possibly last. Fewer still understood that the very presence of their life-giving capital stimulated social unrest at the same time

[54] Elisha A. Talbot, "American Interests in Mexico," *Moody's Magazine,* IX (April 1911), 236–237.

[55] For an example of the conditions faced by American interests see David M. Pletcher, "An American Mining Company in the Mexican Revolutions of 1911–1920," *Journal of Modern History,* XX (March 1948), 19–26.

that it modernized Mexico. For this false sense of security and for the illusion of easy riches they might well thank the promoters who had urged them to invest in Mexican railroads or mines and whose optimistic writings formed the basis of their misconceptions.

II

Civil War General:

William S. Rosecrans

ONE of the first important American promoters in Mexico after the Civil War was William S. Rosecrans, late major general in the Union Army. During the Reconstruction period, as always after a major war, American politics and business were infiltrated by waves of veterans. Rosecrans was one of these uprooted men, a professional soldier discontented with what seemed to be a blighted career. After drifting west to California, he was appointed for a brief time minister to Mexico, and here he recognized the opportunities for promotional work. Fresh from the fields of Murfreesboro and Chickamauga, he volunteered for a command in the army of economic imperialism, and from 1868 to 1873 the cause of American railroading in Mexico was bound up with his name.

To his dismay Rosecrans found politicians, financiers, and journalists less tractable than armies, and he could not order them shot for deserting him in the face of the enemy. His Civil War training, invaluable for some aspects of promotion, proved inadequate in other ways, and some of the qualities which had won him renown on the battlefield foredoomed him to failure in the postwar campaign.

I

William S. Rosecrans was an average product of the nineteenth-century Middle West. His father, descended from English-Dutch immigrants, farmed and managed the village tavern in Homer, Ohio, during the early 1830's while William got the rudiments of an education in a log schoolhouse during a few months of each year. Appointed to West Point by a local congressman, he made a good record and was graduated in 1842. Then followed twelve dull years of teaching military engineering and building fortifications, before he finally resigned his army commission in 1854 and went into business surveying for coal in western Virginia. Soon he was president of a small coal company.[1]

When the Civil War began, Rosecrans returned to the army as colonel and aide-de-camp to George B. McClellan. He was soon promoted to brigadier general, and in 1862 he was transferred into the western theater as commander of the Army of the Mississippi. Succeeding Don Carlos Buell in command of the Department of the Cumberland, he began a successful and dramatic drive southward from the Cumberland River toward Chattanooga and Georgia. After a bloody battle at Murfreesboro (Stone River), Rosecrans brilliantly outmaneuvered the Confederate, Braxton Bragg, in southeastern Tennessee and, following a cautious advance toward Chattanooga, occupied the city in August 1863.

This was the crest of Rosecrans' military career. Idolized by his soldiers and praised by Lincoln for his successes in Tennessee,

[1] Two brief accounts of Rosecrans' early life and military activities are [L. W. Mulhane], *Memorial of Major-General William Stark Rosecrans* [Columbus, Ohio, 1898], and [John Fitch], *Annals of the Army of the Cumberland: Comprising Biographies, Descriptions of Departments, Accounts of Expeditions, Skirmishes, and Battles, Also Its Police Record of Spies, Smugglers, and Prominent Rebel Emissaries, Together with Anecdotes, Incidents, Poetry, Reminiscenses, etc., and Official Reports of the Battle of Stone River* (Philadelphia, 1864).

he was even sounded out for the presidency. Unfortunately he had made an enemy of Edwin M. Stanton, and his defeat at Chickamauga, south of Chattanooga, on September 19–20 gave the vindictive secretary of war an opportunity to break him. General (later President) James A. Garfield, who was Rosecrans' chief of staff during the battle, has been accused of partial responsibility for his removal because of disloyal reports about Rosecrans to friends in Washington, and the sharp criticism of Charles A. Dana, then acting assistant secretary of war, doubtless strengthened Stanton's decision. In October, Rosecrans was transferred to a less important theater and later even removed from this command.

The question of Rosecrans' military ability became a political football as Garfield rose to prominence in politics, and it has not been completely settled to this day. Grant called him disobedient, but this opinion may not be significant, since Rosecrans and Grant disliked each other heartily. On first acquaintance Garfield found Rosecrans "a man of very decided and muscular thoughts and with the rare . . . quality of having his mind made up on every important question." After Chickamauga, Dana wrote that he lacked administrative ability, went off on tangents, and lost the confidence of his officers and men. A biographer of Garfield, trying to reconcile these contradictions, has produced this complex characterization of Rosecrans:

Outwardly testy and choleric, seldom troubling himself to put his opinions in tactful form, seemingly impulsive, certainly warmhearted in both his likes and dislikes, the idol of his officers and men, Rosecrans was in fact one of the most cautious of men, with a certain inertia of will which made him very slow in making up his mind or in taking any important step. Having once decided, however, he never doubted his judgment, and without turning back, placed all his cards on the correctness of an opinion which he had reached with infinite caution and pains.[2]

[2] Robert Granville Caldwell, *James A. Garfield, Party Chieftain* (New York, 1931), pp. 106–107; see also Theodore Clark Smith, *The*

Some of these qualities were later to reappear in Mexico City.

Since many persons thought Rosecrans unfairly treated after Chickamauga, he had considerable political "availability" after the war. Even before he left the army, he refused nomination for the governorship of Ohio, and he might have had other rewards, had he not preferred to move to California in 1867. During the following summer, however, Secretary of State Seward offered him the position of minister to Mexico, and he accepted. On December 2 he arrived in Mexico City with his wife, family, and aged mother-in-law. He found the legation in the hands of an able chargé d'affaires, Edward Lee Plumb, and the two men, soon to be bitter rivals in railroad promotion, took each other's measure briefly before Plumb left for home.[3]

During the few months of Rosecrans' residence in Mexico as American minister, he formed a low opinion of the Juárez government. He thought that it spoke for only a small minority —"neither the intellect nor the conscience of this people, far less its business and prosperity"—and called it weak, vacillating, foolish, and corrupt. Furthermore, the government seemed to him really anti-American at heart. No matter what its protestations, he told Seward, it "will base its policy on the low passions and prejudices of the Mexicans and has no firm intention of opening the country to emigration [*sic*] from the United States, any further than circumstances and public sentiment compel it." For this xenophobia he blamed Sebastián Lerdo de Tejada, who, he felt, imposed on Juárez the motto: "Mexico for me and the Mexicans." Perhaps the clue to Rosecrans' prejudice against the Juárez government may be found in the fact that he was a devout Roman Catholic, for on one occasion he declared that the government had persecuted "the religion of the people," and

---

Life and Letters of James Abram Garfield (New Haven, Conn., 1925), I, 272.

[3] William S. Rosecrans to William T. Hunter, Washington, Aug. 12, 1868, Rosecrans to William H. Seward, Mexico City, Dec. 10, 1868, no. 9, State Dept., Despatches, Mexico, XXXV.

on another occasion he accused Juárez of truckling simultan-
eously to anti-Americanism in Mexico and anticlericalism in the
United States.[4]

Because of the lamentable political condition of Mexico, Rosecrans expected Europe to invite the United States to intervene
and restore order, and he repeatedly warned Seward that the
American government must formulate a definite policy before
this happened. At no time did he go so far as to recommend an
armed invasion, but he urged the State Department to encourage
Mexican conservatives, Imperialists, and European residents,
since these would welcome American intervention. Meanwhile
he suggested that the department expand the American consular
organization in Mexico and grant a monthly subsidy of $100 or
$150 to the struggling local American newspaper, the *Two Re-
publics.*[5]

Most often Rosecrans gave wholehearted and explicit support to peaceful economic penetration by railroad construction.
As he later admitted, he talked railroads to Mexican leaders of
all political stamps, and in his dispatches of the spring of 1869
the subject bulked larger and larger. On March 10 he urged that
the southwestern railroads be pushed to the Mexican border as
fast as possible. On March 28 he added that Americans ought
to build one or two trunk lines from the Gulf of Mexico into
the heart of the country, perhaps from the secondary ports of
Tampico or Tuxpan and Antón Lizardo. Obviously this would
have meant competition with the British-owned Mexican Railway from Veracruz. "Pushing American enterprise up to, and
within Mexico wherever it can profitably go . . ." he declared,
"will give us advantages which force and money alone would

[4] Rosecrans to Seward, Mexico City, Feb. 8, 10, 28, March 22, 1869,
nos. 31, 35, 39½, *ibid.* It is strange that Rosecrans apparently felt no
antipathy to the *puros*, or anti-Juárez extreme liberals, who were more
anticlerical than the government itself.

[5] Rosecrans to Seward, Mexico City, Jan. 10, Feb. 28, March 10, 1869,
nos. 20, 35, *ibid.*

hardly procure. It would give us a peaceful conquest of the country." [6]

About two weeks later, on April 10, he presented the new secretary of state, Hamilton Fish, with four alternatives in Mexican policy: abandon Mexico to disintegration; create support for the Juárez cabinet; help "the true 'Constitutionalists' " (apparently the anti-Juárez liberals) to gain power; or conquer and occupy the country. Assuming that the second and third alternatives would be preferable, in that order, he went on to suggest an elaborate program of railroad expansion, including the possible purchase of the Mexican Railway. Ostensibly to test the attitude of the Mexican government toward American railroad enterprises, Rosecrans sent two petitions to the Mexican Congress for construction of railroads, one from Tampico or Tuxpan to Mexico City and the other from Antón Lizardo to Cuernavaca, with the privilege of extension to the Pacific. [7]

The general was not given much time in which to combine diplomacy and promotion, for the incoming president, Grant, who disliked him, had not even waited for inauguration before informing the Mexican government of his intention to recall Rosecrans. Early in May the minister learned of this intention from the newspapers, and to his chagrin a letter of recall soon arrived from Secretary Fish. Since the "sickly season" was approaching in Veracruz, Rosecrans remained in Mexico City for two months with his family, ignoring his successor, Thomas H. Nelson, as much as possible and making plans to put his petitions through the next session of Congress. Later he published a letter which he addressed to Juárez at this time. It contained no hint of his former prejudice against the government and suggested that American capital for public works and immigrants for colonization would both be forthcoming if Mexico could

[6] Rosecrans to Hunter, Mexico City, March 10, 1869, Rosecrans to Elihu B. Washburne, March 28, 1869, *ibid.*

[7] Rosecrans to Hamilton Fish, Mexico City, April 10, 28, 1869, nos. 43, 46, 55, *ibid.*

eradicate the prevailing impressions of insecurity and anti-Americanism in Mexico. And how better could the Mexican Congress create a proper impression than by approving the two concessions then before it? [8]

Minister of *Relaciones* Sebastián Lerdo de Tejada replied for the government with information about Mexican colonization laws and with encouraging generalities about Mexico's "most sincere and practical desire . . . to favor the greatest possible development of mercantile, industrial, and railroad interests, in the relations of the citizens of Mexico and the United States." [9] Full of plans, Rosecrans left Mexico City in mid-July with his family, to begin the long trip to Acapulco and San Francisco.

II

The idea of a transcontinental railroad from the Gulf of Mexico to the Pacific, passing through or near the capital city, was nothing new to Mexicans. As early as 1849 their Congress had authorized such a road, beginning at Veracruz, and during the next twenty years the government granted at least half a dozen different interoceanic concessions through the central part of the country, as well as others across the Isthmus of Tehuantepec to the south and across Sonora to the northwest. At the end of the French Intervention only one central Mexican project, the railroad from Veracruz to Mexico City, had made any progress. Rather than compete with this partly finished railroad, Rosecrans decided to concentrate his efforts on a line

[8] Adam Badeau, *Grant in Peace: From Appomattox to Mount Mac-Gregor* (Hartford, Conn., 1887), pp. 154–155; Rosecrans to Fish, Mexico City, May 10, 1869, no. 58, State Dept., Despatches, Mexico, XXXV; Rosecrans to Benito Juárez, Mexico City, May 28, 1869, in *El General Rosecrans, la "Doctrina Monroe," el "destino manifesto," y el ferrocarril de Tuxpan al Pacífico* (México, 1870), pp. 12–15.

[9] Sebastián Lerdo de Tejada to Rosecrans, Mexico City, June 14, July 10, 1869, "The National Interoceanic Railway Company of General Rosecrans," General Records of the Department of State, Record Group 59, Accession 161, U.S. Bureau of Archives (hereafter cited as Interoceanic Company Papers).

running northeast from Mexico City to the port of Tuxpan, near which several colonies of Confederate refugees had settled after the Civil War.

Others had the same idea, but at first none offered serious competition. Late in 1867 Abdón Morales Montenegro and R. da Cunha Reis secured a concession for a railroad from Mexico City to the Tuxpan River, but Rosecrans either bought them out or persuaded them to support his project.[10] In the summer of 1869 an Englishman, Edmund Stephenson, announced an ingenious plan for the construction of a whole railroad system, extending to both coasts and to the Rio Grande as well. He proposed universal military conscription from which the upper classes could secure exemption only by buying shares in a national railroad company—a rather visionary procedure in bribe-ridden Mexico. At first Stephenson tried to discourage Rosecrans from competing, but by the spring of 1870 Stephenson was convinced of the general's good faith and pledged him his support.[11]

When Rosecrans returned to the United States in July 1869, he left behind him three agents to represent him in his dealings with the Mexican government: Anthony D. Richards, James Smith, and Joseph Brennan. These men petitioned Congress for a concession to build a railroad and telegraph from the Gulf coast near Tampico or Tuxpan to the Pacific coast at or near the Río de las Balsas. For over a year they lobbied, trying to win over the deputies with personal interviews, the reprinting of letters from Rosecrans, and other propaganda. They probably

[10] A letter from Montenegro to Rosecrans, April 15, 1870, and an unsigned statement of money and shares of stock paid to R. da Cunha Reis, dated Feb. 4, 1869, are contained in *ibid.*

[11] Edmund Stephenson to Thomas H. Nelson, Aug. 31, 1869, State Dept., Despatches, Mexico, XXXVII; Stephenson to Rosecrans, Mexico City, Oct. 8, 1869, April 4, 1870, Interoceanic Company Papers. The most comprehensive summary of the minor railroad projects which competed with Rosecrans is in Cosío Villegas, *Historia moderna de México*, II, 698–711.

published the pamphlet which appeared at this time containing a full description of the proposed railroad. According to a map the main line was to run somewhat northwest of Mexico City, with a branch to the capital, another to Querétaro, and perhaps others along the way. The railroad was to transport countless interior goods to foreign markets, rescue miners from the monopoly of domestic smelters, and otherwise directly benefit six states and the Federal District. At this time Rosecrans supplemented the railroad project with a proposal for a national bank of discount, deposit, loans, and general circulation which would relieve the credit shortage in Mexico, expand the currency, and "supply the temporary void created by exporting, until the general exports of the country can be increased by the construction of railroads and other [transportation] facilities." [12] Mexico certainly needed such a bank, but the railroad project proved more than enough to occupy Rosecrans, and he wrote little more of his broader plan.

The general's three agents in Mexico found the going rough from the beginning. "If you could only hear the remarks, objections & doubts which I hear in my daily discussions & conversations with our Diputados . . . !" wrote Richards. "I run after them constantly day & night, & only by hammering reason into their heads, I succeed in persuading them that their objections & doubts do not correspond with the enlightenment of the nineteenth century." After the bitter argument in 1868 over the exasperating entanglements of the Mexican Railway concession Congress could scarcely be blamed for hesitating to grant another extensive set of privileges. Some of the opposition originated with supporters of the Mexican Railway, and Brennan suggested to his chief that he offer to buy out the British share-

[12] [William Stark Rosecrans], *Mexico* (n.p., [1870]), pamphlet in New York Public Library, pp. 5–11. Rosecrans proposed that his bank take over the operation of all Mexican mints. See also Manuel Fernando Soto, *Proyecto de comunicación interoceánica por el centro de la República mexicana* (México, 1869), *passim*.

holders, taking the precaution of softening them up first by persuading the government to stop their annual subsidy or by spreading rumors of revolution. As he remarked sarcastically, "A fine fat Englishman loves revolutions he do." [13]

The congressional debates brought out many of the leading arguments which were later elaborated for and against the Rosecrans project. In brief, the opponents of the concession called it a bad bargain, granting a virtual monopoly of operations over an important part of Mexico to a group of foreigners, and hated Yankees at that. "We are the hare about to be mangled in the coils of the devouring boa," lamented one deputy, as he predicted that Americans would use any pretext to gain control over Mexico and capitalize it as they had California. Another added that the government would lose over 3,000,000 pesos by the proposed contract in exemptions from import duties and from the tax on exported capital, as well as by the cession of unoccupied lands to the railroad company. Furthermore, he insisted, Mexico did not contain enough public lands for the grant specified in the contract, and the cession would lead to the forfeiture of countless imperfect titles. A third deputy denied the right of the government to prevent rival Mexican organizations from beginning competing concessions.[14]

Against these arguments Rosecrans' friend, Gabriel Mancera, cited the experiences of foreign countries in railroad building. The French government had relieved private companies of all responsibility for grading and masonry work and had guaranteed a minimum return of 5 per cent on railroad investments. From 1850 to 1857, while the French railroad system expanded, French commerce had trebled. In the United States, Mancera said, railroad mileage had increased 400 per cent from 1851 to

[13] Anthony Richards to Rosecrans, Mexico City, March 10, 1870, Joseph Brennan to Rosecrans, Baltimore, March 6, 1870, Interoceanic Company Papers.

[14] México, *Diario de los debates: Quinto congreso constitucional de la Unión* (México, 1871), I, 281, 284, 296, 918.

1868, and goods transported had risen 1,000 per cent and population 50 per cent. He and a colleague denied that the government sought to create a monopoly and freely invited other
promoters to submit favorable plans. A third speaker proposed
to exorcise the specter of American penetration by attracting
colonists from Europe. "Let us make ourselves strong by the
same means that the Americans have employed," he advised.
"Fortunately . . . we have a long period in which to strengthen
ourselves. Considerable time will pass before the Americans
can populate the vast territories which the Pacific railroad
crosses." [15]

Rosecrans and his agents also found support among the advisers of President Juárez. From the beginning Matías Romero,
then minister of *hacienda,* threw his influence in favor of the
Tuxpan railroad project. "We are going to have this matter
. . . pushed during the present session," he wrote in September 1870. "We will not give up no matter how great may be the
obstacle we may find in our way." [16] Long before this he had
offered the facilities of his department for the translation and
editing of Rosecrans' pamphlets. It was probably due to Romero's efforts that Juárez himself sent a formal invitation to
Rosecrans on January 27, 1870: "I shall be truly pleased to have
the capitalist promoters to which you refer come and invest
part of their riches in the development of industrial enterprise
here, thus tightening the bonds of brotherhood which shall
unite the two Republics by the very identity of their democratic institutions." [17] Loath to take chances with unpredictable
Mexican politics, Rosecrans also wrote a fulsome letter to Porfirio Díaz, beginning in true Hispanic style: "Without having

[15] *Ibid.,* I, 282–285, 293, 296.
[16] Matías Romero to Rosecrans, Mexico City, Sept. 18, 24, 1870, Jan. 9,
1871, Interoceanic Company Papers.
[17] Benito Juárez to Rosecrans, Jan. 27, 1870, Copiadores, Archivo
Juárez, Biblioteca Nacional, Mexico City. See also Richards to Rosecrans,
Mexico City, April 9, 1870, Interoceanic Company Papers.

seen [you], I salute you as one of God's noblest works, an honest man, an incorruptible patriot and a worthy soldier of freedom." "God's noblest work" answered in kind, pledging his friendship and thanking Rosecrans from his "Mexican heart" for his interest in the country. Díaz also promised help to Richards in putting the concession through Congress.[18]

By December 1870 the congressional opposition was resigned to the inevitable, and in the usual end-of-session rush the Tuxpan concession was finally passed. Many of the terms were routine and unobjectionable: free importation of construction materials for twenty years, special rates for government employees, provision for governmental approvement of plans, and a statement of the purely Mexican nature of the organization. The contract, however, contained one important flaw: it retained a grant of public lands (10,000 acres per kilometer of railroad) as the principal method of government subsidy. Several deputies had pointed out that the government had lost control of nearly all public lands in central Mexico and that any attempt to investigate faulty titles would cause widespread resentment among landholders and very probably rebellion. Since this situation seems to have been generally recognized in Congress, the provision represented either bad faith or muddled wishful thinking.[19]

While the long debate was proceeding to its unsatisfactory

[18] Rosecrans to Porfirio Díaz, New York, Nov. 9, 1870, in Alberto María Carreño, ed., *Archivo del General Porfirio Díaz: Memorias y documentos* (México, 1947–), IX, 45–46; Díaz to Rosecrans, Mexico City, Dec. 8, 1870, Richards to Rosecrans, Mexico City, Sept. 24, 1870, Interoceanic Company Papers.

[19] México, *Diario de los debates: Quinto congreso*, III, 666–671; México, Secretaría de fomento, *Legislación sobre ferrocarriles: Colección de leyes, decretos, disposiciones, resoluciones y documentos importantes sobre caminos de fierro arreglada en el archivo de la secretaría de fomento* (México, 1882–1885), I, 1191–1200 (hereafter cited as México, *Legislación sobre ferrocarriles*). It must be noted that the concessionaires themselves requested land grants (Soto, *Proyecto de comunicación interoceánica*, pp. 12–13).

conclusion, Rosecrans began his campaign for financial support in the United States, drawing up a memorial to the United States Congress and traveling five thousand miles through St. Louis, Cincinnati, Indianapolis, and Columbus to New York and Washington to re-establish contact with old acquaintances. The letters which he wrote during 1869 and 1870 and later published in publicity leaflets reflect enthusiasm for his project and not a little anxiety about a possible revolution in Mexico which, he feared, might frighten away American capital. He wrote to Juárez that it was impossible to express the difficulty of convincing Americans that Mexico had actually entered upon the road of modern progress, and in February 1870 he urged prompt approval of the concession as material proof of the nation's genuine interest in public works.[20]

Lacking concrete terms at first to present to his prospective backers, Rosecrans had to rely on his facile pen. His memorial to the United States Congress described the bountiful and varied riches of Mexico, hitherto little developed by her scattered population, five-eighths Indian. Before Mexico could exploit her riches, he added, she must have railroads and an adequate currency, and whoever supplied these would profit thereby, for "the trade and commerce of eight millions of people, formerly in other hands, is a business prize worthy [of] national attention, especially when it is considered that their imports . . . might be readily doubled in ten years." Specifically he asked Congress for authority to organize a "Banco nacional de México" and a "Compañía del ferrocarril nacional de México." Declarations of organization and subscription as well as regular reports were to be filed with the secretary of state—apparently only for publicity purposes, since he requested no subsidy.

Rosecrans' appeals to the investing public were couched in similar terms. An open letter to the people of the United States

[20] *El General W. S. Rosecrans y el ferrocarril de Tuxpan al Pacífico* (México, 1870), pp. 11-12, 14-17.

described British economic interests in Mexico and Central America, advocated more governmental support for American investments, and called Daniel Webster from his grave to witness that our most serious border problem lay to the south, where a suffering sister republic awaited the outstretched hand of friendship. Similar letters must have gone out to many acquaintances and others aware of his Civil War reputation, for he later reprinted page after page of well-wishing replies from William H. Seward, Salmon P. Chase, Caleb Cushing, John Jacob Astor, W. H. Aspinwall, Robert Schenck, Rutherford B. Hayes, and other notables.[21]

However flattering might be the autographs of these political and financial titans, they did not promise much material aid. In the end Rosecrans found his principal support in the person of a Colorado railroadman, as yet comparatively unknown—General William J. Palmer, creator of the Denver and Rio Grande Railroad. During the Civil War, Palmer had served as colonel under Rosecrans at Murfreesboro and Chickamauga. After the war he became an engineer for the Kansas Pacific Railroad, and in 1867 he was sent out to survey possible routes to the Pacific. His report of this expedition, published in the following year, contained a long panegyric about potential profits in New Mexico and Chihuahua; and he began to trace mental blueprints of a direct line from Denver to Mexico City by way of El Paso. Unable to carry out these elaborate plans within the Kansas Pacific organization, he broke away and founded his own company in 1870 and 1871 with British and Dutch capital. Construction was expected to be so difficult in the central Rockies that for the sake of speed and economy he and his directors adopted a narrow gauge of three feet instead of the accepted Eastern standard, 4 feet 8½ inches.

As Rosecrans later told General Ramón Corona, he spent nearly all of 1871 in canvassing railroad promoters without

[21] *Ibid.*, pp. 26–28; *El General Rosecrans, la "Doctrina Monroe," el "destino manifesto,"* pp. 8–9, 16–33.

receiving anything more substantial than good wishes. Finally
J. Edgar Thomson, president of the Pennsylvania Railroad,
directed him to General Palmer, his close friend and protégé.
On Thanksgiving Day, Palmer and Rosecrans met in Denver for
"satisfactory discussions," at the end of which Palmer promised
financial support if certain conditions were met. At once Rosecrans sent off an enthusiastic telegram and a letter to President
Juárez. In these he promised to complete the railroad "probably within four years" if Juárez would omit the formal
requirement of depositing a bond (*fianza*) with the Mexican
government and extend the time limits of the 1870 concession.
Palmer also desired greater freedom in choosing the Pacific
terminus of the line and in locating north-south branches, and
it was clear that the original interoceanic route was secondary
in his mind to a line connecting El Paso and Mexico City, which
the original concession had not mentioned at all (see Map 2).

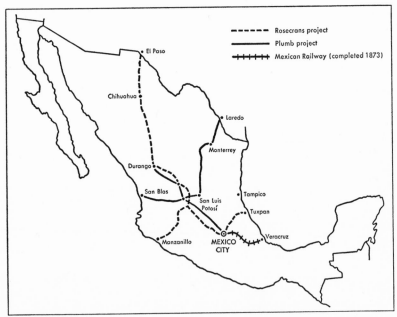

Map 2. The Rosecrans and Plumb railroad projects about 1872

As yet, nothing was said about the gauge of the railroad or the illusory land grant.[22]

Apparently without waiting for a reply from Mexico, Rosecrans signed a contract with Palmer, William A. Bell of London, and the Union Contract Company of Philadelphia, the construction company for the main line of the Denver and Rio Grande Railroad. By this contract Palmer and his powerful friends in the Pennsylvania Railroad system agreed to furnish funds for a reconnoitering expedition to Mexico. If business prospects and topography seemed favorable and if the Mexican government agreed to the necessary terms by the end of 1872, the Union Contract Company would undertake to construct a railroad system with Rosecrans in general supervision.[23] In Mexico, Juárez approved Rosecrans' actions, and on December 28 the Mexican Congress formally transferred the Richards-Smith-Brennan concession to the general. The Mexican president explained that he did not have the power to modify the terms of the concession without the prior approval of Congress, but he promised to "support all modifications not injurious to the interests of Mexico." [24]

During March and April 1872 General Palmer traveled in person down the west coast to the Mexican front, while another

[22] John S. Fisher, *A Builder of the West: The Life of General William Jackson Palmer* (Caldwell, Idaho, 1939), *passim; Ferrocarriles: Carta del General W. S. Rosecranz [sic] al General Ramón Corona y contestación de este señor* (México, 1872), pp. 8–9; Rosecrans to Juárez, Denver, Dec. 3, 1871, Mexico City, May 1872, Interoceanic Company Papers.

[23] Among the members of the Union Contract Company, Rosecrans listed J. Edgar Thomson, Thomas A. Scott, Samuel M. Felton, Mathew Baird, and others (Frank A. Knapp, Jr., "Precursors of American Investment in Mexican Railroads," *Pacific Historical Review*, XXI [Feb. 1952], 56–57).

[24] México, *Legislación sobre ferrocarriles*, II, 86. The correspondence with Juárez is mentioned in a letter of Rosecrans, April 28, 1873, in *Diario oficial*, April 29, 1873, p. 3, and also in various letters in the Interoceanic Company Papers.

party of Coloradoans went overland to examine the probable railroad route. Landing at Manzanillo, Palmer had to endure the grueling coach ride to Mexico City and could observe at first hand Mexico's need for railroads. He arrived in Mexico at a delicate moment: the Juárez government was still engaged in restoring order after Díaz' abortive revolution of La Noria, and the administration's precarious control of Congress was further threatened by angry debates over Matías Romero's newly introduced bills to reform the tariff and tax systems. Several times rebels and bandits threatened the safety of the Colorado engineers, and while exploring a possible railroad route between Toluca and Morelia, Palmer himself was grazed by a bullet. These experiences, however, did not diminish his enthusiasm, and he left Mexico in good spirits, although a little doubtful of Rosecrans' influence over the Mexican government.[25]

Rosecrans might well have shared Palmer's misgivings, for the Colorado railroadman had extended his list of necessary modifications as a result of the preliminary surveys. For one thing, the engineers quickly discovered the virtual nonexistence of public lands in central Mexico, and their journey through the sparsely populated North made them wonder whether the railroad could develop any profitable local traffic. In May, Rosecrans wrote to Juárez that it was up to the government to make up for the lack of lands with bonds, franchises, and exemptions —"solemn, abundant, and spontaneous manifestations of National, State, Municipal & individual aid and good will, affording guarantees that the work is the favorite child of the whole Mexican people." Specifically, he wanted a regular subsidy per kilometer, payable in cash or bonds. Rosecrans still did not mention gauges in his letter, but it is clear from other writings of this period that Palmer had committed him to a narrow gauge of .914 kilometers, similar to that of the Denver and Rio Grande

[25] Fisher, *Builder of the West*, pp. 217–222; Nelson to Fish, Mexico City, May 1, 1872, no. 563, State Dept., Despatches, Mexico, XLV.

Railroad, which had not been specified in the original concession.[26]

To make matters worse, Rosecrans' path was now barred by a number of rival promoters, each with his supporters in the Congress which must approve the general's proposed modifications. The Mexican Railway had not yet given up hope of extending its lines beyond Mexico City or of monopolizing the Gulf of Mexico trade. Robert B. Gorsuch, an American, was working for an international line. Edmund Stephenson was active once again. René Masson, a French journalist, had received concessions extending from Veracruz to Acapulco. Simon Stevens was beseeching government support for a railroad or canal in faraway Tehuantepec. More serious to Rosecrans than any of these, was the competition of Edward Lee Plumb, whose activities will be discussed in the next chapter. For the present it is enough to say that Plumb represented the International Railroad of Texas and proposed to construct an international line somewhat east of Palmer's, running from Laredo, Texas, to San Blas on the Mexican Pacific coast, with branches to Mexico City and Durango. Plumb had been in and out of Mexico for nearly twenty years, and since he had many friends in the Mexican government, he was in a position to offer strong opposition. He brought his project to Mexico in September 1871, and although he did not make formal overtures to the government until about a year later, his presence in Mexico City must have considerably alarmed Rosecrans.

III

When Rosecrans encountered any obstacle to his plans, his automatic reaction was to write to a newspaper or publish a

[26] Rosecrans to Juárez, Mexico City, May 1872, Interoceanic Company Papers; [Anthony Richards], *México necesita atraerse el capital extranjero para construir sus ferrocarriles y los medios que para conseguirlo propone el General William S. Rosecrans* (México, 1872), pp. 16 ff., 46–47.

pamphlet in which letters from his numerous correspondents
might bolster his optimism and confound his opponents. He
and his agents, especially Richards, put forth voluminous propaganda from 1870 to 1873. In Mexico the principal aim of this
propaganda was to persuade the government to revise the terms
of the 1870 concession along the lines which Palmer had indicated. Rosecrans and Richards began with the premise that no
nation can develop commercially or intellectually without good
communications between its center and its frontiers. Rome had
built her highways; the Lombard cities and the Hanseatic League
had explored their sea lanes; Mexico must construct railroads. A
network of railroad lines, they prophesied, would not only
stimulate industry, mining, agriculture, and foreign and domestic trade, but would also make possible the suppression of banditry and the civil warfare which had always weakened the
nation. As Rosecrans put it in a letter, "The sweetest hymn sung
and the most grateful to Mexico's ears will be the whistle of the
locomotives . . . which will say to her people: Peace, Abun-
dance, Prosperity and Glory!" [27]

It was unfortunate, as one pamphlet pointed out, that the great
European capital surpluses were already tied up in overseas
speculation, and, therefore, Mexico must turn to the United
States. But how could she hope to attract investments from New
York, Philadelphia, and Boston in competition with her neighbors of Central and South America after a civil war which had
destroyed virtually all faith in her national credit? Obviously
the Mexican government must convince the Americans not only
that their investments would be as safe in Mexico as at home,
but also that they would bring greater returns south of the border. Rosecrans and Richards pointed out that Mexico enjoyed
certain unrealized advantages: a reputation for inexhaustible
natural richness, a geographical location athwart the most direct

[27] Letter of Rosecrans, Mexico City, May 14, 1872, in *El federalista*,
May 16, 1872, p. 3. See also *El General W. S. Rosecrans y el ferrocarril*,
pp. 3–7, 20–25.

ocean trade route between Europe and the Far East, and a population of over eight million diligent, hospitable, and intelligent people. The national government might capitalize these advantages by proclaiming to the world and especially to the United States its sincere desire to support any projects which would develop the national wealth. Specifically the pamphleteers urged both Federal and State governments to pass general laws standardizing railroad concessions.

Even before the formulation of a general policy, they continued, the Mexican government could show its true colors to foreign investors by granting a cash subsidy to the Rosecrans railroad project. Other countries had set the example of official subsidies: Australia had promised one company 97,000 acres of land per mile of construction; the United States had granted a total of 228,171,929 acres of land; Great Britain had guaranteed $2,000,000 for a system of narrow-gauge lines in India; and the governments of Chile, Peru, Argentina, Brazil, Japan, and Egypt had all subsidized their railroads. These astonishing sacrifices, said Richards, indicated a sincere realization that Progress is the law of Nature. Since Mexico did not boast sufficient public lands to follow the example of Australia and the United States, the American backers were asking a subsidy of 10,000 pesos per kilometer in 6 per cent bonds for the main east-west line, to be issued only after the completion of the section to which they pertained. Estimating that the initial line from Mexico City to the Pacific would be 900 kilometers long, he calculated the total issue of bonds at 9,000,000 pesos, yielding interest of 360,000 pesos a year. This last amount the Mexican government could easily afford, and by the time the principal fell due, the increased trade and prosperity brought by the railroad would have filled the treasury.

Rosecrans and his cohorts devoted special attention to the advantages of narrow-gauge railroads—a point of great importance, since the nearly completed Mexican Railway used the standard gauge of 1.435 meters (4 feet 8½ inches), and Plumb was promising to make no changes. At great length Rosecrans argued that the narrow-gauge track would be much cheaper to lay and maintain and that its use would not greatly inconvenience Mexico. The initial cost of construction would be 30 per cent less than that of a standard-gauge line; thus the United States, with 62,000 miles of standard-gauge track, had squandered fully $818,400,000 through lack of foresight, and the American people were paying $172,800,000 too much each year in passenger and freight charges. In operating her modest 900-kilometer line to the Pacific, Mexico might hope to save 2,067,000 pesos a year by adopting the narrow gauge. Santiago Méndez, a Mexican engineer who supported Rosecrans, described in detail the success of the midget Festiniog Railway in Wales, which ran over rough country similar to that of western Mexico.[28]

Both in Mexico and in the United States, Rosecrans proclaimed that his railroad would inaugurate a new era of greater prosperity and friendlier relations than ever before. He assured suspicious Mexican nationalists that since 1848 the United States had felt only sympathy toward her neighbor and hinted broadly that since the North had won the Civil War its politicians had no intention of annexing any territory that might strengthen the South. An open letter from Rosecrans to the American people suggested a more liberal interpretation for two old shibboleths of our Latin American policy. The Monroe Doctrine ought to promote brotherliness in the Western Hemisphere, until "the citizens of all [its nations] can move freely from one country to another, with as much liberty as if they were traveling through the States of their own country." Similarly, under the inspiration of "manifest destiny" Americans ought to "spread through the whole Western Continent . . . the influence of light, order, industry, and civilization, mixing these elements with those which already exist in the various sections, and leaving their inhabitants . . . in complete liberty

[28] *El General W. S. Rosecrans y el ferrocarril*, pp. 7, 11–12; [Richards], *México necesita atraerse el capital*, pp. 4–7, 10, 14–20, 37–41.

to choose the methods of government which suit them best." [29]

The airy propaganda of Rosecrans and his agents, together with congressional debates on the 1870 concession and the proposed modifications, plunged Mexico into a controversy about railroads in general, American railroad promoters, and the Rosecrans project in particular. Enthusiastically, suspiciously, scornfully, fearfully, journalists dipped pen in ink to attack or defend, and *la cuestión del ferrocarril* became a major issue of the Juárez and Lerdo administrations.

A Mexican article of faith after 1867 was the veneration of *mejoras materiales*—machinery, public works, and industrial establishments, which had made England and the United States powerful and the lack of which had prostrated Mexico before the French. Consequently nearly all writers admitted the pressing need for railroads. As Julio Zarate wrote in *El siglo diez y nueve* in 1872, "*Mejoras materiales* are destined to change the face of the nation. . . . It is an absolute duty to contribute to the realization of all those projects which will bring national greatness." The Mexican Railway would soon effect an economic and social revolution in eastern Mexico; why not spread its benefits to other parts of the country? Furthermore, the completion of this pioneer railroad would soon throw thousands on the labor market; a new railroad would provide work for them and reassure businessmen that the economic future of the country was secure. Another writer predicted an annual increase of $214,000,000 in the national income.[30]

Granted the need for a second railroad, many accepted Rosecrans' statement that Americans must build it. Some, like Emilio Velasco, felt that the United States already possessed enough

[29] *El General W. S. Rosecrans y el ferrocarril*, pp. 7–9; *El General Rosecrans, la "Doctrina Monroe," el "destino manifesto,"* pp. 10–11. See also Rosecrans' statement against filibusters, printed in *El siglo diez y nueve*, March 2, 1872, p. 3.

[30] Julio Zarate, "Mejoras materiales," *El siglo diez y nueve*, March 7, 1872, p. 1; "La cuestión de actualidad," broadside distributed with *ibid.*, Oct. 29, 1872. See also a supplement for Nov. 4, 1872.

power to force her will upon Mexico, although the friendly
Grant administration showed no disposition to do so. For a time
Mexico might close the door to American enterprise, but the
Americans, expansionists by nature, would eventually burst
through all feeble Mexican barriers and might then assuage their
wrath with Mexican territory. Mexican policy should "furnish
a vast field for American activity, so that the expansive force of
that people will show itself in industry and commerce, not in
the acquisition of territory. . . . The greater the interests
which United States citizens have in Mexico, the greater guarantees we shall have of our own independence." Until these
American interests could develop, however, Mexico must take
care to prevent the establishment of shaky or dishonest enterprises whose collapse might embitter her powerful neighbor.[31]

Keeping in mind this precaution, some Mexican writers
scrutinized the Rosecrans project and found it good. According to an unsigned article in the *Diario oficial* during 1870, Rosecrans was considered unanimously "as an honorable man and a
practical and intelligent engineer." Others pointed with awe at
the illustrious names which graced the board of directors of the
Union Contract Company. An article in *El demócrata* remarked that in contrast Plumb's International Railroad of Texas
was less soundly organized and was affiliated with annexationists.[32] Other writers defended the proposed cash subsidy and
the narrow gauge in terms similar to the Rosecrans pamphlets.

It is important to note that these and other opinions appeared
not only in the minor newspapers around the fringe of Mexican
politics, but also in the powerful *Siglo diez y nueve* and in the
Diario oficial, the voice of the government itself. Letters of en-

[31] Emilio Velasco, "Empresas americanas en México," *ibid.*, Feb. 14,
1872, p. 1.

[32] *Diario oficial*, April 12, 1870, p. 2: "La cuestión de actualidad,"
passim. The article in *El demócrata* is quoted in México, *Diario de los
debates: Sexto congreso constitucional de la Unión* (México, 1873), III,
511–513.

couragement from Juárez, Lerdo, and Romero have already been cited. Congress was expected to be compliant, for when the deputies approved the 1870 concession, they had filed out of the chamber, embraced the waiting Richards, and told him to inform his chief "that if at any time you wish any addition, ammendments [*sic*] or further concessions, that they are willing & will grant whatever you desire of them." [33]

Thus Rosecrans can hardly be blamed for anticipating a short campaign and eventual victory. As at Chickamauga, however, appearances were deceptive. The scattered opposition of 1870 and 1871 grew and coalesced, especially as it became obvious that the enthusiasm of some government officials had cooled. Hostile letters began to appear more and more frequently in nominally friendly newspapers. Then the editorial policy of the papers shifted, and when Rosecrans resigned in 1873, very few writers were giving him any but the most heavily qualified support.

In general Rosecrans' opponents argued against him on two fundamental grounds: that as an American he intended to compromise Mexican sovereignty and that as a businessman he drove too hard a bargain. When Rosecrans was appointed minister in 1868, the jingoistic New York *Herald* and even several moderate American newspapers had alarmed Mexicans by urging him to establish an American protectorate over Mexico. Just as Seward's stand against Maximilian and his friendly visit to Mexico in 1869 had failed to allay all suspicions of his motives, so also Rosecrans' peaceable behavior as minister left behind a residue of mistrust. Some deputies opposed the original land-grant concession of 1870 on the ground that Americans would use the inevitable disputes over land titles as an excuse for armed intervention. Late in 1872 a deputy inquired why Palmer and Rosecrans had begun an informal survey of the proposed route with-

[33] Richards to Rosecrans, Mexico City, Dec. 10, 1870, Interoceanic Company Papers.

out informing the government and suggested that they might be preparing maps for the American army.[34]

Most congressmen and journalists accepted Rosecrans' project as a business proposition rather than as the advance guard of military aggression, but some questioned the solidity of his backing in the United States. Suspicion of this sort was only natural after the scandalous collapse of General John C. Frémont's fraudulent Memphis, El Paso, and Pacific Railroad in 1870 and the revelations concerning the Crédit Mobilier and other disgraces of the Grant period which were beginning to appear in American newspapers during 1872 and 1873. In the latter year the old war horse of the Reform, Guillermo Prieto, declared in a series of editorials that his original enthusiasm for the Rosecrans project had turned to disgust when he saw the general resort to the same advertising methods as those used for the promotion of Holloway ointment or Jacks bitters. It made him think of the frauds of John Law in France. Prieto also warned that the railroad might benefit the United States more than Mexico. Instead of watering the thirsty Mexican soil, he said, the Union Contract Company may build "an aqueduct to lead the water over our heads without letting a single drop fall to our lips." Exploitation, not invasion, was his bête noire.[35]

Others objected vociferously to nearly all the proposed terms of the concession. Manuel Payno, who had fiercely attacked the Mexican Railway in 1868, opposed the subsidy and challenged Rosecrans to produce evidence that Britain had ever granted money for this purpose. Emilio Velasco agreed that the need for railroads north and west of Mexico City justified a subsidy, but he felt that none should be granted for a line northeast to Tuxpan, as that would compete with the Mexican Railway and was,

[34] Francisco G. Cosmes, *Historia general de Méjico: Continuación a la de Don Niceto de Zamacois* (4 vols., numbered XIX–XXIII; Barcelona and México, 1901–1903), XX, 353–363; México, *Diario de los debates: Quinto congreso*, I, 296, *Sexto congreso*, III, 472.

[35] *El siglo diez y nueve*, June 27, 28, 29, 1873, pp. 1–2.

therefore, less necessary.[36] To judge from the volume of editorials on the subject, the most objectionable feature of Rosecrans' project was the narrow gauge. Payno was willing to concede that narrow-gauge construction might cost 45 per cent less than that of standard gauge, but Vicente Manero predicted that the saving would be counterbalanced by endless inconveniences: the difficulty of adapting the line to new inventions, the virtual impossibility of using mule teams for animal power, and the necessity of frequently renewing the light ballast.[37]

Although Rosecrans prided himself on his diplomacy and knowledge of the Mexican temperament, it is evident that he antagonized some journalists by his very obvious impatience to secure the necessary modifications and begin work. Just before the project collapsed, Espiridión Carreón remarked that his company was evidently determined to secure legality at all costs, "now insisting that the President pass upon details which are not in his power, now appealing to the legislative body . . . [for] decisions which depend on the President, now drilling into the Law in search of absurd theories which will hide the infractions that it has committed, or perhaps taking up the sententious and decisive style of a superior who believes himself infallible." Carreón denied that the 1870 contract allowed Rosecrans the free choice of gauge. He and others repeatedly reminded Rosecrans that until he paid a bond of 200,000 pesos to the government his contract was not valid, no matter how much time and money he spent surveying the proposed route meanwhile.[38] Thus the opposition press editorialized, and skilled Mexican cartoonists pilloried the plump, bustling figure of the

[36] *Ibid.*, June 6, 10, Dec. 19, 1872.

[37] *Ibid.*, Dec. 19, 1872, p. 1; Vicente E. Manero, *Apuntes históricos sobre ferrocarriles con alguna observaciones que presenta a sus conciudadanos el Ingeniero Vicente E. Manero* (México, 1872), pp. 15–17. A convenient modern summary of Mexican arguments about the narrow gauge and the probable cost of the project is in Cosío Villegas, *Historia moderna de México*, II, 718–725.

[38] *El siglo diez y nueve*, May 13, 19, 26, June 10, 1873, p. 1.

American general, with his long nose, his little eyes, and his sly
ingratiating smile.[39]

IV

It is difficult to fix the exact moment at which Rosecrans
passed over the crest of his popularity in Mexico and began the
long descent. Certainly in the spring of 1872 he cherished the
most optimistic hopes. When General Palmer returned to the
United States in May, leaving behind a corps of engineers to
continue preliminary surveying work, he secured promises for
sufficient capital to construct the first three hundred kilometers,
even without a Mexican subsidy. During the spring Juárez had
once more promised aid to Rosecrans.

Consequently in April he allowed Anthony Richards to petition Congress formally for the necessary modifications in the
1870 concession. The petition requested a cash subsidy instead
of the impractical land grant, listed about ten interior cities to
which branches might be built, and sought permission to extend
one or more of these branch lines to the American border. It
also specified a narrow gauge and suggested cash subsidies of
10,000 pesos per kilometer for the original east-west line and
5,000 per kilometer for the branches, but it stipulated that any
extension to the border would be unsubsidized. During the next
six weeks the general pressed both Lerdo and Blas Balcárcel, secretary of *fomento,* (development) to support his petition.[40]
Rosecrans sent out similar letters to congressmen and governors
of the states through which he expected his railroad to pass,
warning them that if Congress failed to act promptly the whole

[39] One cartoon showed Rosecrans displaying to officials a model
locomotive with pesos for wheels: "Notice, gentlemen, the advantages
offered by the narrow gauge. —It is true, General, that one sight of your
rolling stock will convince *anyone* that your enterprise is the best"
(*El padre Cobos,* May 14, 1873).

[40] *Ferrocarriles: Carta del General Rosecranz* [*sic*], pp. 10–11; *Diario
oficial,* April 29, 1873, p. 3; México, *Diario de los debates: Sexto congreso,*
II, 274.

project might be indefinitely delayed. As his rival, Plumb, suspected, Rosecrans hoped by "a sudden coup" to commit Congress to support his plan.[41]

Although Plumb began at once to lobby among the deputies against the proposed modifications, Gabriel Mancera and others put up a good fight for them in Congress. At the time the administration's majority was extremely slender, and the spring session ended without any action; but the permanent deputation continued to discuss the question, and on July 4 its committee on industry submitted a report on the project which was as favorable as if Rosecrans himself had written it. The committee recited the benefits which Mexico might expect to receive from railroads and recommended that 700,000 pesos be set aside annually for the project.[42] This report aroused some interest, and Rosecrans scurried to and fro, scratching off letters and articles, pushing the preliminary surveys, and preparing for a final drive in September.[43]

On July 18 came a sudden break in his fortunes. President Juárez, already ailing, suffered a heart attack and died, and while newspapers eulogized the fallen hero, Sebastián Lerdo de Tejada, legal successor to the presidency, quietly took office. Since Lerdo had already supported Rosecrans' project in cordial terms, there is no reason to believe that his accession set back the general's hopes, but the wily politician had also encouraged Plumb, who now decided that the time was ripe for

[41] Copies of Rosecrans' letters of this period are in the Interoceanic Company Papers. See also Edward Lee Plumb to John Sanford Barnes, Mexico City, April 26, May 29, 1872, nos. 89, 97, Papers of Edward Lee Plumb, IX, Division of Manuscripts, Library of Congress (hereafter cited as Plumb Papers).

[42] México, *Ferrocarriles en México: Dictamen de la comisión de industria de la diputación permanente sobre las modificaciones pedidas al decreto de 10 de diciembre de 1870 relativo a la concesión de un ferrocarril de golfo al Pacífico* (México, 1872), *passim*. See also Cosío Villegas, *Historia moderna de México*, II, 715–716.

[43] Plumb to Barnes, Mexico City, July 29, 1872, no. 121, Plumb Papers, IX.

positive action in behalf of his own project. On August 17 Plumb inserted in the *Two Republics* a preliminary announcement that the International Railroad of Texas intended to apply for a railroad concession to the Rio Grande.

This unwelcome news spoiled Rosecrans' timing and stung him into tactlessness. On the same day as the announcement he wrote Plumb a blunt note demanding to know whether his action was bona fide and whether his company was informed of Rosecrans' prior concession. Well aware of the general's unconsolidated position, Plumb calmly answered in the affirmative. A few days later Rosecrans dispatched a longer note to Minister of *Fomento* Balcárcel—less peremptory in tone but still too insistent for the Mexican taste—in which he reminded the minister of the efforts which he had made, "using my time and my money, sacrificing my health and even my personal security," and all to promote Mexican interests on the strength of the friendship of the Juárez government. He asked Balcárcel to point out to Lerdo that Juárez had not kept his promise to recommend the amendment of the Tuxpan concession at the opening of the spring session of Congress, but that, nevertheless, Palmer and his American allies were prepared to advance enough money to construct three hundred kilometers of railroad. Balcárcel replied urbanely that Juárez had indeed submitted the concession to Congress on May 16 and that after the end of the session the committee on industry had submitted a report.[44]

In September, Plumb petitioned the Mexican government for a standard-gauge concession with a subsidy of 9,500 pesos per kilometer and published a pamphlet describing in detail his project and his company. Plumb's petition produced renewed activity in the Rosecrans camp—another ill-considered protest to Balcárcel, reminding him of Juárez' promises and the 40,000

[44] Rosecrans to Plumb, Mexico City, Aug. 17, 1872, Plumb to Rosecrans, Aug. 19, 1872, *ibid.*; Rosecrans to Balcárcel, Mexico City, Aug 20, 1872, Balcárcel to Rosecrans, Mexico City, Aug. 24, 1872 (English translation), Interoceanic Company Papers.

pesos which Palmer had spent on preliminary surveys. Balcárcel replied with some asperity that Rosecrans' concession was
not exclusive, that in any case he would forfeit it unless he paid
the required bond by December 17, and that the government
would not recognize any surveys made without officially appointed experts. Rosecrans apparently realized his misstep, for
his next letter was more conciliatory, but the damage was
done.[45]

As the deputies gathered for the autumn session of Congress,
both adversaries girded themselves for the "battle of the gauges,"
as it came to be called. Rosecrans, who possessed an ampler supply of funds, sent out agents to procure favorable resolutions
from the state legislatures, got up popular petitions, and kept a
corps of writers to supply "filler" for every newspaper that
would print it. After Congress convened, he caused copies of
his supporting newspapers to be circulated every day in the
meeting hall. Plumb accused the Rosecrans group of forging
signatures on the petitions, and he suspected that many of the
state resolutions were bogus.[46]

Since some congressmen still feared that the Union Contract
Company was a mere paper organization, Rosecrans obtained
from Palmer a list of 154 subscribers, whose total capital assets exceeded $40,000,000, and a guarantee of funds for the bond from
Duncan Sherman and Company, a leading New York banking
house. On October 21 a telegram arrived from Thomas A. Scott,
G. M. Pullman, and others promising money for immediate construction costs. Rosecrans circulated this telegram in such a
manner as to make it appear that the American consul general,
Julius A. Skilton, and the secretary of legation, Porter C. Bliss,

[45] Most of this correspondence was published in *El siglo diez y nueve*,
Oct. 22, 1872, pp. 2–3. Two unpublished letters, one from Rosecrans
dated Oct. 16 and another from Balcárcel dated Oct. 18, are in the
Interoceanic Company Papers.

[46] Plumb to D. P. Barhydt, Mexico City, Feb. 14, 1873, no. 215, Plumb
Papers, XI.

had vouched for the resources of these men and of the Union Contract Company.[47]

After a talk with Lerdo in mid-October, Rosecrans was confident that he would push through the new concession,[48] but, nevertheless, for over two months the railroad question raged in the Mexican Congress. On October 3 the first committee on industries delivered another favorable report on the Rosecrans project, but the appearance of the Plumb petition prevented acceptance of this report. In succeeding debates the Rosecrans supporters argued that subsidies for their project would cost the government 3,000,000 pesos less than for the Plumb line. (Rosecrans had whittled his subsidy down to 8,000 pesos a kilometer.) They played up his promise to complete his railroad to the Pacific in four years, since Plumb was vague on this point, and proved that the general's higher freight rates would be offset by a rebate of 30 per cent on Mexican products. Furthermore, added his supporters, although both promoters represented American concerns, the International Company was the creature of land-hungry Texans.

On their side, the Plumb supporters protested that Rosecrans' railroad would run into sparsely populated Colorado instead of leading directly toward the Mississippi Valley and the Northeast. Others rang the familiar changes on the narrow gauge and accused Rosecrans of fraud for not paying his bond before requesting new terms. All in all, as one deputy remarked, the debates brought out every kind of "heated expression, pompous phrases, high-sounding terms, poetic style, and exaggerated declamation" without settling the matter in the slightest, for at the end of the session the exasperated deputies simply authorized the

[47] Rosecrans to Balcárcel, Mexico City, Nov. 14, 1872, J. Edgar Thomson, S. M. Felton, and L. W. Meyer to Porter C. Bliss, Nov. 19, [1872], Interoceanic Company Papers; *El siglo diez y nueve*, Oct. 28, 1872, p. 3; Plumb to Barhydt, Oct. 22, 1872, no. 156, Plumb Papers, X.

[48] Rosecrans to Gabriel Mancera, Mexico City, Oct. 15, 1872, Interoceanic Company Papers.

president to negotiate new terms subject to congressional approval. Meanwhile, the old time limit for the payment of the bond remained.[49]

Observing the congressional deadlock from a distance, General Palmer decided to go to Mexico and talk to Lerdo himself. Consul General Skilton met Palmer at Orizaba on the recently inaugurated Mexican Railway and informed him that the government had not even accepted a bond, "that Lerdo was against us, [and] that a number of people surrounding him wanted to be bought off." A personal report by Rosecrans further depressed Palmer, and on January 2 he wrote: "The General as usual has been constantly led on by his hopes. Evidently we should have had someone here all along. If the good old Indian, Juárez, were still here it would no doubt be very different." [50]

During the next few weeks Palmer pulled every wire in Mexico City that he could reach. Seeing that Rosecrans had tried to join forces with a local project for a narrow-gauge railroad from Mexico City to Toluca and Cuautitlán, he visited the president of that company, Mariano Riva Palacio, a powerful figure in the state of Mexico. He talked to Lerdo, whom he found friendly but noncommittal. He even rubbed shoulders with the rebel forces of Porfirio Díaz, then plotting to overthrow Lerdo as he had plotted against Juárez. None of these wires ever led anywhere, but the very activity seemed to reassure Palmer, and he returned home in February, giving Rosecrans another chance in the next session of Congress.[51]

Left to his own devices, Rosecrans once again resorted to pen and ink. During succeeding months he delivered a barrage of

[49] México, *Diario de los debates: Sexto congreso,* III, 111–120, 262–267, 304–305, 393–394, 470–476, 500–506, 507, 544–556, 622, *et passim.* For the final resolution see pp. 768–769.

[50] Fisher, *Builder of the West,* p. 223.

[51] Plumb to Barnes, Mexico City, Dec. 28, 1872, no. 190, Plumb Papers, XI; Fisher, *Builder of the West,* pp. 223–225.

protests and arguments to local newspapers and engaged the minister of *fomento*, Blas Balcárcel, in a spectacularly futile artillery duel over the problem of the overdue bond. The government insisted on the complicated provisions of the original contract: Rosecrans must name Mexican guarantors who could be easily held for the bond if the company failed to fulfill its obligations. Rosecrans offered a loan of 200,000 pesos instead and finally, with many sighs, set out to obtain the required guarantors, long after the passage of the deadline. Even then Balcárcel refused to accept Rosecrans' appraisals of the guarantors' landed property and placed numerous other petty obstacles in his way.

Meanwhile the government tried to persuade Rosecrans and Plumb to pool their resources in one project for the good of Mexico. On February 13 Balcárcel, Plumb, and a representative of the Mexican Railway confronted the general with their plan. Taken by surprise, Rosecrans marked time for over an hour in rambling, halting Spanish, until finally his lawyer rescued him by suggesting that the whole plan be communicated in writing. Being more at home with a pen in his hand, Rosecrans successfully stalled off the proposed merger in subsequent letters, probably because the joint line would logically have retained the standard gauge, which Palmer absolutely refused to consider.[52]

Whether Rosecrans realized it, in the spring of 1873 his sands were rapidly running out. When Congress convened again in April, he submitted a new petition, reciting the old arguments about gauge, subsidy, and bond, and at the end of the month

[52] Correspondence of Rosecrans and Palmer with Balcárcel may be found in two pamphlets, *Actual estado del asunto del ferrocarril interoceánico* (México, 1873) and *El ferrocarril interoceánico: Ultimas comunicaciones cambiadas entre el señor ministro de fomento y el concesionario* (México, 1873), and also in *Diario oficial*, May 20, 1873, pp. 2–3, and June 1, p. 2. For an account by Plumb of the meeting of Feb. 13 see Plumb to Barhydt, Mexico City, Feb. 14, 1873, no. 218, Plumb Papers, XI.

he won a last small triumph in the customary favorable report by the first committee on industry.[53] The continued impasse on the floor of the Chamber of Deputies, however, again attracted Palmer's attention in the United States, and on April 24 he arrived at Veracruz with blood in his eye. Finding, as he had anticipated, that Rosecrans had completely alienated the government, he confronted his old commander and took him to task for mismanagement and tactlessness. There was a stormy interview between the two men, and Rosecrans offered to resign. Palmer accepted his offer at once and took charge of the project himself, still hoping to save the day. On May 15 Rosecrans, once again relieved from command, stepped on board the train for Veracruz. United States Minister Nelson considerately saw him off at the station, but neither Palmer nor any of Rosecrans' Mexican ex-allies was there to take leave of him.[54]

After landing at New Orleans, Rosecrans traveled about the United States for a while, making disgruntled and indiscreet pronouncements about American capital and influence in Mexico, and finally returned to his home in California.[55] For some years he retained his interest in American-Mexican economic contacts and in 1878 did a little surveying for the Sonora Railway between Guaymas and the border, but although he admired the Díaz administration, he did not attempt any further promotion work.

In 1880 he finally entered politics as a Democratic representa-

[53] México, *Dictamen que la comisión primera de industria presenta al congreso de la Unión sobre la reciente solicitud del cesionario de la concesión otorgada el 10 de diciembre de 1870 para el establecimiento de un ferrocarril interoceánico* (México, 1873), *passim.*

[54] Fisher, *Builder of the West, pp.* 230–231; Plumb to Hunter, Mexico City, May 16, 1873, Plumb Collection.

[55] According to dispatches received in Mexico, Rosecrans told journalists in New Orleans "that all distinguished classes of Mexican society . . . would gladly accept the protection of the United States, as the best means of securing peace and security there . . . [and] that the conquest of Mexico would be the easiest thing in the world" (*El siglo diez y nueve,* June 24, 1873, p. 3).

tive from California and soon became chairman of the military affairs committee in recognition of his Civil War record; but his most memorable action in Congress was an ungracious opposition to a bill for placing his old enemy, Grant, on the retired list. It was only appropriate that years later, after he had left Congress, there should be a similarly bitter argument over placing his name on the list. After a residence of eight years in Washington as registrar of the treasury under Cleveland and Harrison, Rosecrans spent his last days in the rough but easy-going ranch life of southern California, where he had foresightedly bought 14,000 acres of sagebrush and cacti immediately after the Civil War. There he died in 1898.[56]

V

After Rosecrans left Mexico City in 1873, General Palmer stayed behind to see what he could salvage from the wreckage of the project. His experiences soon made him appreciate some of the obstacles against which his agent had vainly striven, and after several weeks of lobbying he too left Mexico empty-handed. At the end of May, Lerdo granted a concession to Edward Lee Plumb for railroads to the Pacific coast and the American border, but by autumn the Panic of 1873 had dried up American sources of capital, and Palmer wrote feelingly that he was "as anxious now *not* to hear of success" as he had been before to obtain it.[57] As long as the depression lasted, no promotional ventures in Mexico could expect to make much progress.

Not until 1880 did the Palmer interests secure a satisfactory railroad concession from the Mexican government, and by that time conditions on both sides of the border had considerably changed. In Mexico, Díaz had replaced Lerdo as president, and in the United States the Atchison, Topeka, and Santa Fe Railroad had blocked Palmer's Denver and Rio Grande Railroad from access to El Paso. Consequently, under the concession of

[56] [Mulhane], *Memorial of Rosecrans*, pp. 23–31.
[57] Fisher, *Builder of the West*, pp. 231–236.

1880 Palmer agreed to construct a shorter line from Mexico City to Laredo, Texas—approximately the route which had been originally proposed by his old rival Plumb. In only one respect did Palmer hold to his original plan: the railroad was to have a narrow gauge. Construction began at both ends of the route in 1881 and continued slowly for three years, until Palmer ran out of funds. After two years of stagnation and a reorganization in 1886 work began again, and the completed line was opened to the public in 1888 (see Map 1).[58]

Thus, although the Rosecrans project survived the downfall of its creator, years passed before others carried out his plans. Why did he fail? Many groups in Mexico were unfriendly or openly opposed to his project: conservatives and anti-Juárez liberals, ultranationalists who wanted no dealings with foreigners, businessmen and politicians who were interested in rival railroad projects, and pro-European interests which feared lest the railroad bring in competitors from the north.

It was Lerdo, however, who actually canceled the Rosecrans concession, and for a fuller explanation of the general's failure this fact must be examined. Plumb guessed that Lerdo used the bond argument simply as an excuse to get rid of the project with as little public clamor as possible and that his real reason lay deeper.[59] Most Mexican historians have identified this deeper reason as anti-Americanism and have attributed to him the motto "Between strength and weakness let us preserve the desert." For example, both Francisco Cosmes and Ricardo García Granados agree that Lerdo wished to develop an interior network of railroads before building any lines to the American border and

[58] *Ibid.*, chap. xiii; Fred W. Powell, *The Railroads of Mexico* (Boston, 1921), chaps. xii–xvi; L. L. Waters, *Steel Trails to Santa Fe* (Lawrence, Kansas, 1950), chaps. iii, iv. It turned out that the critics of Palmer's narrow gauge were right after all, since the line's small-sized rolling stock proved inadequate. Shortly after 1900 the whole line was converted to standard gauge.

[59] Plumb to Barhydt, Mexico City, Feb. 14, 1873, no. 217, Plumb Papers, XI.

that he preferred to use European or Mexican capital for that purpose.[60]

In the next chapter the history of the Plumb project will be used to test this hypothesis further. For the present it is enough to say that in the most recent account of the Lerdo administration Daniel Cosío Villegas disagrees with both Plumb and the earlier Mexican historians. Rosecrans, he declares, brought his failure on himself by refusing to fulfill his obligations (especially in the matter of the bond) until the government agreed to accept his proposed changes, such as the narrow gauge.[61]

Whether Lerdo balked at American capital in general or at Rosecrans' terms in particular, the circumstances clearly demanded the tact and patience of a seasoned diplomat, and Rosecrans was no Talleyrand. The *doyen* of the State Department, old William Hunter, who had watched diplomats come and go since 1827, called him "rash and even reckless," and Plumb's correspondence is full of criticism. He thought the general's claims of narrow-gauge economies fantastic to the point of insanity and called Rosecrans' letters to newspapers "altogether too patronizing as to this people not to be offensive." When the general declared that Mexico was even more backward than Egypt in railroad building, Plumb wrote that this was the "most damaging communication (to himself) that he has yet published." [62]

Worst of all, Rosecrans tactlessly allowed himself to be identified with opposition groups in Congress, and during the last six months of his campaign he even took to attacking the government directly. In November, Anthony Richards accused Lerdo of "aiding from interested motives to defeat the Rosecrans bill

[60] Cosmes, *Historia de Méjico*, XX, 253–264, 282; Ricardo García Granados, *Historia de México desde la restauración de la república en 1867 hasta la caida de Porfirio Díaz* (México, [1912?]–1928), I, 117–118.

[61] Cosío Villegas, *Historia moderna de México*, II, 730–731.

[62] Hunter to Plumb, April 15, 1873, Plumb Collection; Plumb to Barnes, Mexico City, April 26, May 16, June 28, 1872, nos. 91, 95, 110, Plumb Papers, IX.

in Congress." Although Rosecrans soon wrote to the *Diario oficial* disavowing this statement, his attacks continued through the winter, and Plumb wrote that Balcárcel had found the general's account of the joint meeting of February 13 both inaccurate and insulting. For a while Plumb felt a grudging admiration for his rival's energy, but he soon began to worry about the growth of anti-American prejudices, and six months after the general's departure he told a friend that "the prejudice they [Rosecrans and Palmer together] have inflicted upon American interests is almost beyond calculation." [63]

Rosecrans' railroad career in Mexico, promisingly begun, seemed to end as so much sound and fury, signifying nothing. Equipped with a mental blueprint of transcontinental travel, his wartime reputation, and boundless enthusiasm, he erected an impressive edifice of concessions and letters of recommendation, only to see it fall about his ears, because his superstructure had overstrained the weak foundation. He was temperamentally the wrong man for the job, and he attempted it at the wrong time, with the United States rocking on the brink of a depression. Nonetheless, he left his mark on American-Mexican economic relations, whether for good or bad. Not only did he help to divert Mexican attention from British to American capital; his profuse and widely read propaganda created a picture of inexhaustible Mexican resources and life-giving American capital which could not be forgotten, either north or south of the border. Rosecrans' dreams were the dreams of the next generation, and his optimistic rhetoric served as a literary model for many years to come.

[63] Plumb to Barnes, Mexico City, Oct. 30, 1872, no. 164, Plumb to Barhydt, Mexico City, March 25, 1873, no. 235, Plumb to Pearsall, Mexico City, Nov. 22, 1873, no. 296, *ibid.*, X–XII.

III

Diplomat: Edward Lee Plumb

DURING the latter part of the nineteenth century the United States Foreign Service offered an easy approach to promotional activities. Many ministers and consuls, appointed from the ranks of loyal party members after a successful election, went directly from business or professional surroundings to their new posts, unimpeded by careerist scruples and well aware that the next administration would probably replace them. Often they regarded business contacts as part of the rewards of office. As officials representing a nation renowned for economic prowess, they brought with them an aura of infallibility, so that progressive native leaders sometimes entrusted important and delicate projects to an American minister whom they would not have looked at twice in his original role of small-town editor or businessman.

The last chapter related the promotional career of one ex-diplomat in Mexico. General Rosecrans, however, was not enough of a diplomat to make a good promoter. A far better example of diplomacy turned to the uses of American business was the career of his rival, Edward Lee Plumb. Plumb had several of the basic requirements of both diplomacy and promotion: patience, tact, a smooth tongue, and a fondness for personal acquaintanceships. While still in his twenties, he tried his hand at promoting a Mexican mining company, and when this disintegrated, he filled minor diplomatic posts in Mexico and Cuba between 1861 and 1869. After his resignation from the Foreign Service he became a railroad promoter and set out to capitalize his wide circle of friendships with Mexican officials. A combination of unlucky circumstances, however, delayed the realization of his railroad project until others had crowded him out of the spotlight. As a result, although he was one of the first Americans in the mid-nineteenth century to appreciate the potentialities of Mexico, he is virtually unknown today.[1]

I

Edward Lee Plumb was born on July 17, 1827, at Gowanda, New York, a small town near Buffalo. His father gave him a good business education, and after an apprenticeship in a large mercantile house in Hartford, Connecticut, he emerged at twenty-one with a reputation for integrity and a "rather remarkable business capacity for one of his age." [2] On February 22, 1849, he set out for California to seek his fortune near the gold fields. After a year or so in San Francisco, he became interested in Mexico and applied to President Millard Fillmore for a consular appointment, but in vain, for apparently no vacancy existed. Even without the desired appointment, Mexico seems to have attracted the young man more than California, for early

[1] Fortunately Plumb left behind many of the business letters which he received and drafts of the letters which he sent. These have been gathered in two collections: the Papers of Edward Lee Plumb, Division of Manuscripts, Library of Congress, Washington, D.C., and the Edward Lee Plumb Collection, Special Collections Division, Stanford University Libraries, Stanford, Calif. These are cited as Plumb Papers and Plumb Collection respectively.

[2] Ralph Plumb to N. K. Hall, Gowanda, N.Y., March 27, 1851, letter file in U.S. Bureau of Archives, Washington, D.C. This file contains further correspondence respecting Plumb's application for a consular appointment. The Plumb Papers contain a "Journal of a Voyage from New York to San Francisco around Cape Horn, 1849."

in 1854 he made an exploratory trip southward, to see what business opportunities he could uncover.

In March, Plumb landed at Acapulco to find himself in the midst of a revolution, for several weeks earlier General Juan Alvarez, the local military chieftain, had "pronounced" against Mexico's perennial dictator, Antonio López de Santa Anna. Undismayed by the confusion of a military camp, Plumb made friends with the rebel leaders and traveled about the west coast, observing mineral deposits. After several weeks he went inland to Mexico City to petition Santa Anna for a formal prospecting concession, but he shrewdly kept up his friendships in the rebel camp, so that when Alvarez' junta replaced Santa Anna, the change had no effect on Plumb's project. In the United States he managed to attract the attention of a group of Eastern businessmen, and on October 5, 1855, the Mexican Pacific Coal and Iron Mining and Land Company was incorporated in New York with a capital of $4,000,000. Unlike the *conquistadores* and most of their successors in Mexico, Plumb was more interested in iron and coal deposits than in precious metals, but he also hoped to develop other Mexican resources, such as copper, lead, cotton, coffee, cacao, tobacco, and tropical woods.[3]

One of Plumb's first concerns was to make a thorough reconnaissance of western Mexico as soon as possible and locate exploitation tracts under the terms of the concession, so as to be able to sell stock. During the dry season (winter) of 1856-1857 the young promoter led a small party of geologists and surveyors from Veracruz to Mexico City and westward to the Pacific coast through the state of Guerrero, in which Plumb hoped to

---

[3] An account of Plumb's relations with Santa Anna is contained in an unsigned and undated letter, Plumb Papers, XIV. Volume I of the Plumb Papers contains a copy of the original concession and of the company charter. See also "Stock History of the Late *Mexican Pacific Coal and Iron Mining Company*—Showing the Reasons for Basis Used in Present *Mexican Pacific Company*," undated paper in *ibid.*, V; *Preliminary Prospectus of the Mexican Pacific Coal and Iron Mining and Land Company* (New York, 1856), *passim*.

concentrate most of the company's operations. After two or three months of prospecting the group stumbled almost by accident on exactly the combination of resources which the company seemed to require: a vein of iron ore near the Pacific coast, running up to one hundred feet wide, a short road to a fine little harbor five miles away, and plenty of limestone and hardwood fuel nearby. After staking out a claim to the deposit, Plumb and his men made their way back to Mexico City to announce the claim to the Mexican government. On July 16, 1856, Plumb returned to New York City, having traveled 8,519 miles over a period of nine months.[4]

For a year or two the affairs of the young company seemed to flourish, and a prospectus, issued in 1858 and probably written by Plumb, announced confidently that the modest sum of $30,000 would suffice to keep eight Americans and one hundred Mexicans in the mines for one year, during which time they could take out 1,200 tons of ore and thus finance another year's operations. But despite Plumb's optimism months and years passed, and the company sent out neither miners nor explorers. Undoubtedly the War of Reform and later the French Intervention frightened off potential investors, and, as the young promoter gradually came to realize, the American directors of the company managed its finances in a loose and careless fashion. They began by issuing too much stock for gifts to American subscribers and Mexican officials, and after a reorganization in 1857 the new officers took to bickering. The company lingered on into the 1860's, issuing occasional plans and reports, but the true state of affairs is revealed by the fact that no member of Plumb's exploring party ever received his full pay.[5]

[4] David M. Pletcher, "A Prospecting Expedition across Central Mexico, 1856–57," *Pacific Historical Review*, XXI (Feb. 1952), 21–41.

[5] "Stock History of the Late *Mexican Pacific Coal and Iron Mining Company*," *passim*, Plumb Papers, V; "*Grants of the Mexican Pacific Co. in Mexico*," New York, Aug. 1863, *ibid.*, VI. Volumes V and VI contain extensive correspondence between Plumb and Theodore Olcott regarding the company's finances.

Long before the final disappearance of the Mexican Pacific Company, Plumb, seeing no immediate prospect of success in promotional ventures, took a position in the American legation in Mexico City as translator and interpreter. Between 1861 and 1865 he served in various capacities, now in Mexico City, now in Washington, helping to maintain a thin line of communications between the hard-pressed governments of Juárez and Lincoln. Late in 1866 he accompanied a newly appointed minister, Lewis Campbell, as far as Veracruz, but when Plumb's new chief discovered that the French and the Mexicans were still fighting in eastern Mexico, he prudently withdrew to New Orleans, to Plumb's disgust. After an "enforced and mortifying sojourn" there lasting over seven months, Campbell was dismissed, and Secretary Seward instructed Plumb to proceed to Mexico City as chargé d'affaires. On the journey inland from Veracruz he experienced the final indignity of being robbed by bandits.[6]

As the only fully accredited foreign diplomat in Mexico City, Plumb had an unusually good opportunity to observe the distress and confusion of the times, and he made more friends and exerted more influence than any chargé could expect under ordinary circumstances. Although Foreign Minister Sebastián Lerdo de Tejada had warned Americans not to intervene to protect European nationals who had supported the French Intervention, Plumb and Lerdo became such good friends that the American chargé often served as "trouble shooter" for distressed Europeans. Once he even helped to forestall British armed violence by prompt intervention when the commander of H.M.S. "Chanticleer," exasperated by difficulties with the port

[6] A general account of the futile Campbell mission is found in E. P. Oberholtzer, *A History of the United States since the Civil War* (New York, 1917–1937), I, 512–514. See also Plumb to J. S. Mackie, Havana, Nov. 22, 1866, Plumb to Charles Sumner, New Orleans, Jan. 28, Aug. 15, 1867, Plumb to E. H. Saulnier, Orizaba, Oct. 3, 1867, Plumb Papers, VII.

authorities of Mazatlán, blockaded and threatened to bombard the town.[7]

Plumb deserved to be promoted to minister, and friends at home, such as J. Edgar Thomson and Caleb Cushing, tried to use their influence for him at Washington, but something went wrong, and in 1868 General Rosecrans was appointed instead. Plumb stayed on to receive the new minister, but when Rosecrans invited him to become permanent secretary, he understandably refused, and at the end of the year he left for home.[8] As already noted, Rosecrans kept the legation only a few months, for in the following spring President Grant replaced him with Thomas H. Nelson. Plumb doubtless hoped for this appointment, but although he knew both Grant and Orville E. Babcock, the president's private secretary, he was offered only the somewhat inferior position of consul general at Havana. After a little hesitation he accepted, and from June to December of 1869 he served creditably in his new post, submitting a series of well-informed reports on the rebellion for independence which had recently broken out on the island. In December he resigned his post and returned to the United States.[9]

The letters and dispatches which Plumb wrote during his early years in Mexico set forth in microcosm the confusion of aims in the policy of the United States toward its weak and divided neighbor. During the years of the French Intervention, as Mexi-

[7] Plumb to Sebastián Lerdo de Tejada, Mexico City, Oct. 18, 1867, Jan. 22, 1868, Lerdo to Plumb, Mexico City, Oct. 26, 1867, March 11, 1868, Plumb to R. S. Chew, Oct. 10, 1867, Plumb to William H. Seward, Nov. 7, 1867, Jan. 24, March 28, 1868, State Dept., Despatches, Mexico, XXXI, XXXII.

[8] J. Edgar Thomson to Plumb, Philadelphia, July 9, 1867, Caleb Cushing to Plumb, Washington, July 15, 1867, George Earl Church to Plumb, Sept. 11, 1867, Plumb Collection; New York *Herald*, June 20, 1867; William S. Rosecrans to Seward, Mexico City, Dec. 10, 1868, State Dept., Despatches, Mexico, XXXV.

[9] Plumb's letters from Cuba are scattered through both the Plumb Papers and the Plumb Collection.

can independence flickered in the wind, Lincoln and Seward could not quite make up their minds whether the United States ought to protect Juárez or peacefully take over part of Mexico's territory. Like them, Plumb wavered between sympathy and imperialism. In 1855 he predicted that the tide of Manifest Destiny would sweep as far as the Isthmus of Tehuantepec, producing "one race . . . one language—the same purpose, a preference for the same form of government with an universal liberality—and perhaps more than all the thousand ties of continued, intimate commercial intercourse and unlimited facility of communication." [10] The theme of an irresistible Manifest Destiny recurred in his official reports from time to time.

Lower California interested Plumb particularly, because he anticipated that Britain might acquire the Hawaiian Islands, throwing the United States back upon two defensible ports in California and one in Oregon. When the French finally entered Mexico City in 1863, Plumb suggested to Seward the outright military occupation of the peninsula as a defense measure, and in 1862 and later in 1866 he proposed to Senator Charles Sumner that the American government pay interest for five years on the Mexican debt in return for the cession of Lower California. This, he felt, would be the only way "to keep Mexico from falling into our hands to be with its inferior and heterogeneous population the source of untold political difficulties to us." [11]

At the same time the young diplomat editorialized for an independent Mexico and breathed encouragement to the harassed Juárez. For example, late in 1862, before the American government had decided what to do about Juárez, Matías Romero believed that one of Plumb's articles in the New York *Times* had stiffened Seward's resistance to Napoleon. During the following

[10] Plumb [to Albert H. Plumb, a brother], New York, April 29, 1855, Plumb Papers, I.

[11] Plumb to Sumner, Washington, Feb. 10, 1862, and New York, Jan. 3, 1866, Plumb to Seward, New York, July 2–3, 1863, "Memorandum: Policy of the United States as regards Mexico," *ibid.*, VI, VII.

April, four months before he recommended to Seward the seizure of Lower California, Plumb wrote to Juárez expressing confidence in Mexico's final victory "under the leadership of one who has proved himself so exalted, so pure, so constant and so able as Your Excellency." On another occasion he served as intermediary between the Mexican government and a group of American financial magnates in a vain effort to persuade Jay Cooke to float a Mexican loan of fifty or a hundred million dollars.[12]

As Juárez and the Mexican liberals overpowered Maximilian, thoughts of territorial annexation gradually disappeared from Plumb's writings. In June 1867, while still languishing in New Orleans, he suggested once again to Seward that the United States might have to acquire a small portion of Mexico soon and eventually perhaps all of it.[13] A long letter of July 26 to Senator Sumner, however, argued that Americans must not use force to hasten the eventual union. The following passage epitomizes Plumb's attitude toward Mexico after the French Intervention and the basic assumption upon which his later promotional plans rested:

Now as to how far the Spanish American race is capable of success-fully establishing themselves under the republican institutions they have copied from ours, is a question yet to be solved. Certainly now, no *other* institutions can be adopted in their place, and, in the case of Mexico, they have either to succeed in maintaining by themselves at least a tolerable degree of stability, tranquility and security under them, or the task will devolve upon us. Is it not better to leave them alone for a time to try whether they can succeed (hitherto they have never really been free from a malign European influence, diplomatic, clerical, and pecuniary), or, at most, only to "help them to help

---

[12] Plumb to Benito Juárez, April 1863, and New York, Oct. 9, 1865, *ibid.*, VI. Both the Plumb Papers and the Plumb Collection contain many letters between Matías Romero and Plumb concerning the loan and various schemes for securing munitions for Juárez.

[13] Plumb to Seward, New Orleans, June 26, 1867, Plumb Collection.

themselves"? In those five words, I think, lies our true Mexican policy. . . .

Peace with Mexico, the best advantage of its commerce, full opportunity for our Citizens to safely engage in the industrial development of that country, and the future mingling of the destinies of the two countries by a natural, peaceful process, instead of by violent, illegitimate means, is what we want, as the subject appears to me. . . . If we have their trade and development meanwhile we need not hasten the greater event. Their people and their religion can better remain under a distinct but sympathetic nationality as long as possible.[14]

This was often the expressed hope and, it is fair to believe, often also the real hope of American promoters—that they might "help Mexicans to help themselves," enjoy "the best advantage" of Mexican commerce and industrial development, and forestall "the greater event" of annexation by strengthening "a distinct but sympathetic nationality." It remains to be seen whether Plumb and his successors found it possible to fulfill these hopes.

II

Plumb was forty-two years old when he left the Foreign Service and, after casting about for employment, turned to railroad promotion in Mexico. He had always been interested in the growth of railroads, and while chargé in Mexico City he had had many chances to observe and report on the congressional battle over the revalidation of the Mexican Railway concession. In general he defended the generous terms which Juárez granted to the repentant concessionaires, for he believed that Mexico was "suffocating, commercially speaking, for the want of the conclusion of this road, and the construction of lines hence into the interior." It was obvious to him that Mexico must look to American leadership in railroad matters.[15]

[14] Plumb to Sumner, New Orleans, July 26, 1867, Plumb Papers, VII.
[15] Plumb to J. Edgar Thomson, Mexico City, Dec. 8, 1867, *ibid.*; Plumb to Seward, Mexico City, Dec. 13, 1867, April 21, Nov. 14, 1868, State Dept., Despatches, Mexico, XXXI, XXXII, XXXIV.

One day in the summer of 1871 a friend casually introduced Plumb to John Sanford Barnes, the president of the International Railroad Company of Texas. This company, one of a network of railroads which appeared almost overnight in that state during the Reconstruction period, had been formed by a group of "thoroughly loyal Northern men" to build a line across the state from Fulton, Arkansas, to San Antonio and Laredo. (Early in 1872, after beginning construction in Texas, the International Company merged with the Houston and Great Northern Railroad, in order to secure an outlet on the Gulf coast. Thereafter the company was known as the International and Great Northern.) Upon being introduced to Plumb, Barnes sought his advice on a railroad extension to the Mexican Pacific coast. Within three weeks Plumb had agreed to represent the International Company in Mexico for an annual salary of $6,000. On August 10 he received his official commission as agent of the company, and on September 1 he arrived in Mexico City to begin operations.[16]

Although the details of Plumb's new project changed from time to time, its principal features were as follows. The company planned to lay two main lines of track, crossing Mexico at right angles to each other: one stretching in a broad arc from Laredo on the Rio Grande southwest to San Blas on the Pacific, the other running through the heart of central Mexico from Mexico City northwest to Durango, with short branches to Guanajuato and Morelia. The city of Lagos was to be the junction point of the two lines (see Map 2). Neither the Mexico City–San Blas nor the Mexico City–Laredo route was very direct, but even so

[16] John S. Barnes to Plumb, New York, July 25, Aug. 9, 1871, Plumb to Barnes, July 31, Aug. 9, 10, 1871, Plumb to H. A. Johnston, March 21, 1872, Plumb Papers, VII, IX. The decision must have been sudden, for Plumb was planning to accompany George Earl Church to Bolivia (George Earl Church to Plumb, Providence, R.I., June 5, 1871, Plumb Collection). For an account of the origins of the International Railroad Company see St. Clair Griffin Reed, *A History of Texas Railroads and of Transportation Conditions under Spain and Mexico and the Republic and the State* (Houston, Texas, [1941]), pp. 315–317.

the rail distance to the United States was shorter than along Rose-crans' line to El Paso. Later Plumb suggested that the Laredo-Pacific line run farther north across the flat Bolsón de Mapimi, up the fertile Nazas Valley, and through Durango to the port of Mazatlán.[17]

To build these railroads, Plumb counted on the support of a company capitalized at $50,000,000, with an immediate sub-scription of from $2,000,000 to $5,000,000. He eventually asked the Mexican government for a subsidy of 9,000 pesos per kilo-meter, payable in installments as sections were completed, and other indirect subsidies in the form of tax exemptions. For his part, he agreed to begin construction at Mexico City on a line to the Pacific coast first of all and to maintain the standard gauge of 4 feet 8½ inches, which was used by the Mexican Railway to Veracruz. As he later wrote to a company officer, however, he presumed that his mission had a broader purpose than simply cultivating short-run profits. "It was rather, to do what could prudently be done, to stimulate the construction of the Mexican portion of what is destined to become a great through line . . . [from] the commanding central city of St. Louis . . . [to] the City of Mexico . . . and the Pacific Ocean, at a port within the region of tropical supplies." [18]

Plumb's campaign opened auspiciously. When he arrived in Mexico City, Minister Thomas H. Nelson and Consul Julius Skilton met him at the depot, and he dined with the Nelsons that evening. Next day he called on Ignacio Mariscal and Matías Romero, the day after that on President Juárez and his family at Chapultepec. Later he talked to Sebastián Lerdo de Tejada, Blas Balcárcel, and other acquaintances from the old days. With each one he left a copy of Poor's *Manual of the Railroads* as

[17] *Proyecto del ferrocarril internacional sometido al Congreso de la Unión* (México, 1872), p. 15 *et passim;* Plumb to Barnes, Mexico City, Dec. 23, 1871, Jan. 29, 1872, Plumb Papers, VIII.

[18] Plumb to Barnes, Mexico City, Sept. 29, 1871, Plumb to Thomas W. Pearsall, New York, March 21, 1874, Plumb Papers, XII; Knapp, "Pre-cursors of American Investment," p. 52.

"statistical fertilizer" for his project, and he was careful to repeat his visits from time to time.[19]

Although *simpatía* and private man-to-man contacts were vital to business with Latin Americans, Plumb did not depend on these alone. Occasionally he placed informative articles in leading newspapers, especially after Rosecrans appeared on the scene, but Plumb used the press more unobtrusively than the general. He obliged his friends with favors such as obtaining books for them in the United States. He joined learned societies such as the Sociedad Lancastriana (to promote education), the Sociedad Filarmónica, and the Sociedad Mexicana de Geografía y Estadística. The promotional work which the gregarious Plumb enjoyed most of all, to judge from his letters, was that of giving huge breakfasts and banquets, usually at the Tivoli de San Cosme, the leading restaurant of the time. Within three weeks of his arrival he had entertained at breakfast Minister Nelson and the principal businessmen of the capital. On the last day of the year he entertained the Nelsons, the Mariscals, the Romeros, and the Skiltons, following up with fifty personal calls on New Year's Day. In January and February he invited practically the whole upper echelon of the Mexican government to two enormous breakfasts at San Cosme. Since he ran short of money in March, he had to postpone a similar banquet for the newspapermen of the capital until April 24.[20]

After his initial talks with Juárez and his cabinet ministers Plumb began to cherish hopes that the company might soon begin surveys to determine the terminal point on the Rio Grande and actual construction at the Mexico City end of the line. When Congress met in mid-September an alliance of the followers of Juárez and Lerdo constituted a large majority among the mem-

[19] Plumb to Barnes, Mexico City, Sept. 9, 19, 1871, Plumb Papers, VIII; Knapp, "Precursors of American Investment," p. 52.

[20] Plumb to William T. Hunter, Mexico City, June 28, 1872, Plumb Collection; Plumb to Barnes, Mexico City, Sept. 19, 1871, Jan. 29, Feb. 26, April 24, 1872, Plumb Papers, VIII, IX; Plumb to Mrs. Grace B. Bristed, Mexico City, Jan. 5, 1872, Plumb Collection.

bers, and the way toward a formal concession seemed clear. Almost at once the first obstacle appeared—the unsuccessful but dangerous revolt of Porfirio Díaz. Tactfully Plumb refrained from pressing the disturbed officials and allowed the autumn session of Congress to pass without presenting his petition.[21]

By the beginning of the spring session the administration's majority in Congress had dwindled, and competition was appearing from other quarters. When Plumb first took up his promotional work, he was well aware that others hoped to build American-Mexican railroad lines. One of these was Robert B. Gorsuch, an engineer of considerable experience in Mexico who claimed to have the support of a group of American capitalists in New York and the South. Gorsuch called on Plumb the day after his arrival in Mexico City and described his project in lofty terms, but Plumb shrewdly calculated that he did not enjoy the confidence of Mexican officials and was too unbusinesslike to have much chance of success.[22] Another promoter, Simon Stevens, was seeking English capital for a railroad across the Isthmus of Tehuantepec, but Plumb and Romero agreed that the International Company's route offered more benefits to Mexico. Stevens failed to obtain support in England, and in the end Plumb generously intervened to help him secure an extension from the Mexican government.[23] The man who was to be Plumb's most formidable rival, William S. Rosecrans, was even then planning a reconnoitering expedition for the narrow-gauge project of the Union Contract Company, but he and his engineers were still

[21] Plumb to Barnes, Mexico City, Sept. 19, 29, Oct. 9, 24, Nov. 9, Dec. 18, 1871, Plumb Papers, VIII; Plumb to H. Hall, Mexico City, Oct. 30, 1871, Plumb Collection.

[22] Plumb to Barnes, Mexico City, Sept. 9, 19, 1871, Plumb Papers, VIII. At the same time Gorsuch was corresponding with Rosecrans, encouraging him (Robert B. Gorsuch to William S. Rosecrans, Oct. 29, 1871, Interoceanic Company Papers).

[23] Plumb to Barnes, Havana, Aug. 22, 1871, and Mexico City, Nov. 9, 1871, June 5, 1872, Plumb Papers, VIII, IX.

in the United States, and Plumb apparently knew little about them.

During the winter of 1871–1872 Plumb began to detect opposition from officials of the British-owned Mexican Railway, which was then completing its Veracruz line by constructing a difficult section through the mountains and ravines west of Córdoba. In October, Guillermo Barron, one of its directors and a leading representative of Anglo-Mexican capital, assured Plumb that the company had no immediate intention of building an extension west of Mexico City and would be willing to cooperate with the International Company in this region. Plumb did not quite believe Barron and was anxious to secure his concession in order to oblige the Mexican Railway to join forces with him or give up the extension altogether.[24]

Plumb's early campaign against these rivals was somewhat hampered by signs of halfheartedness among his own supporters in the International Company. Alarmed at the expenses of his publicity campaign during the winter, Thomas W. Pearsall, the company treasurer, suggested economy to Plumb, since the money was needed for railroad construction in Texas. Plumb replied in a tone of sorrowful reproach that the project could not be lightly thrown aside at this point "without personal disgrace and American discredit." The activities of the International Company and perhaps of all American companies in the field of Mexican railroads, "one of the most profitable on the Continent," would be greatly damaged. On April 6 he received a letter of credit for £1,000.[25]

This was well, for all indications seemed to require renewed efforts in the spring session of Congress. For one thing, during February the influential pro-Lerdist newspaper, *El siglo diez y nueve*, printed a series of editorials in support of railroad con-

[24] Plumb to Barnes, Mexico City, Oct. 25, 1871, Feb. 6, 1872, *ibid.*, VIII.
[25] D. P. Barhydt to Plumb, New York, Dec. 8, 1871, Pearsall to Plumb, New York, Feb. 27, 1872, Plumb to Pearsall, Mexico City, March 20, 1872, Plumb to Barhydt, April 13, 1872, *ibid.*, VII, IX.

struction.[26] Even more important, on April 23 General Rosecrans arrived in Mexico City to begin his campaign. Plumb had followed his earlier activities from a distance, but he showed little alarm until he learned that J. Edgar Thomson of the Pennsylvania Railroad and Thomas A. Scott of the Texas and Pacific were both allied with Palmer and Rosecrans. As he told Barnes, he regarded Scott as slippery and unreliable, and he added that Europeans in Mexico City identified the Texas and Pacific with the notorious railroad project of General Frémont, which had just ruined many French investors.[27]

Whatever Plumb may have felt about Rosecrans' American backing, the general's whirlwind campaign in the Mexican press and Congress during 1872 made his immediate intentions clear enough. Along with his windy disquisitions on the civilizing mission of railroads and the advantages of the narrow gauge, he delivered an occasional blast at Plumb during the spring and summer, and in the autumn session of Congress his supporters denounced the International Company at exhausting length. As already noted, Rosecrans argued that Plumb's company was too weak to begin construction at once and that Barnes was secretly an annexationist.[28] Perhaps in view of Pearsall's earlier advice to economize, the first charge had some foundation, but no evidence has been found to support the second.

[26] *El siglo diez y nueve*, Feb. 10, 14, 16, 1872. Emilio Velasco assured Plumb that his favorable editorial of Feb. 14 represented the views of Lerdo and his followers (Plumb to Barnes, Mexico City, Feb. 14, 1872, Plumb Papers, VIII).

[27] Plumb to Church, Mexico City, Jan. 29, 1872, Plumb Collection; Plumb to Barnes, Mexico City, Jan. 29, April 13, 1872, Plumb Papers, VIII, IX.

[28] See, for example, an article in *El demócrata* quoted by Manuel Blanco in the congressional debates (México, *Diario de los debates: Sexto congreso*, III, 511–513). A contemporary cartoon, satirizing Rosecrans' eagerness to begin work, showed Lerdo and Balcárcel quizzing Plumb, Barron, and the general: "When can you begin the railroad?" Plumb: "Within four years and—a little." Barron: "Within a hundred." Rosecrans: "At once." Lerdo: "Well, the matter requires reflection" (*El padre Cobos*, no date, Plumb Collection).

Confronted with the energetic, self-confident Rosecrans, Plumb continued his original policy of winning friends by direct interviews and social contacts. The death of Juárez in July was a lucky break for him, he thought, for his friend Lerdo now succeeded to the presidency. He reminded a friend at home of the many times that they had remarked, "If only Mr. Lerdo was at the head of the government," and in August he wrote to William Hunter of the State Department: "Mr. Lerdo is taking a deep interest in our project, and with his active aid I think I can safely count, now, upon favorable action at the coming session of Congress." [29] Accordingly he submitted a formal petition for a concession in September, and "the battle of the gauges" began in earnest.

Although the main action was fought on the floor of the Mexican Congress, both sides made every effort to bring up reinforcements from the United States. As shown in the preceding chapter, Rosecrans secured a list of prominent names in support of his project and by means of misrepresentation tried to make it appear that the American legation in Mexico approved it as well. On his side, Plumb suggested that Barnes obtain letters of recommendation for the company from President Grant and Secretary of State Fish if possible. Later he asked Barnes to hint to Grant that any criticism of Mexico in the annual message to Congress might hurt the company's chances.[30]

Although Plumb's personal relations with his rivals were chilly, he and his company made some effort to join forces with them, in order to end the sterile debate. Barnes, Palmer, and their subordinates met on one occasion in the United States but

[29] Plumb to William Henry Hurlbert, Mexico City, July 30, 1872, Plumb to Hunter, Mexico City, Aug. 23, 1872, Plumb Collection. Romero was still friendly to Rosecrans, however, and seemed to think that both projects could be carried through (Plumb to Barhydt, Nov. 13, 1872, Plumb Papers, X).

[30] Plumb to Barnes, Mexico City, July 13, Oct. 30, 1872, Plumb Papers, IX, X; Plumb to Hall, Mexico City, Aug. 24, 1872, Plumb Collection.

broke off negotiations after Palmer had refused to abandon his narrow gauge. In December, Plumb proposed joint action to the officials of the newly completed Mexican Railway. It has been noted that in February the Mexican government called all three groups together, but that Rosecrans refused to co-operate with the others. Plumb said as little as possible, hoping to let the general hang himself, for he too wanted to remain independent as long as possible.[31]

Indeed, Rosecrans was now perceptibly losing ground in the spring of 1873, but the increasing scarcity of money in the United States and the possibility of rivalry with the Mexican Railway alarmed Barnes so much that he instructed Plumb not to press for a concession if it would mean competing directly with the English company. Once again Plumb protested that withdrawal would seriously embarrass Lerdo before the country and ruin the company's chances for even a limited concession in the future. Still, in view of the general uncertainty in both countries, he agreed to postpone further activities and sit out the spring session of Congress.[32]

In the end it was Palmer who forced Plumb's hand. After Rosecrans' resignation from the Union Contract Company in May, the Denver railroadman took charge of the project and launched a sudden pressure campaign with the aid of a determined bloc of antiadministration deputies who argued that Palmer was the only promoter who was prepared to begin construction work at once. In order to stifle this argument and retain the support of the Lerdo administration, Plumb immediately laid another set of formal proposals before the cabinet, and on May 31 he wrote to Barnes that he had concluded a formal agreement with Lerdo. Whatever the feelings of the Interna-

[31] Plumb to Barhydt, Mexico City, Sept. 14, 1872, Jan. 29, Feb. 14, 1873, Plumb to Barnes, Dec. 2, 14, 1872, Barnes to Plumb, New York, Sept. 27, Dec. 6, 1872, Plumb Papers, X, XI.

[32] Barnes to Plumb, New York, Feb. 3, April 24, 1873, Plumb to Barnes, Mexico City, March 1, May 16, 1873, *ibid.*, XI.

tional Company's directors, they accepted the *fait accompli* and approved the contract.[33]

III

Despite the ominous forewarnings of financial distress in the United States, Plumb spent the summer of 1873 in a glow of optimism. In August he wrote to Secretary of State Fish from New York predicting an eventual trade of $200,000,000 a year between the United States and Mexico and asking whether the establishment of peaceful relations would not shed as much glory on Grant's second administration as the Treaty of Washington had on the first. As for the International Railroad project, Lerdo had called it "the preferential work of my Administration," partly because of its expected effect on border troubles. Plumb concluded from this and other indications that Mexico had completed her "work of political construction" and was ready for "the full and frank opening of the door for American enterprise." [34] Now that the Mexican government had approved his railroad concession, he advised the International Company to furnish evidence of good intentions by chartering a side-wheel steamboat for semimonthly trips between Galveston and Veracruz. If a regular line could be established, Texan influence in Mexican commerce would grow, even before the completion of the International Railroad.[35]

The mere fact that Plumb had secured a formal concession, however, did not obliterate all his old rivals in Mexico. When General Palmer returned to the United States in May, he left his project in the hands of an Irish agent, James Sullivan, who petitioned Congress in September for a concession to build a railroad line from Mexico City to the Pacific and others from

[33] Plumb to Barnes, Mexico City, May 17, 19, 31, June 14, 1873, Galusha Grow to Plumb, New York, Aug. 13, 1873, *ibid.*, XII. For the text of the concession see México, *Legislación sobre ferrocarriles*, II, 224–240.

[34] Plumb to Hamilton Fish, New York, Aug. 15, 1873, Plumb Collection.

[35] Plumb to Pearsall, Mexico City, Sept. 20, 1873, Plumb Papers, XII.

this line to the American border by way of Chihuahua and Monterrey, with a government subsidy of 8,000 pesos per kilometer.[36] Unfortunately for Sullivan, the recent memory of Rosecrans' indiscretion prevented him from making much headway against Plumb.

While Sullivan was drawing up his petition, much more serious opposition appeared from another quarter: a group of fourteen Mexicans and Europeans decided to form a company with Mexican and British financial support to build the Pacific railroad. On September 15 they discussed the matter with Lerdo, and before the end of the month they had presented a formal petition to Congress. The moving force behind *"los Catorce,"* as the group was familiarly called, seems to have been Guillermo Barron and the other Anglo-Mexican directors of the Mexican Railway, and the rest of the group was made up of Mexican nationalists and Europeans who feared that American railroads would bring in other forms of American business and break up their long-time monopoly over Mexican trade.[37]

Although anyone with eyes to read the names of the fourteen would-be promoters could appreciate the cosmopolitan nature of their support, they loudly proclaimed themselves a truly Mexican company and appealed for capital to build "a great

[36] Plumb to Pearsall, Mexico City, Sept. 13, Oct. 1, 1873, *ibid.*; México, *Diario de los debates: Sétimo congreso constitucional de la Unión* (México, 1874), I, 148–160.

[37] Plumb to Pearsall, Mexico City, Sept. 13, 15, Oct. 1, 1873, Plumb Papers, XII; Plumb to Mariscal, Mexico City, Oct. 31, 1873, Plumb Collection. The fourteen promoters were: Antonio Mier y Celis, a very wealthy real-estate owner; Angel Lascuráin, a member of a respectable mercantile house; Esteban Benecke, a highly respected banker; J. M. Landa, brother-in-law of the Escandón family of the Mexican Railway; Pío Bermejillo, a wealthy Spanish landowner; Miguel Rul, an anti-American conservative politician; Pedro de Valle, a wealthy capitalist of a cosmopolitan family; Cayetano Rubio, the Spanish owner of the "Hercules" cotton mills in Querétaro; Carlos Felix, a member of a German importing house; Sebastián Camacho; David Fergusson; Manuel M. Cortina; Miguel Lizardi; and Guillermo Barron (Plumb to Pearsall, Mexico City, Oct. 31, 1873, Plumb Papers, XII).

bridge from New York to one of our Pacific ports"—almost the same language as will be found in the pamphlets of Albert K. Owen and Arthur E. Stilwell. "Of course," wrote Plumb, "it was rather difficult . . . for the Executive to reject the apparent newly born spirit of national enterprise and give the preference to an American company." But even so, he added, the national inferiority complex in business matters would probably have overcome *los Catorce*, had not the full fury of a business depression burst forth in the United States during the fall of 1873.[38] The failure of Scott's Texas and Pacific Railroad in particular discredited all Americans in Mexico. Consequently after a comparatively brief debate Congress withdrew Plumb's concession in November and the government signed a very similar contract with the fourteen.

Far from losing his temper or giving up in despair at this new setback to his plans, Plumb showed obvious relief. By the time American railroad companies could recover from the depression and continue construction in the West and Southwest, Mexicans would have forgotten the resentment stirred up by Rosecrans, and *los Catorce* would have demonstrated their incapacity to lay a mile of track. Plumb reported that the "inefficient and impolitic management" of the Mexican Railway, with which several of the fourteen promoters were identified, had stirred up "an intense feeling of hostility" and that the new railroad was saving the public neither time nor money.[39] The obvious line of action was to wait and see what would happen.

[38] Compañía limitada mexicana para construir el ferrocarril internacional e interoceánico, *Proyecto de concesión del ferrocarril internacional e interoceánico* (México, 1873), pp. i–vii; Plumb to Philip H. Sheridan, New York, March 31, 1874, Plumb Collection. See also Cosío Villegas, *Histoira moderna de México*, II, 735–737.

[39] Plumb to Albert H. Plumb, Mexico City, Oct. 13, 1873, Plumb to Hurlbert, Nov. 22, 1873, Plumb to Walton W. Evans, Dec. 13, 1873, Plumb Collection. Plumb was, however, a little disappointed at Lerdo's easy capitulation (Plumb to Pearsall, Mexico City, Jan. 3, 1874, Plumb Papers, XII).

The management of the International Company, however, being less farsighted than its agent, decided that all was lost and wired Plumb to return home at the end of the year. On the way he traveled through Texas on the International line as far west as San Antonio and promptly sent Minister of *Fomento* Balcárcel a glowing description of the new railroad.[40] In Washington, Plumb set about mending fences in conversations with President Grant, Secretary Fish, Senator Oliver P. Morton, General Sherman, and others. Always he sought to explain Lerdo's withdrawal of the concession in such a way as to preserve the reputation of both company and government, and he added "words of good cheer regarding the steady progress of Mexico in her march toward self government and prosperity." Writing to Andrew D. White, Plumb attempted to soften American denunciations of the recent murder of a Protestant missionary in Mexico: "Are our own skirts as a nation and as a people sufficiently clear for us to do this?" [41]

In the spring and summer of 1874 events began to justify Plumb's patience and hopefulness. Although the United States still wallowed in the trough of the depression, the fourteen Mexican and European promoters were showing unmistakable signs of weakness. Barron and David Fergusson visited London, Paris, and Frankfort in a fruitless search for capital, and the fourteen appealed openly for support in Mexico City with disappointing results. Unable to post a bond with the government as required by their concession, they petitioned Congress for a postponement and for easier terms. But Lerdo had heard the same language from Rosecrans. Disgusted with the feeble showing of *los Catorce*, he refused to listen to their pleas and on May

---

[40] Pearsall to Plumb, New York, [Dec. 31, 1873], Plumb Papers, XII; Plumb to Blas Balcárcel, New York, March 13, 1874, Plumb Collection.
[41] Plumb to Andrew D. White, New York, April 11, 1874, Plumb Collection. For "fence-mending" letters to David A. Wells, Carl Schurz, and others see the same collection.

7 informed Congress that their concession had been nullified. Foster reported: "People are all asking, 'Will Mr. Plumb return?'"[42]

For months Mr. Plumb had awaited just such queries, but he postponed his return to Mexico City until October 25. Meanwhile Palmer's agent, the indefatigable James Sullivan, presented yet another petition for a railroad concession, lowering his subsidy to 4,000 pesos per kilometer and offering a bond of 300,000 pesos in cash. He made no headway whatever. At the same time two allies of Barron, Sebastián Camacho and José A. Mendizabal, petitioned for a restricted concession entirely within central Mexico, to be financed by a lottery. Seeing that this concession would not compete with his and that the International Company could graft its line on the Camacho-Mendizabal stub, Plumb pushed ahead with his own project. The deputies took a dim view of the truncated Mexican project but concluded that if this were the best that Mexican capital could do, Congress would have to support it. December 5 Congress approved the Camacho-Mendizabal concession from Mexico City to León, and a week later the minister of *fomento* granted Plumb another concession from León to the American border.[43]

Plumb was well satisfied with what he called the most generous railroad concession so far granted by Mexico, providing a subsidy of 9,000 pesos per kilometer and postponing construction until the Camacho-Mendizabal line reached León. By that time American capital would surely have recovered from the Panic of 1873. Plumb spent several months in the United States,

[42] John W. Foster to Plumb, Mexico City, March 27, May 11, July 12, 1874, Estanislao Cañedo to Plumb, Mexico City, May 31, 1874, *ibid.*; *El siglo diez y nueve*, July 20, 1874.

[43] Plumb to J. L. Kennedy, Mexico City, Dec. 5, 1874, Plumb Collection; [James Sullivan], *Propuesta de la Compañía unión contract de Pensilvania [sic] para la construcción y explotación de varias vías ferreas en la República mexicana* (México, 1874), *passim*; México, *Diario de los debates: Sétimo congreso*, III, 560–568, 635–637, 705–721, 828–844, 853.

returning to Mexico City in the spring of 1875 to be on hand while Congress discussed his concession. On May 29 it was approved almost unanimously.[44]

For the rest of the year the only serious obstacle to actual construction—aside from the completion of the Camacho-Mendizabal line—seemed to be the depression in the United States. Foster gave every possible support to the Plumb project in a widely publicized speech before the New Orleans chamber of commerce in November, but investors continued to hold back. Since the company had promised to submit a bond of 200,000 pesos to the Mexican government by December 5, Plumb had to make a hasty trip to Mexico City, just before that date and petition for an extension. To his great satisfaction, Lerdo asked no questions and revised the contract to allow an extra year for the presentation of the bond.[45] If no other evidence were available, this circumstance would be almost enough by itself to demonstrate the superiority of Plumb's promotional methods over those of the impetuous Rosecrans.

IV

When the year 1876 began, Plumb seemed about to obtain that favorable conjunction of economic conditions in the United States and political conditions in Mexico for which he had patiently waited since the autumn of 1872. But alas, as prosperity returned to the United States, revolution broke out again in Mexico, and by the end of the year his assiduously cultivated

[44] Plumb to Kennedy, Mexico City, Dec. 15, 26, 1874, Plumb to Mrs. Bristed, Mexico City, Dec. 31, 1874, Plumb to Samuel Sloan, May 30, June 9, 1875, Plumb Collection; *Two Republics*, June 9, 1875. The text of Plumb's concession is reprinted in México, *Diario de los debates: Sétimo congreso*, IV, 347–354. The subsidy was later reduced to 9,000 pesos.

[45] Plumb to Barnes, New Orleans, Nov. 19, 1875, Plumb to Foster, Mexico City, Dec. 8, 1875, Plumb Collection; Plumb to Balcárcel, Mexico City, Dec. 1, 1875, Plumb Papers, XII.

friend, Sebastián Lerdo de Tejada, found himself discredited, out of power, and an exile.

At the beginning of the uprising Plumb minimized its effects and hopefully assured his correspondents that it would soon blow over, leaving constitutional government stronger than ever. In April he thought that Foster's pessimistic dispatches showed a lack of experience with Mexican civil disturbances, and he wrote a long letter to Secretary of State Fish, urging him not to be too hasty in recognizing any *de facto* government. Dissatisfied elements in Mexico welcomed the confusion of revolutions, he said, and European merchants could secure great reductions in duties and other advantages by contributing money to rebel leaders. If Europeans liked to fish in troubled waters, it would seem an obvious policy for the United States to keep the waters still.[46] He did not need to add that still waters would benefit one American enterprise in particular.

Lest Americans interpret the revolt as the beginning of a new civil war, Plumb put pressure on New York newspapers to publish encouraging editorials and made use of his friend George Earl Church in England to insert anti-Díaz propaganda in the London *Daily Telegraph*.[47] By early summer, the uprising seemed to have died out. Foster returned home to deliver speeches in the Hayes presidential campaign, and Plumb took a vacation at the Philadelphia Centennial Exposition. To be sure, on September 26 Díaz issued a decree nullifying any Lerdo concession "which may result in burden to the nation," [48] but not until late in October did the doomed Lerdo regime show any obvious signs of weakness. At that time the sudden opposition

[46] Plumb to Mariscal, New York, April 2, 1876, Plumb to Elijah Ward, New York, April 2, 1876, Plumb to Fish, New York, April 4, 1876, Plumb Collection.

[47] Plumb to Foster, New York, May 20, 23, 1876, Plumb to Lerdo, New York, May 20, 1876, *ibid*.

[48] Foster to Plumb, Mexico City, June 27, 29, 1876, Plumb to Foster, Bryn Mawr, Pa., July 3, 1876, *ibid*.

of the chief justice of the supreme court, José María Iglesias, split the government in two, and by the end of the year Díaz' reinvigorated armies had swept before them Lerdistas and Iglesistas alike. The International project disappeared in the dust of battle: Plumb, who had hurried to Mexico in October, read Díaz' proclamation against foreign concessions and concluded that the jig was up, at least for the time being. On December 9 he left for Veracruz, Havana, and New Orleans, postponing his project indefinitely.[49]

For many months after his precipitate departure from Mexico, Plumb regarded the new regime of Porfirio Díaz as shallowly grounded in principles, feeble, and apt to be overturned at any moment. Believing that Lerdo would surely regain power soon, he resigned himself to the delay and set about to protect his project by cultivating friendly relations with the government in exile. After fleeing from Mexico by way of Acapulco and Panama, Lerdo arrived in New York on February 11 with General Mariano Escobedo and Manuel Romero Rubio. Plumb called on him as soon as possible, offering his services as guide, and within two weeks he had shown the deposed president many of the principal tourist sights of the city: the railroad stations, Brooklyn Bridge, the Astor Library, Cooper Institute, Stewart's and Tiffany's stores, and others.

In April, Plumb, Lerdo, and Romero Rubio visited Philadelphia, Harrisburg, Johnstown, and Pittsburgh to inspect the facilities of the Pennsylvania Railroad and the principal ironworks. A similar visit to the New England mills at Boston, Lowell, and Lawrence was proposed, but news from Mexico prevented the trip, and although Plumb hoped to take Lerdo to Texas to see the International lines, the exiled president remained in New York. Whenever possible, Plumb introduced him to

---

[49] Plumb to Hurlbert, Mexico City, Oct. 27, 29, 1876, Plumb to Hall, Mexico City, Dec. 8, 1876, and New York, Jan. 5, 1877, *ibid*. See also a statement on the revolution in Plumb's handwriting in Plumb Papers, XIII.

influential politicians, industrialists, and journalists, obviously hoping to impress the Mexican with his many contacts and with the industrial potential of the United States.[50]

While he shepherded the little group of Mexican exiles around the American business centers, Plumb bent every effort to persuade the American State Department not to recognize the Díaz government. During January and February he bombarded Fish with letters and late in March suggested to Assistant Secretary of State F. W. Seward the impropriety of condoning "a desperate revolutionary outbreak like the present in Mexico, especially when it is probable . . . that it will be replaced by the restoration of the legitimate Constitutional order, which alone can give any hope of future tranquility or of the increase of our commercial relations with that country." [51] The Díaz government and its American supporters blamed Plumb very largely for the American delay in recognition, but they doubtless exaggerated his influence on the government, for the waiting policy of Hayes and Evarts was mostly determined by conditions on the Rio Grande border.[52]

Gradually Plumb realized that Lerdo could never return to power. For over a year after the flight from Mexico, General Escobedo loyally intrigued for his master and gathered troops

[50] Plumb to Hurlbert, New York, Feb. 16, 1877, Plumb to Hall, New York, Feb. 17, 1877, Plumb to Albert H. Plumb, Feb. 18, 1877, Plumb to R. S. Hayes, New York, March 26, 1877, Plumb to Benjamin E. Bates, New York, April 10, 1877, Mackie to Plumb, April 11, 1877, Plumb to Mackie, New York, April 12, 1877, Plumb to Edward Atkinson, New York, April 23, 1877, Plumb Collection.

[51] Plumb to Fish, New York, Jan. 8, 1877, and Washington, Jan. 29, Feb. 2, 6, "Correspondence of Hamilton Fish," CXVIII, Papers of Hamilton Fish, Division of Manuscripts, Library of Congress; Plumb to F. W. Seward, New York, March 24, 1877, Plumb Collection. Plumb also talked directly to F. W. Seward and William Hunter (Plumb to Lerdo, Washington, April 4, 1877, *ibid.*).

[52] Gregg, *Influence of Border Troubles,* pp. 35–36; Callahan, *American Foreign Policy in Mexican Relations,* p. 384; Chicago *Tribune,* Dec. 17, 1877, p. 2.

on the Rio Grande frontier, but after his capture in Coahuila and the dispersal of his troops, the only lasting effect of his labors was increased border tension. Meanwhile Lerdo lived on peacefully in New York, rising at noon, as Plumb remarked sadly, and showing no qualities of leadership in a crisis. Plumb did not make clear exactly what he thought the Mexican leader should do—perhaps no more than encourage the United States to intervene and unseat Díaz. But in the spring of 1878, far from seeking American aid, Lerdo issued a protest against the American policy of pursuing Indians across the border, and at that moment Plumb abandoned his cause for good.[53]

During these bitter years Plumb's optimistic hopes for the peaceful regeneration of Mexico through American investment gave way once again to his former conviction that the United States must use force to restore order. Before he had been home for a month, he wrote to Editor W. H. Hurlbert of the New York *World* that the fate of Mexico, "that land . . . of peace and pure delight, where majestic order never reigns," must serve as a warning to those Americans who advocated civil war over the Hayes-Tilden election. In the following October he told a former minister to Mexico, Thomas H. Nelson, that "the overthrow of Lerdo" was more than a simple change of rulers. It was "the irreparable destruction of the fabric of constitutional development in that country." An almost-completed constitutional edifice, twenty years in the building, "was in an hour of madness and delirium destroyed by the very party which had erected it." The revolution had set back American-Mexican relations twenty years too, he added, and obliged the Hayes regime to protect American interests by violating the Mexican border.[54]

[53] Knapp, *Sebastián Lerdo de Tejada*, pp. 257–258, 261 note; Plumb to Thomas H. Nelson, New York, Oct. 11, 1877, Plumb to Ulysses S. Grant, Washington, May 29, 1878, Plumb Collection.

[54] Plumb to Hurlbert, New York, Jan. 12, 1877, Plumb to Nelson, New York, Oct. 11, 1877, Plumb Collection.

When Hayes and Evarts finally recognized Díaz in the spring of 1878, Plumb sank from depression into despair. Writing to ex-President Grant, Plumb referred briefly to "the supineness of the Mexican constitutional party" and deplored the weak relinquishment by the United States of all conditions which Hayes had formerly asked in return for recognition. Not only was the recognition too late to save Díaz from overthrow, but it would antagonize the few remaining Constitutionalists, "the only party from which we have anything to hope." As he had written earlier to Nelson, he expected Díaz to give way to some proclerical, anti-American dictator.[55] But the future was to be quite different, for the despairing Plumb had failed to consider that Díaz, an opportunist from the beginning of his career, might annex both pro-American and proclerical sentiment in Mexico as weapons against his remaining enemies.

Clearly Plumb believed that he would have carried through his project if Lerdo had continued in power for another presidential term. If he was right, what becomes of the conviction held by some Mexican historians that Lerdo was opposed to the use of American capital and to railroad connections between the United States and central Mexico? The slightest encouragement to Plumb would seem inconsistent with anti-Americanism, for from the beginning the International Company of Texas proposed a line to the northern border, and Mexicans considered Texas as the center of annexationist spirit in the United States.

Frank A. Knapp, Jr., has offered another explanation of Lerdo's railroad policy which best fits his apparently shifting behavior toward Plumb: that Lerdo would grant concessions and even subsidies to Americans in all sincerity, as far as his funds would allow, but that he preferred to use Mexican or European capital if possible. "Certainly," Knapp adds, "when it came to a choice of either sacrificing the national dignity by making diplomatic or other advances to Mexico's European

[55] Plumb to Grant, Washington, May 29, 1878, Plumb to Nelson, Oct. 11, 1877, *ibid.*

creditors or turning toward United States capital, he never hesitated to take the second alternative." [56] Daniel Cosío Villegas agrees that Lerdo's railroad policy cannot fairly be called anti-American and points out that of Lerdo's eighteen railroad concessions eight were granted to Americans, and five of these ran to the American border.[57] It appears, therefore, that Lerdo would have continued to support Plumb wholeheartedly if he had remained in power.

V

The story of Edward Lee Plumb's career might well end in 1878, the symbol of patience unrewarded, had not the promoter returned to Mexico a few years later to play a subsidiary role in one of the secondary railroad companies of the Díaz period. Since he left behind few records of his actions, the story of this project can be little more than an epilogue to the rest of his life.

Between 1878 and 1881 several factors complicated the railroad question in northern Mexico, making it almost impossible for a relatively obscure promoter such as Plumb and a relatively small railroad company such as the International and Great Northern to retain a leading position. In the first place, as already brought out, Porfirio Díaz became actively interested in the use of American capital and in September 1880 granted liberal concessions to the Mexican Central and Mexican National Railroad companies for lines from Mexico City to El Paso and Laredo respectively. Secondly, the state of Texas became the scene of a battle royal and then a truce between two of the greatest railroad magnates of the time, Collis P. Huntington and Jay Gould.

Having tied California securely in a network of Southern Pacific lines during the early 1870's Huntington turned east at Fort Yuma in 1877 and pushed his track to the Texas border against the vain opposition of Thomas A. Scott and the Texas and Pacific Railroad. At the same time Gould, who had plun-

[56] Knapp, *Sebastián Lerdo de Tejada*, pp. 203, 205, 211.
[57] Cosío Villegas, *Historia moderna de México*, II, 741–742.

dered and almost wrecked the Erie Railroad in the East, turned to speculation in Western lines and bought up the Wabash, the Missouri Pacific, the Missouri, Kansas, and Texas, and several smaller lines, one of which was Plumb's old company, the International and Great Northern. By the end of 1880 the two railroad barons faced each other suspiciously across the plains of western Texas.[58]

Both Huntington and Gould began to build parallel lines across the wastes east of El Paso, and for a few months a railroad war seemed inevitable, but, as often happened in American business history of the period, ruinous competition gave way to compromise and co-operation. On November 26, 1881, the rivals agreed to join their main lines at El Paso and pool their earnings from through traffic between New Orleans and the Pacific coast. Then both of them turned to face a common rival, the Atchison, Topeka, and Santa Fe, and the fighting shifted to a new front, more remote from Mexico.[59]

In the contest for control of the Texas railroads the unrealized Mexican concessions naturally played a very minor part. Late in 1880 officials in some of the Gould lines began to talk of extensions from Mexico, and in January 1881 Plumb sold all his rights in the International concession to the Gould system.[60] By this time, however, Gould had decided to support the Mexican project of ex-President Grant, which will be described in another chapter. Losing interest in Plumb's concession, he made no objection when, on June 7, 1881, a Huntington subsidiary, the International Construction Company, secured a concession from the Mexican government extending from Piedras Negras on the

[58] Robert E. Riegel, *The Story of the Western Railroads* (New York, 1926), chaps. xi–xii; Reed, *History of Texas Railroads*, pp. 202–203.

[59] Riegel, *Story of the Western Railroads*, pp. 172–173, 182–183; Clarence R. Wharton, *History of Texas* (Dallas, Texas, 1935), pp. 408–409; Chicago *Tribune*, Nov. 29, 1881, p. 6.

[60] Pearsall to Plumb, New York, Jan. 15, 1881, Plumb Collection. Letters from the presidents of some of the Gould lines, showing interest in construction in Mexico are found in the same collection.

Rio Grande (opposite Eagle Pass, Texas) to the Pacific coast south of Mazatlán—a route very similar to that of Plumb's earliest project, except that it did not lead to Mexico City. Since the concessionaires agreed to do without a governmental subsidy, the construction dates and other conditions were made very liberal. The Huntington interests received other concessions later and on December 9, 1882, organized the Mexican International Company to unify the various grants.[61]

By this time the Mexican Central and Mexican National Railroads had pre-empted the best north-south routes to Mexico City, but the resources of northern Mexico and the west coast still offered a tempting goal. The Mexican International Company began construction at the American end of its line in 1883. By January 1884 the line had reached the mining center of Monclova, Coahuila, and in 1888 it crossed the Mexican Central at Torreón, a newly built city on the east edge of Durango state. On October 1, 1892, the railroad was opened for service as far as the city of Durango (see Map 1).[62]

From about 1881 to April 15, 1889, or, in other words, during most of this period of slow construction Plumb was vice-president of the Mexican International Railroad Company. Since he left behind only a few letters and papers dating from this period in his life, it is impossible to say exactly how much influence he had in determining company policy; but much of Huntington's attention was occupied by the consolidation of his American lines and competition with the Atchison, Topeka, and Santa Fe, and it is reasonable to suppose that he relied heavily on Plumb's extensive experience in Mexico. During much of this time

[61] Powell, *Railroads of Mexico*, p. 137; typed memorandum, dated Dec. 5, 1888, describing the Mexican International Railroad, Plumb Papers, XIV; Dublán and Lozano, *Legislación mexicana*, XIV, 800–808.

[62] Powell, *Railroads of Mexico*, pp. 137–138; Mexican International Railroad Company, *Annual Report of the Mexican International Railroad Company for the Year Ending December 31, 1892* (New York, 1893), pp. 3–4.

Plumb's old rival, Robert B. Gorsuch, served the company as chief engineer, and the two became close friends.[63] It would be interesting to know exactly how Plumb buried the hatchet with the Díaz administration, against which he had unsuccessfully propagandized in 1876.

When the company opened its 540 miles of main-line track to Durango in 1892, three years after Plumb's resignation, it also controlled two active coal-mining companies, the Coahuila Coal Company and the Alamo Coal Company, with extensive holdings in Mexico's best coal fields along the Sabinas River, which were counted on to furnish the railroad with profitable and dependable business. The opening of silver-lead smelters at Velardeña, Monclova, and elsewhere in northern Mexico during the 1890's furnished a market for coal and further traffic for the railroad, and a branch line to the cotton fields of Tlahualilo added a supply of agricultural products. The company eventually extended its main line from Durango northwest to Tepehuanes to tap the lumber-producing areas on the east slopes of the Sierra Madre Occidental, but the rough mountain country prevented the railroad from reaching its original goal, the Pacific coast.[64]

From the organization of the company to the end of the Díaz period the Mexican International Railroad earned regular profits from this varied traffic in coal, ores, and agricultural products. The gross earnings per mile increased from 612.37 pesos in 1884, the first year of partial operations, to 4,518.67 pesos in 1892, when the line was opened to Durango. After a brief falling-off in the Panic of 1893, the earnings began to rise once more, and in the financial year of 1909-1910 they reached the figure of 9,822.57 pesos. During about the same period the

[63] Gorsuch to Plumb, Mexico City, Sept. 3, 1888, Plumb Papers, XIV.
[64] Memorandum on the Coahuila and Alamo Coal Companies, Dec. 5, 1888, *ibid*. The annual reports of the Mexican International Railroad give some information as to the source of traffic.

average gross returns per mile of American railroads rose from
$6,657 to $11,021.[65] As in the case of all other Mexican enterprises, however, comparative figures of earnings must be interpreted with care, for by 1910 the American dollar was worth
more than twice as much as the Mexican peso.

In spite of economies in operation, the declining value of the
peso drained away much of the profits, and there is no evidence
to indicate that the stockholders of the Mexican International
Railroad ever received any dividends. By 1903 the company had
almost exhausted its power to issue mortgage bonds for improvements and extensions, and in that year its stockholders sold a
controlling block of shares to a rival, the newly reorganized
Mexican National Railroad. Neither company, however, could
stand the strain of competition, and in 1909 both lines became
part of the National Railroads of Mexico, a system controlled
by the Mexican government. In this network the Mexican International lines practically lost their separate identity.[66]

Edward Lee Plumb, the original promoter of the International project, followed all these developments with the detachment of old age. After his retirement from the company in 1889
he traveled in Europe for his health and then settled down to
live quietly in New York and Washington until his death at the
age of eighty-four on April 18, 1912. He left behind few
writings from this period of his life and no comments whatever
on the fate of his Mexican project. If this meant that he washed
his hands of Mexican railroads, not many would blame him,
for he had spent over thirteen years of his life planning and

[65] A table of earnings for the period 1884–1910 is contained in Mexican
International Railroad Company, *Annual Report, 1910*, p. 10. The figures
for American railroads represent annual averages for the periods 1891–
1895 and 1906–1910. See U.S. Bureau of the Census, *Statistical Abstract of
the United States, 1947* (Washington, 1947), p. 520.

[66] Fernando González Roa, *El problema ferrocarrilero y la compañia de
los Ferrocarriles nacionales de México* (México, 1915), pp. 100–101;
Jaime Gurza, *La política ferrocarrilera del gobierno* (México, 1911), pp.
21, 40, *et passim*.

building a railroad which never really reached its goal. In spite of his genuine talents as a diplomat and publicist, he suffered to some degree from the same tendency toward over-enthusiasm and self-hypnosis as General Rosecrans, and it is hard to believe that the fall of Lerdo and the loss of Plumb's initial advantage were responsible by themselves for the mediocre success of his project. Perhaps no one could have achieved the golden results which he had confidently predicted so many times.

IV

Utopian Reformer:
Albert Kimsey Owen

IN the spring of 1881, when Plumb was about to enter the employment of Collis P. Huntington and begin construction of his long-planned Mexican International line, another and even more ambitious railroad blueprint lay on the drawing table. Its architect, Albert Kimsey Owen, was both a businessman and a reformer, who hoped to build a railroad from the Rio Grande to the Gulf of California with the aid of American capital and the labor of colonists living along the line of track in semisocialist settlements.[1] Thus, while a new transcontinental line opened the riches of the Far East to American trade, a new society would appear in northwest Mexico to teach men how best to use the new wealth. Owen had even less success than Plumb. For about a decade a few score colonists made their homes on the shores of the Gulf of California, "to eat mush and dream of Utopia,"[2]

[1] Albert K. Owen was not related to the more famous social reformer, Robert Owen. By an interesting coincidence, Robert Owen was also drawn to Mexico as a site for colonization and in 1828 vainly petitioned the Mexican government for a land grant in Texas and Coahuila. See José C. Valadés, *Topolobampo: La metropoli socialista de Occidente* (Mexico, [1939]), pp. 20–26.

[2] *Mexican Financier*, Aug. 23, 1890, p. 584.

but the railroad to the Orient was never laid, and soon the settlers began to quarrel with each other. By the turn of the century most of them had given up and gone home.

I

Albert Kimsey Owen's early life prepared him in some degree for both parts of his dual career as railroad promoter and Utopian colonizer. Born about 1840 in Chester, Pennsylvania, Owen traveled all over the United States and Europe with his brother and his father, a Quaker physician. For a time he is said to have lived in New Harmony, Indiana, where the decline of Robert Owen's experiment should have impressed him with the difficulties of colonization. At the age of about thirty he became a surveyor and civil engineer. In 1868 he visited Mexico for the first time, apparently out of curiosity about resources and possibilities for colonization, but he saw no more than the tropical coast line of Veracruz and concluded that it would be unhealthful for settlers. Four years later he entered Mexico again, this time by way of Chihuahua, as a surveyor in the party of General William J. Palmer, who had recently decided to finance the Rosecrans railroad project and wished to examine its prospects for himself.[3]

Although no record exists of Owen's contribution to the Palmer surveying expedition, there is no doubt that the expedition set the course of Owen's life. Already interested in the Mexican west coast when he set out, he learned from Indians along the way of an immense lake called Ohuira (Enchanted Place) lying along the coast in the midst of a fertile plain. His curiosity was aroused, and, leaving the Palmer party, he set off toward the Pacific with guides, after writing a preliminary letter

[3] Albert Kimsey Owen, *Integral Co-operation: Its Practical Application* (New York, [1885]), pp. 199 ff.; New York *Tribune*, Dec. 19, 1886, as quoted in Albert Kimsey Owen, ed., *Extracts from Newspapers Explanatory of the Credit Foncier Company* (New York, [1887]), p. 20; Valadés, *Topolobampo*, pp. 14–15.

to Dr. Benjamin R. Carman, a resident of Mazatlán who owned
much of the land around the "lake." The journey over the Sierra
Madre and down the valley of the Fuerte River stimulated
Owen's romantic imagination to such a degree that when he
finally arrived on the shores of Ohuira at midnight in late September 1872 he stood speechless, wrapped up in a blanket
against the chill, and vowed to himself that here he would
create a great seaport for the ships of the world.[4]

What he had found was not a lake at all but a long arm of
the sea consisting of an inner and an outer bay, connected by a
narrow strait and protected from storms by headlands and
islands. The harbor had been known only locally until in 1869
the American government sent Commander William T. Truxton and the sloop of war "Jamestown" to survey the outer harbor at Carman's request. He reported that the harbor contained
plenty of room for vessels of the deepest draft. Provided with
many of Truxton's findings, Owen spent several weeks exploring the lands around the two bays and laying out plans in his
mind for the buildings, stores, docks, plazas, and schools of a
great port and railroad terminus. From the natives of the region
he adopted the name Topolobampo (Hidden Water) for the
harbor.[5]

Returning to the United States, Owen put his ideas on paper
and in May 1873 submitted them to a convention of state
governors in Atlanta, Georgia, hoping to attract Southern commercial interests with the lure of Mexican trade outlets. A
pamphlet of his described a great trunk line running from Norfolk, "the most commanding commercial position along the
whole Atlantic seaboard of the United States," through Austin,

[4] Valadés, *Topolobampo*, pp. 15–18. A letter from Carman to Owen,
Mazatlán, Aug. 17, 1872, refers to an earlier letter by Owen ([Albert
Kimsey Owen], *The Austin-Topolobampo Pacific Railroad Route*
[Washington, 1879?], p. 44).

[5] [Owen], *Austin-Topolobampo Pacific Railroad Route*, pp. 41–45, 47–
49; Valadés, *Topolobampo*, pp. 18–19. The name seems to be a corruption
of an Indian name Topolcampo.

Texas, to Topolobampo. With such a railroad and five years of peace, he maintained, Mexican commerce would increase from less than 50,000,000 pesos a year to 200,000,000 pesos. The country's vast resources, including the "untold ores of Lower California," and the possibility of cutting the time of New York–San Francisco trips to eight and a half days were additional arguments of importance. In 1874 he persuaded Governor James L. Kemper of Virginia and the state legislature to charter a "Southern Settlement Society" for the foundation of colonies along the railroad route, but soon the business depression which had begun a year earlier convinced Owen that he must appeal for funds on a national scale, and he turned to the United States government for aid.[6]

From December 1874 to February 1879 Owen waged a campaign of pamphleteering and personal lobbying in an effort to persuade the president and Congress to sponsor his project. As he remarked later, whenever he spoke to Americans about Mexico, he encountered an almost unanimous opinion "that Mexico was composed of a series of sterile, unsurmountable cordilleras." [7] Fortunately he succeeded in arousing the interest of President Grant, and according to Owen's account the president even agreed to send three or four engineers to survey the railroad route if Owen could secure the prior approval of the Mexican government. He immediately laid his project before Ignacio Mariscal, the Mexican minister, who consulted the Lerdo government. On May 22, 1875, the minister of *fomento* gave his formal approval. No government engineers ever appeared to survey the route, however, for apparently Grant had made his offer contingent upon the approval of Congress.[8]

[6] [Owen], *Austin-Topolobampo Pacific Railroad Route*, pp. 25–40; Sanford A. Mosk, "A Railroad to Utopia," *Southwestern Social Science Quarterly*, XX (Dec. 1939), 244.

[7] Speech of Owen at a banquet, May 2, 1880, as quoted in Valadés, *Topolobampo*, p. 34.

[8] *Ibid.*, pp. 34–35. It is worth noting that even at the height of the border crisis in 1878 the suspicious Manuel Zamacona fully approved of

When Owen submitted his first proposals to Congress, he appealed for support both to Southerners and to followers of the Greenback movement, then at its height. Owen was already a Greenbacker in good standing, for in 1873 he had organized the first Greenback Club in Pennsylvania, and he served as delegate to every one of the party's national conventions. Now he asked Congress to authorize construction of a "great Southern trans-oceanic and international air line" from Norfolk to Presidio del Norte on the Rio Grande and issue a special series of treasury notes to pay all expenses. He proposed to retire the notes gradually with the net earnings of the railroad and then to charge moderate tolls for maintenance only. Conservatives, however, were repelled by the Greenback provisions, liberals by the fear of another Crédit Mobilier. Furthermore, the smoldering border controversy with Mexico inspired very natural doubts of that government's co-operation. Consequently Owen's sponsorship bill never became law, although it was favorably reported from committees and debates on the floor of the next two Congresses with strong support from the press.[9]

At this point, temporarily discouraged over the failure of his railroad bills, Owen turned his attention to another project. This was a plan to drain Lake Texcoco, one of a chain of lakes on the outskirts of Mexico City which occupied valuable land and made the city unhealthful. Time and again the Spanish and

---

Owen's railroad project (*ibid.*, p. 36). José Valadés has singled out Owen from other American promoters of the period as the only one free from speculative or annexationist interests (Valadés, *El porfirismo: Nacimiento,* p. 348).

[9] Mosk, "Railroad to Utopia," pp. 243–248. See also the following pamphlets by Owen, which contain pertinent documents from this period: *The Great Southern Trans-oceanic and Inter-federal Air-Line Asia to Europe via Mexico and the Southern States: Memorial of A. K. Owen* [Chester, Pa., 1874], and *The Great Southern Trans-oceanic and International Air-Line Asia to Europe via Mexico and the Southern States: Supplementary to a Memorial of A. K. Owen, C.E.* [Chester, Pa., 1874]. See also the pamphlet *Austin-Topolobampo Pacific Railroad Route,* cited above.

Mexican governments had tried to cut adequate drainage ditches or tunnels through the surrounding mountains to lower levels but had always stopped short of success.[10] In April 1879, during one of Owen's business trips to Mexico City, a leading lawyer and politician, Miguel Hidalgo y Terán, persuaded him to examine the most recently excavated tunnel. He returned to the United States somewhat interested in the engineering aspects of the problem and later discussed terms with Díaz. On May 31 Díaz agreed to Owen's plan for financing the undertaking, and during the summer Owen made a thorough survey of the ground and somehow managed to interest a few financial backers in the United States. In early October he returned to Mexico to see the necessary legislation put through Congress.

The engineering aspects of the plan were rather closely modeled on an unsuccessful attempt of the early seventeenth century. Estimating that the water of Lake Texcoco would evaporate in 320 days and leave a bed of mud if the lake were not fed by streams, Owen proposed simply to allow the force of gravity to carry off, by way of an open canal, as much water as the streams brought in. This canal, from the center of the lake to the old Huehuetoca cut, would be 29 miles long, and a depth of six feet would be maintained in the canal the year round, in order that it might be used for commerce. Owen estimated that 16,000 persons or their equivalent in machinery could excavate such a canal in the volcanic rock of the area within 313 days, at a total cost of about $3,000,000 for labor and management, but not including tools or construction materials.[11]

To defray the immediate costs of labor, Owen fell back upon

[10] A brief account of the principal attempts is contained in Matías Romero, *Mexico and the United States: A Study of Subjects Affecting Their Political, Commercial, and Social Relations, Made with a View to Their Promotion* (New York, 1898), pp. 266–280.

[11] [Albert Kimsey Owen], *The Texcoco-Huehuetoca Canal: Proposed as a Basis on Which to Issue Treasury Money and to Inaugurate a National System to Multiply and Diversify Home Industries* (Philadelphia, 1880), pp. 16–18, 118–120.

the Greenbacker's cure-all, a special issue of "Treasury money" in small denominations and a series of 5 per cent bonds costing as low as five pesos, in which Mexican laborers would be encouraged to lay away their savings after the manner of French peasants. The bonds would also be used to pay the nine commissioner-engineers who were to undertake the project. In this manner, Owen told Díaz, he and his fellow commissioners proposed to put Mexican credit to use and thus cause it to be respected abroad.[12] Within six years the tolls on the canal and adjacent road, together with taxes of city properties and royalties from soda and salt manufacture in the lake bed, would yield $4,872,000, and immediate benefits to the Valley of Mexico would total $30,000,000. In defending his proposals he cited Greenbackers and other authorities in the United States and many examples of state-controlled economic enterprises, especially in Europe.[13] Obviously, however, he failed to take into consideration the marginal existence of the Mexican peon, who had no conception of surplus capital, of investment, or in many cases even of cash payment. Nor did he realize the utter lack of confidence at home and abroad in any securities bearing the seal of the Mexican government.

Owen's drainage project collapsed as quickly as it had been built up. In the autumn of 1879 he rounded up support among Mexican officials, and when he returned to the United States at the end of the year, Díaz reiterated his eagerness to see Mexican credit "made useful to the people," although he told Owen that the foreign population of Mexico City had protested against the issue of Treasury money. During the next six months Owen completed the organization of an American syndicate for the work, headed by General Alfred A. T. Tarbert, and late in the summer the two sailed for Mexico in the "City of Vera Cruz."

[12] Albert Kimsey Owen to Porfirio Díaz, Mexico City, Oct. 23, 1879, *ibid.*, pp. 19–28.

[13] *Ibid.*, pp. 25, 43–52, 55–57.

They never reached their destination, for on August 29 the ship foundered off Daytona, Florida, and nearly all on board were lost. After twenty-two hours in the water, buffeted by wreckage but holding fast to $400 in a sack tied around his neck, Owen crawled on shore, more dead than alive. As soon as he had recovered, he proceeded to reorganize his syndicate, with Ulysses S. Grant, Jr., the son of the ex-president, at its head, but he soon learned that the Díaz government was in the process of re-establishing relations with France, in order to negotiate a debt contracted with the Franco-Egyptian Bank of Paris. Under the circumstances Owen's inflationary plan no longer appealed to the Mexicans.[14]

It is possible that Owen had considered returning to his Topolobampo project even before the collapse of his plans for draining Lake Texcoco, for Jose C. Valadés writes that he spent part of the autumn of 1880 in London, setting forth his plans for an ideal city. In any case he quickly remodeled his Texcoco syndicate and on March 8, 1881, incorporated the Texas, Topolobampo, and Pacific Railway and Telegraph Company, filling out its roster of officials with associates and friends of ex-President Grant, who, despite his failure to win nomination for a third term during the preceding year, was nonetheless a figure of considerable stature in the business world.[15] On the day after the incorporation of the company one of its directors, George

[14] *Credit Foncier of Sinaloa* (newspaper), Aug. 1, 1892, p. 363; New York *Tribune*, Sept. 5, 1880, pp. 1–2; *ibid.*, Dec. 19, 1886, as cited in Owen, *Extracts from Newspapers*, p. 21.

[15] Valadés, *Topolobampo*, p. 42. From 1881 to 1886 the president of the company was ex-Senator William Windom, of Minnesota. As a hard-money Republican, he was a strange colleague for the Greenbacker Owen. A complete list of officers and directors is contained in Alexander Dwight Anderson, *The American and Mexican Pacific Railway or Transcontinental Short Line* (Washington, 1883), p. 2. Díaz later told Arthur E. Stilwell that General Grant was president of the company for a brief time, but no corroboration of this has been found (Arthur E. Stilwell, *Forty Years of Business Life* [New York, 1926?], p. 17).

W. Simmons, set out for Mexico to examine the proposed route
of the railroad. He and his party were much impressed with the
beauty of Topolobampo harbor, the fertility of the nearby
Fuerte Valley, and the varied resources of the sierras to the east.
Before they left the state of Sinaloa, they began to buy up lands
for the company, and on their return trip they outlined a pro-
visional route for the railroad survey.[16]

Nothing now remained but to secure a formal concession from
the Mexican government. The ever-watchful Mexican minister,
Manuel Zamacona, observed the incorporation of the Texas,
Topolobampo, and Pacific Company with a few misgivings, and

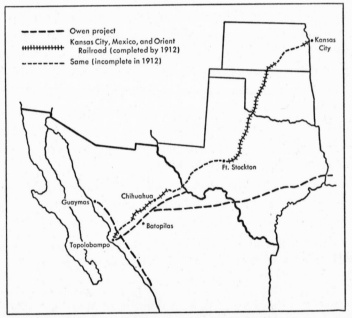

Map 3. The Owen and Stilwell projects

[16] Texas, Topolobampo, and Pacific Railroad and Telegraph Company,
*Reports of Geo. W. Simmons, Jr., Dr. B. R. Carman, and John E. Price,
Esq., upon the Route of a Railroad from Topolobampo Bay, on the Gulf
of California, to Piedras Negras, on the Rio Grande* (Boston, 1881),
pp. 3–22.

he sent his government the full background of all its officials, noting how the sons of ex-President Grant were exploiting their father's name and calling attention to the presence among the directors of the notorious General Ben Butler, who had annoyed the Mexican government with inflated damage claims.[17] Nevertheless, on June 13, 1881, President González of Mexico awarded to the company a contract for the construction of a main railroad line from Piedras Negras on the Rio Grande to Topolobampo, with branches to Mazatlán, to Alamos, Sonora, and to Presidio del Norte, Chihuahua (see Map 3). Construction work must begin within sixty days after official approval of the company's plans, and during each succeeding two-year period the company must complete 150 kilometers, or 100 kilometers in mountainous country. The whole line must be finished in ten years. For all construction except that of the third branch line the government promised a subsidy of 5,000 pesos per kilometer, in addition to certain tax exemptions.[18]

II

Before continuing the narrative account of Owen's railroad project it is necessary to examine the many articles and pamphlets which he published between 1873 and the mid-1880's, in order to understand his intentions and the principal bases of his appeal to American investors. Although his propaganda is obviously very similar to that of General Rosecrans, it was directed more to American than to Mexican readers. Unlike the general, Owen easily secured from the Mexican government the terms which he wanted, but he did not enjoy the financial backing of an American corporation like the Denver and Rio Grande Railroad. Consequently Owen and several associates, such as Alexander D. Anderson and George W. Simmons, filled pamphlets and periodicals with fluent, oratorical prose and

[17] Valadés, *Topolobampo*, pp. 44–45.
[18] Dublán and Lozano, *Legislación mexicana*, XIV, 826–838.

pages of statistics directed not only at the general public but also at any special economic groups whose interests they thought they could identify with a transcontinental railroad.

Like Rosecrans, Owen and his associates argued the vital necessity of good communications for national development. To him a country's roads were "tests of the degree of its civilization" and "the veins and arteries of the body-politic." Just as the greatness of Greece had begun with its control over the Armenian-Caucasian trade route to the Far East (an interpretation which many historians would dispute), so also the growth of the Inca civilization had paralleled the development of the Andean highway. In America and Australia the railroads had changed sterile lands to fertile, in India and Russia they were repeating the process. The United States had solved "the Indian and Mormon difficulties" and brought border outlaws under civil authority by building the Pacific Railroad. "In fact," he went on enthusiastically, "railway enterprise is a cure for the social and political problems of modern life. Poverty, revolution, brigandage, religious persecution, and social singularities disappear before this all-powerful agent. Where armies and legislation are powerless, the locomotive-engine does not fail of success." [19]

Not content with outtalking Rosecrans on the civilizing mission of the railroad, Owen and Anderson went beyond him also in emphasizing the broad international scope of their project. In one pamphlet Owen urged that just as Europe was paying increased attention to the "Eastern Question" of trade with Asia by way of Turkey and the Near East so also the United States must concern herself with the "Western Question" of trade with the Far East by way of Mexico. Anderson called American

[19] Albert Kimsey Owen, *The Topolobampo Pacific* [Chester, Pa., 1878?], *passim;* Owen, *The Great Southern Air-Line: Supplementary to a Memorial,* pp. 4–5; [Owen], *Austin-Topolobampo Pacific Railroad Route,* pp. 16–17.

trade with countries bordering on the Pacific Ocean the "weak side of our foreign commerce," since it accounted for only 4 per cent of their total trade. "The time has now come," he continued, "when the industries of the United States should be diversified. . . . But Europe prefers to purchase our raw material and manufacture for herself and other parts of the world. We must, rather, look to the countries and islands surrounding the Pacific, which are deficient in manufactures and which will gladly buy of us when the Pacific is adequately bridged over with steamship lines." [20]

Naturally the same argument could be used in support of the Union Pacific–Central Pacific Railroads and the other transcontinental lines which lay entirely within American territory. Therefore Owen and his fellow writers went to great lengths to prove that the total land-sea distance from the Atlantic seaboard to the principal Pacific trade centers was shorter by way of Topolobampo than by way of San Francisco. When Owen appeared before congressional committees in the 1870's, he brought with him maps, chalk, and pieces of string with which to lay out comparative distances and prove that Topolobampo was truly "the apex of the great commercial V on the Pacific, for not only the United States but for Canada and Nova Scotia." All American cities to the east and southeast of St. Paul, Minnesota, he demonstrated, were closer by land to the Mexican than to the California port. In answer to the criticism that Topolobampo lay too far south for trade with north and central Pacific countries, especially China and Japan, Anderson argued that "the star of empire . . . has recently been deflected from the Orient towards those great and fertile islands of the South Pacific—Australia and New Zealand." His pamphlets were profusely illustrated with maps demonstrating every conceivable advantage of distance which Topolobampo possessed, and

[20] [Owen], *Austin-Topolobampo Pacific Railroad Route*, pp. 25–26; Anderson, *American and Mexican Pacific Railroad*, pp. 71–75.

wherever possible he cited winds and ocean currents to strengthen his case.[21]

An important part of Owen's publicity campaign dealt with the qualifications of the harbor of Topolobampo for the role of world entrepôt which he had proposed for it. On the basis of surveys by Commander Truxton in 1869 and by Commander George Dewey in 1874 and 1875, Owen maintained that the inner harbor was completely landlocked and that ships in the outer harbor would feel only northwest and southwest winds. A few strategically placed buoys would make both bays more accessible than "most of the harbors on the coast of the United States south of Boston." Over the sandbar at the entrance of the outer harbor Owen claimed to have found a wide channel of six or seven fathoms, and both harbors together contained twelve square miles of water over twenty-one feet deep—twice as much anchorage area as in San Diego and almost as much as in the harbor of Greater New York. George W. Simmons, who had also visited Topolobampo, reported that there was plenty of high, well-drained land for a city site as well as enough stone in the region to fill in certain marshy sections on the north shore.[22]

Hardly less vital to Owen's success than a deep harbor at Topolobampo was a practicable route over the Sierra Madre for his railroad. In the absence of a complete formal survey, he published optimistic estimates by those who had traveled over the proposed line. Professor George A. Koenig, for example, wrote of a crossing made in December 1870 and described the descent from Churo, at the crest of the Sierra, as "hardly comparable to the descent of the Union Pacific Railroad into the Sacramento valley regarding difficulty and cost of construction." [23] In 1877 John O. Keim estimated that 150 miles of railroad in the Sierra

[21] [Owen], *Austin-Topolobampo Pacific Railroad Route*, pp. 14–16; Anderson, *American and Mexican Pacific Railroad*, pp. 61–64, 71–75.

[22] Anderson, *American and Mexican Pacific Railroad*, pp. 53–57.

[23] Quoted in Mosk, "Railroad to Utopia," p. 247.

section would cost $8,750,000 to construct, and the whole line about $25,000,000. Four years later, after an examination of the Sierra section, Frederick G. Fitch estimated construction costs at an average of $25,000 per mile for 250 miles.[24]

For the purposes of this study the most significant portions of Owen's publicity efforts, and certainly the most flowery, were those which dealt with the resources of Mexico, especially that part of the country adjacent to the proposed railroad line. In 1875 Owen told Congress: "In all the world there is not another land so rich as Mexico. It is one vast mass of mineral, metal, pastoral, and agricultural wealth. California was always considered the worst section of the Mexican territories; yet, behold the enormous wealth and influence it has attained inside of twenty years." So saying, he launched into an enumeration of Mexico's export products, both mineral and agricultural. He praised her streams as "capable of great waterpower," her climate, her textile mills, "perhaps the nearest complete, in machinery, in their appointments, and in ornamented grounds, on this continent," and her interior trade, estimated at $400,000,000. In another place he declared solemnly: "Mexico awaits development. Every influential and moneyed man there will give his assistance and his protection to the organization that comes among them to work." [25] Anderson kept pace with Owen in his writings, as in his statement, quoted in the Introduction, that Mexico would become the India, Cuba, Brazil, Italy, and Troy of the United States.

There is no need to point out the exaggeration in such generalized proclamations as these. Prospective investors probably paid more attention to specific data on the sections through which Owen's railroad was to pass, especially Chihuahua and

[24] John O. Keim in *Railway Age*, II (1877), 1572, as cited in *ibid.*, p. 246; Texas, Topolobampo, and Pacific Railroad and Telegraph Company, *Reports*, p. 43.

[25] [Owen], *Austin-Topolobampo Pacific Railroad Route*, pp. 19-21, 31.

Sinaloa. Here too the publicists were generous with superlatives. In the Sierra Madre, wrote Owen, "the minerals and metals embrace almost every variety known to commerce—petroleum, quick-silver, onyx, and coal being among the most recent developments." The silver deposits of nearby Batopilas, controlled by Alexander Robey Shepherd after 1879, were "metals and not ores" and could be reduced as easily as the copper of Lake Superior. Simmons described coal deposits in the region of Santa Rosa and Piedras Negras and declared that the railroad would pass through "what is acknowledged to be the richest mineral belt in Mexico." Anderson published page after page of testimony concerning mineral deposits, beginning with the writings of Baron von Humboldt, and predicted that any well-developed mine would furnish as much traffic for the railroad as a town of 10,000 people.

Owen and his associates took a similar view of the other resources of northwest Mexico. After passing through the Fuerte Valley on his way home from Topolobampo in 1881, Simmons pronounced it to be the "Garden of Mexico" and described how one progressive Mexican planter had made use of irrigation and dust mulches in growing thousands of acres of cotton, sugar, tobacco, oranges, limes, and other fruits during the dry season. Carman described the small-scale sugar industry of the same area and added that many crops were harvested twice a year. Among the host of quotations which Anderson reprinted, some admitted the dryness of the climate, but others anticipated an agriculture comparable to that of California, and Simmons felt confident that the company could eventually pay for the entire cost of railroad construction with the profits from land sales. As for forests, he declared: "There is wood enough along our line to supply ties for all the railroads in Mexico." Off the coast, added Frederick G. Fitch, the Gulf of California and its islands could furnish oysters, seals, whales, guano, and other resources. As a final inducement Owen suggested that tourists could be attracted to this land of mild climate, where both sunstrokes and fireplaces were unknown.[26]

III

In all this railroad publicity there was very little of Utopian social reform. Owen soon realized, however, that it would be useful if not absolutely necessary to develop his long-cherished plans for a Utopian colony as an adjunct to the railroad project. On December 5, 1882, the Mexican government revised the railroad contract to include the construction of a city on To-polobampo Bay, to be named Ciudad González after the president. According to Valadés, Owen immediately organized a co-operative society for railroad building and colonization and began to issue bonds; but other sources fix a later date for the organization of a formal colonizing company.[27] In any case, events between 1883 and 1885 must surely have convinced Owen that he could not build the railroad without the colony. In the former year he and a party surveyed one hundred miles of the route, and in 1885 a construction company began preliminary grading work, but the company lacked capital for even a few miles of rails. In June of that year all immediate prospects of aid from the Mexican government disappeared when Díaz, returning to office to find an empty treasury, suspended the payment of all railroad subsidies. Partly in order to tap a new source of capital, therefore, and partly to secure himself a dependable supply of American labor for the railroad,

[26] United States, 48th Congress, 1st Session, *House Executive Document 86;* Joseph Nimmo, Jr., *Trade between Mexico and the United States* (Washington, 1884), Appendix IV, p. 60; Texas, Topolobampo, and Pacific Railroad and Telegraph Company, *Reports,* pp. 8–10, 16–17, 25–26; Anderson, *American and Mexican Pacific Railroad,* pp. 22–35, 44–51, 57–60; [Owen], *Austin-Topolobampo Pacific Railroad Route,* pp. 60–66.

[27] Dublán and Lozano, *Legislación mexicana,* XVI, 353–357; Valadés, *Topolobampo,* pp. 45–46.

Owen now publicized his project for a Utopian settlement.[28]

Despite his association with Grant and other pillars of Republican orthodoxy, Owen belonged to that long line of nineteenth-century social reformers who troubled American consciences or, failing that, disturbed American complacency. The world, he declared, was destroying itself by ruthless competition. In 1885 he prophesied impending doom: American cities saturated with "unmixed wickedness and utter moral depravity," Cuba "decaying . . . sinking into death," Britain "fast becoming one vast prison-swamp of reeking pestilence, physical and moral." [29] In the United States 5,000 millionaires owned one-fifth of the country's wealth, and 21,000,000 men and women were reduced to poverty by rents, taxes, interest, fares, freightage, expressage, and commissions. As a later journalist reported, Owen accused reformers of "all chasing, to the exclusion of every other consideration, some liquor law, some tariff legislation . . . each riding to death his or her own little hobby-horse." [30] Movements for labor reform such as the Knights of Labor, of which he was once a member, had become "puppets in the hands of the politicians." In any case he believed strikes to be wrong, "because they excite the worst passions of all concerned . . . [and] because each strike unites the incorporated classes into a closer and more tyrannical compact." [31]

Owen proposed to solve the problems of competition with what he called "integral co-operation." One of his followers concisely summarized his goals as follows:

[28] Mosk, "Railroad to Utopia," pp. 250–251.
[29] Albert Kimsey Owen, *The Credit Foncier of Sinaloa* [n.p., 1885], pp. 54–55.
[30] Albert Kimsey Owen, *The Problems of the Hour* (New York, [1897]), *passim;* "The Topolobampo Colony," *Harper's Weekly,* XXXI (July 2, 1887), 475.
[31] The description of the Knights of Labor was written by an unidentified member of the Credit Foncier Company. See *Credit Foncier of Sinaloa,* Dec. 1, 1888, p. 54; Albert Kimsey Owen, *Integral Co-operation at Work* (New York, [1890–1891]), I, 51.

Is it not plain as the sun at noon that the only way out of this industrial quagmire is for the people everywhere in small bodies to "pool" and carry on their *own* industries by themselves or *for* themselves; to unite their means, become their own capitalists, employ their own capital in their own labors, and keep and divide equitably among themselves, the *entire* fruit of those labors. . . . Is it asked how? The answer is, by forming over the whole country, in every country or every state, numbers of integral co-operative towns and cities—each of which will own and work its surrounding farmlands . . . —will own and work its own factories; own and work its *public utilities;* every appliance which the people of the city need for the convenience of all.[32]

As Owen put it himself, each community must have full control of its soil, manufactures, means of communication, and medium of exchange, as "the muscles, bones, sinews, and heart" of its body. At the same time the individual must be guaranteed that portion of income which results from his labor, since "all wealth is created by labor intelligently co-operating with the land and the natural elements." [33]

Because of the failure of Brook Farm, Red Bank, and other communal experiments surrounded by the old, imperfect society and because of the relatively high cost of land in the United States, Owen explained that he preferred to create his first model colony in Mexico. He recognized, however, that the Mexico of his day fell far short of co-operative ideals. He declared:

Her people go to more expense and suffer greater tortures in their wish to live separate lives than any conspicuous people of our time. . . . Her native people are scattered into small and insignificant

[32] William H. Muller, *The New Departure: A Description of Pacific Colony* (New York, [1886]), p. 27; see also *Credit Foncier of Sinaloa,* Jan. 1, 1889, p. 63.

[33] Quoted in Leopold Katscher, "Owen's Topolobampo Colony, Mexico," *American Journal of Sociology,* XII (Sept. 1906), 147, 149. Except where otherwise stated, the description of Owen's plans which follows is based on Katscher's somewhat longer exposition, *ibid.,* pp. 152–167.

communities, each tries to act for him or herself without consulting with, or a consideration for, anyone else, thing, or group, and hence he and she readily become enslaved to those few persons of foreign blood who have made a business of associating themselves, their moneys, and experiences into business firms or houses and into military and political cliques.[34]

Nevertheless, Mexico was his chosen site.

When it came to drawing up a specific plan of action, Owen borrowed widely and unashamedly from a variety of sources. His central organization, a kind of super–public utility corporation called the Credit Foncier Company of Sinaloa, was based on the joint-stock principle, almost as old as capitalism itself. His industrial organization and part of his housing system had as model the Godin iron and brass foundries and the "Familistère" or "Social Palace" at Guise, in France. Agricultural production imitated the bonanza farming of the Dakotas in co-operative use of machinery, distribution the Rochdale co-operative stores. The scrip which he proposed to substitute for money was directly suggested by the communal construction of a market house on the island of Guernsey. Two contemporary reformers, Henry George and Theodor Hertzka, also left traces of their thinking here and there in Owen's plans.[35]

The Credit Foncier Company was the heart and soul of Owen's project. Anyone could become a member by buying at least one share at $10 and by swearing allegiance to the principles of integral co-operation. All colonists were required to be members. The company was authorized to carry on most of the

[34] [Albert Kimsey Owen, Christian J. Hoffman, *et al.*], *Homes and How to Obtain Them: Integral Co-operation, the Solution of the Problem* (Topeka, Kansas, 1890), pp. 45–46. See also New York *Tribune*, Dec. 19, 1886; *Golden Gate*, Jan. 15, 1887. Both are quoted in Owen, *Extracts from Newspapers*, pp. 20, 42.

[35] Mosk, "Railroad to Utopia," p. 251; [Owen *et al.*], *Homes and How to Obtain Them*, pp. 51–52; *New City* (newspaper), Dec. 22, 1892, p. 7; Joyce O. Hertzler, *A History of Utopian Thought* (New York, 1923), pp. 236–244.

functions of economic life: to buy and sell land, to lay out settlements, to build houses, to build and manage railways, shipping lines, utilities, markets, theaters, inns, warehouses, and factories, to operate schools, to administer agricultural affairs, commerce, banking, insurance, and so forth. The management of this powerful organization was vested in ten directors, elected by the members (each member having only one vote, no matter how many shares he held). Under the supervision of a president each of the directors administered one of the ten principal branches of government.

Every family of colonists which wished to hold land was required to pay from $20 to $500 into a land and improvement fund, meet its own traveling expenses, and bring its own bedding, clothes, and furniture. The family would then receive land at the rate of 400 square yards for each share of stock purchased, and the company would build homes as needed (within certain limitations), but neither land nor houses could be mortgaged or transferred to anyone but the company, and then only at the original price. In this manner Owen exorcised the age-old bogies of rent and unearned increment.

The organization of labor was only half communistic, since colonists could work either for themselves or for the company. If a man produced something of his own for sale, he must bring it to the public warehouse, sell it at a fixed price, and receive payment in the form of credit on the company's books. If he worked for the company, he would receive lithographed "credit notes," originally at the rate of $2 a day, and all his expenditures would be placed to his debit on the company books. The system contained none of "the illusive equality of real communism," however. Wages depended upon the amount and quality of work done, and company profits were to be distributed in proportion to the number of shares held. During the early years men worked hard and long each day to keep the colony going, but Owen's ideal was a work week of thirty hours for men and twenty hours for women.

Various other details of Owen's plans reinforce the general impression of a benevolent paternalism, modified by democratic political procedure and lying about halfway between capitalism and socialism. Private property was defined to include clothing, furniture, tools, inventions, and raw materials used in small workshops. Publicly maintained schools were to give free education up to the age of twenty, with special emphasis on "useful, practical occupations." The Mexican government allowed the colony to settle its own internal lawsuits by arbitration, and no attorneys were to be allowed except in external suits. The company paid all physicians yearly salaries and debited individuals for medical care. It also maintained a single newspaper, which was supposed to print every signed communication which it received, in order of arrival. Although many of the colonists came from the "Bible belt" in the United States, there were no churches in the colony, for Owen believed that "as the custodian of our morals, the preserver of peace, the protector of the helpless, and the teacher of the truth, the 'Christian Church' is and has been, a most conspicuous and lamentable failure." [36] Although nonreligious, he and his colleagues were moral enough to forbid gambling—perhaps because it would have required money.

Owen was particularly proud of the elaborate ground plan which he had drawn up for "Ciudad González," or "Pacific City" as it came to be called after González had left office. The city was to have the same area as New York at that time, twenty-nine square miles, but whereas 100,000 acres were allotted to buildings and house gardens, he reserved twice that area for parks and farms. Owen expected to realize $200,000,000 from the sale of land at graduated prices, and with this money he hoped to build all necessary public works and buildings. He laid out broad streets, avenues, and plazas, lined with four to six rows of trees. Not only were industrial plants restricted to cer-

[36] *Credit Foncier of Sinaloa,* Jan. 1, 1891, pp. 58–59. Owen did not outlaw liquor, but since the company bought all goods consumed by the colonists, it could regulate the use of liquor.

tain zones, but also electricity was to be required for cooking purposes, to minimize smoke; and Owen published surprisingly harsh strictures against dogs and horses, for sanitary reasons. Each block of dwellings would be built in common architectural style: a sample sketch showed buildings with Moorish doorways and fat, onion-shaped towers. He planned three types of dwellings: separate houses with gardens, "company dwelling-houses" with a joint kitchen, and "palaces" composed of small apartments for single people.

Such was the blueprint of Owen's Utopia on the shores of Topolobampo Bay. He often repeated the details of organization, management, and operation in his pamphlets, mingled with idealistic rhapsodies such as the long prose poem, "I Love to Dream of an Ideal City," which he wrote in 1893. To judge from their writings, his followers and colonists also partook of their leader's mysticism, for one of their favorite hymns ended with this apostrophe:

> From Dreamland, O city, arise,
> For shadows the substance must be;
> And he who has faith and who tries,
> This beautiful city shall see.

Not unreasonably, a New York newspaper writer commented: "Such is their faith and hope, and having cast religion proper aside, this city of Dreamland has become their cult." [37] But in Sinaloa, as in Brook Farm, New Harmony, Nauvoo, Amana, and Salt Lake City, success required more than faith and hard work.

IV

Between 1883 and 1885 Owen settled the principal details of his colonization project, and on June 9 of the latter year two of his earliest converts began publication of a newspaper, the

[37] "I Love to Dream of an Ideal City" appeared in a supplement to *New City*, Dec. 8, 1893, pp. 1–3, and was also published as a separate pamphlet. The hymn and the comment on it appear in New York *Tribune*, Dec. 19, 1886, as quoted in Owen, *Extracts from Newspapers*, p. 25.

Credit Foncier of Sinaloa, at Hammonton, New Jersey. Like Owen the editors of this newspaper, Edward and Marie Howland, had long been identified with various reform movements. The son of a prominent cotton commission merchant of Charleston, South Carolina, Edward had dabbled unsuccessfully in literature, drifted into the Greenback and Grange movements, and served for a time as master of the New Jersey Grange. Marie had written a popular socialistic novel, *Papa's Own Girl,* based upon her experiences while living in the "Familistère" project in France. Both of them, but especially Marie, possessed boundless enthusiasm, and although Edward was an incurable invalid by the time the colony got under way, they moved to Sinaloa in 1888. After Edward's death there in 1890, Marie stayed on, loyal to Owen through all his troubles. Another of his influential supporters at the beginning was John W. Lovell, a successful New York publisher who had made considerable money from issuing cheap reprint editions and who published several of Owen's Utopian pamphlets.[38] Other early converts were Edwin J. Schellhous, of California; Stephen T. Peet, of Denver, Colorado; and Alvin J. Wilbur, of Greeley, Colorado.

On July 22, 1886, while Owen was making final plans for the organization of his company, the Díaz government revised his concession and required him to establish a colony of at least five hundred families within two years.[39] In September he incorporated the Credit Foncier Company of Sinaloa in Colorado, where he already had a considerable group of followers. According to a formal account which he later issued to the stock-

[38] An account of Edward Howland's life is given in *Credit Foncier of Sinaloa,* Jan. 1, Feb. 1, March 1, April 1, and July 1, 1891. See also Muller, *New Departure,* pp. 22–23; *New City,* Feb. 8, 1893, pp. 7–9; Owen, *Extracts from Newspapers,* p. 19.

[39] Valadés, *Topolobampo,* pp. 47–48. The Mexican Congress approved the concession unanimously in October. See México, *Diario de los debates de la Cámara de diputados: Decimatercera legislatura constitucional de la Unión* (México, 1888–1889), I, 74–79, 203, and *Diario de los debates de la Cámara de senadores* (2 vols. in 1; México, 1887), I–II, 100–101.

holders, the company was to be closely connected with the railroad, and as its shareholders paid their subscriptions, some of the money would be transferred in installments to Senator William Windom, as trustee for the railroad, in payment for the twenty-nine-square-mile site of Pacific City. In October the company paid $10,000 to Windom. Thus Owen did not control the city site himself, nor did the company hold a clear title at the time when settlement began—a fact which caused much misunderstanding among early malcontents in the colony.[40]

In addition to purchasing the city site from the railroad's trustee, the Credit Foncier Company was to construct thirty-five miles of track from the bay to the Fuerte River, in return for half of the stock in the Mexican-American Construction Company, which was building the whole road. Perhaps as a bonus the railroad turned over to the company an extensive tract of land along the shores of the bay. The colonizing company's obligations to the railroad placed a heavy load on the integral co-operators, especially since they also had to purchase materials with which to build their dream city; but Owen was optimistic and announced that as early as September 7 a total of 3,625 adults representing 190 different crafts had subscribed to 15,056 shares of the Credit Foncier Company.[41]

During the autumn and winter of 1886–1887 colonists by the scores streamed to Topolobampo Bay from California, Colorado, and the East. Unfortunately no one had provided shelters, food, or even a supply of fresh water for them in advance on the site of the colony. From the resulting recriminations and counterrecriminations it is hard to learn exactly what happened in the early days or fix the exact responsibility for the premature

[40] *New City*, Dec. 22, 1892, p. 10; Mosk, "Railroad to Utopia," p. 253; [Albert Kimsey Owen], *A Statement to Accompany the Call of Treasurer John W. Lovell for the Payment of the Second Assessment on the Stock of the Credit Foncier Company and for Placing the Equipment Bonds for the Railroad Line from Topolobampo Harbor to the Rio Fuerte Valley* [New York, 1887], pp. 1–3.
[41] [Owen], *Statement*, pp. 1–3; *New City*, Dec. 22, 1892, p. 10.

migrations. Many naturally blamed Owen for his optimistic accounts of the future colony, especially since he was almost the only company official who had actually seen Topolobampo and the Fuerte Valley. On the other hand, Owen blamed Schellhous, Peet, and some of the other directors for misleading the colonists, so that, he said, "against my positive instructions, and, in face of the written order and discipline of the movement, about five hundred of them rushed, pell mell, to Topolobampo before I could stop them." [42] Schellhous himself admitted that the first colonists had come without Owen's knowledge.[43]

Wherever the fault may lie, some of the impetuous Utopians soon regretted their haste, and their complaints nearly wrecked the project at the very outset. The first colonists to arrive, a group from California, took up residence in an old stone fort overlooking the inner strait and pitched tents on the adjacent headlands, where others soon joined them. Owen had just finished his surveys and started back to the United States, but as soon as he learned of the influx of ill-equipped settlers, he retraced his steps, organized the colonists temporarily, and started out again. At Guaymas he met unwelcome reinforcements and told them to go on to the bay, and on his way east he encountered still others. Many of these had brought sums of money with them for supplies, and they had elected a committee en route to buy supplies. By the end of the year between two and three hundred persons had encamped on the shores of Topolobampo Bay.[44]

If the account of the director Schellhous is reliable, the situation of the new colonists was probably no worse than that of the original settlers in much of the American West. Although they were less accustomed to "roughing it" than their ancestors, on

[42] *Ibid.*, Jan. 8, 1893, p. 7.
[43] E. J. Schellhous, *A History of Pioneer Life in Pacific Colony, Topolobampo, Mexico* (San Francisco, 1887), p. 3.
[44] *Credit Foncier of Sinaloa*, July 1, 1892, p. 351; Schellhous, *Pioneer Life in Pacific Colony*, p. 3.

the other hand the Sinaloa climate was mild enough for tents, even in December. Since the country was covered with heavy underbrush and much loose rock on the hills, the Topolobampo colonists had to start with a backbreaking clearing job. According to Schellhous' account, before the end of November they had a two-hundred-loaf bake oven ready for a newly arrived baker, and in succeeding weeks they brought in lumber from Guaymas for a company office, built a stone wharf out into the bay and a wagon road around a mountainous headland toward the interior, and set up a smithy, a kitchen, and a laundry. Later in December a party migrated thirty-five miles overland to lay out a second settlement, Vegaton, on the Fuerte River. A brick kiln was built in the bay colony, and at Vegaton the colonists prepared to turn out sun-dried adobe for buildings. Here they even began a sugar refinery, in anticipation of their principal staple crop. As yet they still lived mostly on food which they had brought with them, but early in 1887 the New York *Sun* reported to its readers that the settlers had celebrated Christmas properly with pudding, fruit cake, oranges, lemonade, and the strains of their own eleven-piece band, playing in the shade of a huge cactus.[45]

Unfortunately by Christmas disease had broken out among the colonists. When a group from Denver arrived in early December, several of the children had measles, and the disease spread to others; one child, sick on arrival, soon died. Presently several cases of smallpox were discovered, and one of the later parties brought in more cases, apparently contracted in Guaymas. According to Schellhous' count, four died of smallpox out of thirteen cases, and two more died later from other causes. The loss of prospective colonists was harmful enough to the enterprise, but even worse was the feeling of disillusionment, uncertainty, and later despair which the sickness spread among some of the healthy majority.

[45] Schellhous, *Pioneer Life in Pacific Colony*, p. 7; New York *Sun*, Jan. 23, 1887, as reprinted in Owen, *Extracts from Newspapers*, pp. 6–9.

Shortly after the first Christmas the lowered morale produced a crisis. Among the later arrivals were several directors of the Credit Foncier Company, Alvin D. Brock and two who are identified simply as Eaton and Hawkins. As Owen later complained, these men had been irregularly elected by various bands of colonists, not by the shareholders as a whole, and in the confusion nonshareholders had been allowed to vote. Whether or not they had planned in advance a "conspiracy to control or to destroy the organization," as Owen believed, Eaton and Hawkins certainly lost no chance to make trouble after their arrival on January 5. At first they refused to pool their supplies with the commissary stores, and after they had explored the city site, they returned to the bay camp with loud charges that Owen had lied to them and must be removed from command.

For a time after this they subsided, and Eaton led a group off to work at Vegaton. According to later pro-Owen testimony, however, Hawkins had started drinking too much mescal on his arrival, and when his son died of smallpox shortly after this, he withdrew into his own hut, drinking more than ever and complaining about Owen to all who would listen. Eventually word came from Vegaton that Eaton had stopped work there and was organizing a police force. This news precipitated a crisis. At a formal meeting the bay colonists asked the two mischief-makers to leave, and in mid-February, after an unseemly wrangle about finances, Eaton, Hawkins, and twenty or thirty others set out for Guaymas.[46] At about the same time Brock resigned his directorship.

Naturally these and other malcontents vented their spleen on Owen in American newspapers. The New York *World* and the New York *Times* printed the accusations of one Nichols, who called Owen a "money-making Socialist," profiting from

[46] Schellhous, *Pioneer Life in Pacific Colony*, pp. 3–6; *New City*, Jan. 8, 1893, p. 7; *Letter of William C. Crooks, M.D., Marie Howland, and John Lovell to the Stockholders of Credit Foncier Company, New York, March 16, 1887* (privately printed).

the misery of his colonists. Early in March a letter to the St. Louis *Globe-Democrat* described women and children on the rocks at Topolobampo imploring God for aid and accused Owen of callously refusing to see sick and destitute colonists who were stranded at Guaymas.[47] Later in the month Brock printed in the Los Angeles *Times* a regular barrage of accusations against Owen and Lovell. They had signed a secret, fraudulent agreement with the railroad company, he said, for control of Mexican concessions. Owen did not really own any of the city site at all. He was deliberately underestimating the cost of irrigation. He knew of the danger of smallpox at Topolobampo but took no precautions. Even the enthusiastic Mrs. Howland did not escape: she was Owen's "eager and too-willing dupe and co-worker in this gigantic swindle." [48]

Owen could not afford to let all these charges go unanswered. Fortunately the majority of the colonists seem to have supported him, for when he and several of the loyal directors arrived at the colony on February 28, they were received with mottoes spelled out in evergreen leaves and scarlet flowers, and the colony band played "Hail, Sinaloa!" composed especially for the occasion. Owen demanded an immediate trial on the charges made against him by Eaton and Hawkins, whereupon a committee elected by the colonists acquitted him and found the others guilty of conspiracy, willful disobedience, and desertion.[49] Earlier in the month he had disposed of Nichols' charges by remarking that he had warned the man not to migrate until the site had been prepared. Somewhat later Mrs. Howland and

[47] Letter of Albert Kimsey Owen to the editor of the New York *Sun*, New York, Feb. 4, 1887, reprinted in Owen, *Extracts from Newspapers*, pp. 46–51; letter to St. Louis *Globe-Democrat* from Nogales, Ariz., March 3, 1887, reprinted in *Crooks, Howland, and Lovell to Stockholders, New York, March 16, 1887*, p. 6.

[48] Reprint from Los Angeles *Times*, date line March 27, 1887, bound with pamphlets on the Owen project in collection of John Crerar Library, Chicago.

[49] Schellhous, *Pioneer Life in Pacific Colony*, pp. 6, 9–10.

two others published a joint letter to the Credit Foncier stock-holders in which they reprinted some of the leading criticisms and countered with their own views of the Hawkins-Eaton imbroglio. Near the end of the letter they published a telegram from the directors in Sinaloa: there were plenty of provisions; 410 healthy colonists were still on the spot, and only 30 had deserted.[50]

V

Undoubtedly the premature migrations of 1886, the inter-necine quarrels, and the bad publicity resulting therefrom pre-vented the colony from growing as Owen had hoped. Groups of new colonists continued to arrive several times a year, but despite his publicity efforts in the United States the newcomers were not enough to counterbalance those who gave up and left. The United States consul at Guaymas, who kept a box score of arrivals and departures, reported that during the first four years some 600 persons went to Topolobampo, but at the end of that time the colony had shrunk to 150.[51] In August 1888 Edward and Marie Howland arrived at Topolobampo with a portable printing press, and from then on the company's official journal, the *Credit Foncier of Sinaloa*, sent back detailed reports on conditions in the colony together with practical suggestions for immigrants, in order that the confusion and disillusionment of 1886–1887 might not be repeated.

[50] Owen to editor of New York *Sun*, New York, Feb. 4, 1887, in Owen, *Extracts from Newspapers*, pp. 46–51; *Crooks, Howland, and Lovell to Stockholders*, New York, March 16, 1887, passim. Later in the year the United States government, stirred by complaints, sent the U.S.S. "Iroquois" to take away any colonists who wished to go. None left. See A. Willard to A. A. Adee, Guaymas, Dec. 14, 1887, U.S. Department of State, Consular Despatches, Guaymas, VII (hereafter cited as State Dept., Consular Despatches).

[51] A. Willard to W. P. Wharton, Guaymas, Nov. 25, 1890, State Dept., Consular Despatches, Guaymas, VIII. This figure agrees fairly well with that of 125 given in the colony's newspaper earlier in the year (*Credit Foncier of Sinaloa*, May 15, 1890, p. 324).

Prospective colonists during these years were required to pay for at least one share of stock per adult, contribute $90 for land rights and provisions, and secure written permission from company headquarters before starting on the trip. Owen and Mrs. Howland furnished lists of supplies which emigrants must bring with them: a year's supply of clothing including three pairs of stout shoes, tents, light furniture, cots, firearms, medicine, soap, and other items of daily use. Most of the colonists came by way of Nogales to Guaymas, using the Atchison, Topeka, and Santa Fe and Sonora Railroads, and completed the journey on one of the coasting vessels that called regularly at Topolobampo. Delays and stopovers were sometimes unavoidable, and the colonists were warned against gamblers, "con men," and other rough characters at Guaymas and Nogales. Sickness and childbirth sometimes complicated the journey, but when the tired emigrants arrived at the bay, the older settlers did their best to welcome them and help them to adjust themselves to the new conditions of life.[52]

From the beginning the plan of colonization called for two types of settlements: a colony on the north shore of Topolobampo Bay which was to be the nucleus of a great railroad terminus and seaport and several agricultural colonies along the lower course of the Fuerte River, about thirty-five miles to the north, which were to construct an irrigation system, produce food for all, and eventually develop a sugar industry (see Map 4). Owen planned to connect the various settlements with his transcontinental railroad, but for the time being the colonists had to be satisfied with a wagon road. The bay colony contained a few semipermanent buildings—an abandoned stone fort, a frame office in which Mrs. Howland published her newspaper, and later a brick customhouse—but nearly all settlers lived in tents, and even those families assigned to space in the old fort

[52] *Credit Foncier of Sinaloa*, Sept. 15, 1888, p. 2, March 1, 1891, p. 95; letter of Albert Kimsey Owen, New York, Sept. 25, 1888, printed as a leaflet.

put up makeshift tents for privacy and protection against rain.

For several years the principal settlement on the river was La Logia, a temporary farm located on land which the colony was buying by installments. All the homes and public buildings here seem to have been tents or simple thatched structures of wattle and cane mats with plain clay floors. Some colonists mitigated the primitive conditions with carpets, mats, furniture, and table linen; and during the rainy season all could enjoy the lush subtropical vines and plants which grew everywhere.[53]

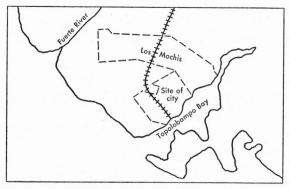

Map 4. Owen's plan of the Topolobampo colony, 1882

Hostile newspaper stories warned prospective emigrants that they would gradually starve to death on musty corn meal, but in reality the colonists ate well enough, although at the unproductive bay colony the diet sometimes grew monotonous— fried fish, turtles, beans, corn bread, syrup, tea, and coffee. At least once a week they received fresh vegetables from La Logia and oftener during the rainy season. In good years the farm settlements produced a variety of vegetables and fruits, and especially in the winter the thickets and underbrush supplied

[53] Among the best descriptions of life in the various settlements are those in the following issues of *Credit Foncier of Sinaloa:* Oct. 1, 1888, pp. 12–13; Feb. 1, 1890, p. 271; May 15, 1890, p. 324; July 15, 1892, p. 353. A leaflet in John Crerar Library contains many photographs of the colonies and settlers dating from 1890 and 1891.

rabbits, quail, deer, and other game. During December and January flocks of ducks migrated along the coast, supplying more eggs than the colonists could eat, but the ducks themselves tasted strongly of fish and had to be cooked with onions to make them palatable. None of the settlements ever had an adequate supply of milk, however, for cattle proved unexpectedly difficult to acclimate, and many of them soon died.[54]

Just as living conditions were primitive but endurable, so the colonists' daily work was hard but often relieved by homemade amusements. According to an account of the daily schedule at La Logia during 1890, the colonists were awakened, sent off to work, and called to dinner by blasts on a horn. Work began soon after sunup, continued until eleven thirty, and was resumed from one to five o'clock. The camp was never quiet, even when the men were away at work, thanks to thousands of birds during the day and crickets, frogs, and an occasional coyote at night, to say nothing of the chatter of children and the noises of everyday household activities.

The older children spent the day in school, for the colonists set up both grade schools and high schools at the principal centers during 1887 and 1888, and at La Logia the schoolhouse was the largest and best building in the settlement. After working all day, the lively minded colonists still had energy enough for dances, argument, and self-entertainment several evenings a week. A lyceum debated such questions as that of raising grapes for wine. (The negative side won.) Owen and other speakers lectured on the Utopia of the future, and a ladies' social culture group taught Spanish and botany. At one of the smaller camps a group of actors even presented scenes from *Julius Caesar.*

---

[54] See the descriptions cited in the preceding note and also *Credit Foncier of Sinaloa,* Dec. 1, 1888, p. 44; Dec. 15, 1888, pp. 52, 55; Jan. 1, 1889, pp. 60–61; Jan. 1, 1890, p. 255; April 1, 1891, pp. 108–109. Owen admitted that in five years at La Logia the colonists got only two good crops (*Two Republics,* May 17, 1892, as cited in Albert Kimsey Owen, *Pacific City Studies* [n.p., n.d.]).

Owen's followers were unusually fond of music: the first colonists in 1886 organized a band, and there are frequent references thereafter to quartets, imported reed organs, and concerts.[55]

Although contemporary reports from the colonies say little about the Mexicans living in the vicinity, it seems clear that the colonists maintained friendly relations on a basis of "live and let live." In the autumn of 1886 the governors of Sinaloa and Sonora sent cordial welcoming letters to Owen, and on at least two occasions during the first four years of settlement the governor of Sinaloa visited the colonies. Mrs. Howland praised the friendliness of the few backward inhabitants of the Topolobampo region, and one Mexican lady, the widow of a *hacendado* near the Fuerte River, sometimes sent food to the settlers at La Logia to vary their diet. Fortunately the colonists were not troublemakers, nor were they prosperous enough to excite the envy of the natives.[56]

Both Owen and his more farsighted colonists recognized that the isolated little settlements could not survive indefinitely without some powerful economic stimulus such as the long-planned transcontinental railroad. After two years of pioneering at Topolobampo by the colonists the railroad had made no progress whatsoever, for the Credit Foncier Company received only $25,119 in cash to September 1, 1888—scarcely enough to keep

[55] *Credit Foncier of Sinaloa*, Feb. 1, 1890, p. 271; Sept. 15, 1888, p. 1; Sept. 1, 1891, p. 189. Many Mexican children attended schools in the colony (*New City*, Feb. 22, 1894, p. 5). Mrs. Howland and her newspaper doubtless passed over some of the seamier aspects of colony life. Although not as humorless as some reformers, she naturally came out strongly for moral, upright living, as in an article describing a boat race between two young men of the colony to determine which one should give up smoking. In the end, to her pleasure, both gave it up (*Credit Foncier of Sinaloa*, Nov. 15, 1888, p. 36).

[56] Luis Torres to Owen, Hermosillo, Sonora, Oct. 22, 1886, Francisco Cañedo to Owen, Culiacán, Sinaloa, Dec. 20, 1886, both reprinted in Owen, *Extracts from Newspapers*, pp. 18–19, 51–52; *Credit Foncier of Sinaloa*, April 15, 1890, p. 309, Oct. 1, 1888, p. 10, Jan. 15, 1889, p. 70.

the colonies going, let alone a surplus for railroad building. In the spring of 1889 Owen visited London in search of support and discussed integral co-operation at some length with William Morris, Annie Besant, and other British reformers. A friend later related that he had secured for Owen introductions to two leading financial houses and that agreements for financial aid had been drawn up and were actually awaiting signature—when the bankers discovered that a "socialistic experiment" was involved. To Owen's bitter disappointment the deals fell through, and he returned home empty-handed.[57]

Later in 1889, however, help came from Christian B. Hoffman, a Kansas businessman who had become interested in the dual project. Hoffman organized a second company to sell stock on the open market to any investors who might like to try for a profit in Mexican lands without incurring the hardships of emigration. This organization, the Kansas Sinaloa Investment (or K.S.I.) Company, also publicized the colony among the discontented farmers of Kansas, "a fertile ground for recruits." The additional capital and encouragement gave Pacific City a new lease on life. On June 6, 1890, the Mexican government granted a revised colonization concession to Owen, and groups of settlers migrated to Sinaloa during 1890 and 1891. The K.S.I. Company bought part of Los Mochis, a large tract of fertile land near the Fuerte River, intending to hold it for the Credit Foncier Company to purchase on easy terms (see Map 4). Colonists began to occupy the new tract, and early in 1891 they began the Herculean task of scraping away dirt with horse-drawn plows and drags to form a seven-mile irrigation ditch leading from the river to the edge of Los Mochis.[58]

[57] *Credit Foncier of Sinaloa*, Jan. 1, 1890, p. 249; Albert K. Owen, "Remarks to the Subscribers," undated pamphlet, p. 8; letter of J. Leon Williams, no date, in *Fortnightly Magazine*, LXXXIX (April 1, 1908), 763.

[58] Mosk, "Railroad to Utopia," pp. 254–256. For an outline of the original relationship between the two companies see [Owen et al.], *Homes and How to Obtain Them*, pp. 6–10.

The railroad project also showed signs of life. In 1891 Owen, Rice, Lovell, and several others organized a new construction company, the Mexican Western Railroad Company, giving the colonists of the Credit Foncier Company an option to do the construction work at wages of $3 a day, to be paid in credits on their company. After the first section of track had been laid from Topolobampo to the river, Owen announced, the Credit Foncier Company would be reorganized and would issue a new set of bonds to pay off its debts to the K.S.I. Company. After that the reorganized company would control all the colony sites; the colonists would lease and operate the railroad; and the artificial equality in wages would cease.[59] On January 6, 1892, Owen negotiated a new railroad contract with the Mexican government, which promised a subsidy in public lands and certain tax exemptions and authorized Owen to operate the railroad for ninety-nine years.[60] Now all he had to do was build it.

VI

Unfortunately the intervention of Hoffman and the K.S.I. Company furnished only temporary relief. It is hard to say whether in time they could have financed the necessary railroad construction, for the new leaders and settlers who represented Hoffman could not get along with the old, and their appearance at Topolobampo simply aggravated the centrifugal tendencies from which the colony already suffered.

The first serious signs of trouble appeared in Sinaloa during the winter of 1891–1892. The preceding year had been a hard one for the colonists despite the work of the K.S.I. Company: crops had been poor, and typhoid fever and malaria had complicated the never-ending, tedious excavation work for the

[59] Letter of Owen in *Two Republics*, May 26, 1891, reprinted as a leaflet; *Credit Foncier of Sinaloa*, Aug. 15, 1891, p. 177, Sept. 1, 1891, pp. 185–186.
[60] Dublán and Lozano, *Legislación mexicana*, XXII, 189–198.

ditch. Owen later accused two miscreants of starting a "whispering campaign" against the company officials. In any case the morale of the ditch workers sank so low that they threatened to strike unless Hoffman and his subordinates were expelled. In February and March 1892 Owen visited the colonies and made several conciliatory speeches, setting forth the principles of integral co-operation once again.[61]

These speeches quieted the murmurings for a while, but curiously enough Owen made use of the ensuing lull to abandon some of the Utopian principles which he had just defended. After a consultation with company delegates he issued a simplified constitution, the "New Definition of the Principles," in which Utopia bowed to Capitalism, and "everything which was not of an essentially business character was simply struck out." Owen and the directors determined to revise the constitution still further so that, although the company would retain control over soil and natural resources, anyone might sell what he produced for any price that he could get and do what he pleased with the income. As one of the directors put it, "If the company succeeds in peacefully solving the questions of land, trade, and means of communication, it will have done everything which, generally speaking, it can do, and more than has been done for long elsewhere." [62]

In any group of reformers an abandonment of original principles is apt to cause trouble. On this occasion Owen's retreat seems to have come too late to do any positive good. According to Valadés, even before the colonists' outburst of 1891–1892 the New York officials of the company had split into two groups, some favoring a socialist colony and others hoping for a great

---

[61] *Credit Foncier of Sinaloa*, July 1, 1891, p. 157; Valadés, *Topolobampo*, p. 60; *New City*, Aug. 8, 1893, p. 1; Katscher, "Owen's Topolobampo Colony," p. 169.

[62] Mosk, "Railroad to Utopia," p. 256; Katscher, "Owen's Topolobampo Colony," pp. 169–170.

city in which men of all parties could find refuge. Both groups now accused Owen of betrayal.[63] To make matters worse, a schism appeared between Owen and Hoffman, and during the summer of 1892 Owen started an effort to buy out the K.S.I. Company, which Hoffman had founded.

A final complication was added at about this time by the appearance of a newcomer, Michael Flürscheim, a well-known German land reformer and follower of Henry George. Attracted by the principles of integral co-operation and the "joint-stock state," Flürscheim invested the much-needed sum of $1,000 in February 1892. When he heard of the "New Definition" and its abandonment of many co-operative features of the original constitution, he appears to have accepted the chances at first, and early in 1893 he even undertook the task of reconciling Owen and Hoffman. Soon, however, he fell out with Owen and joined the Hoffman group.[64]

Thus by the beginning of 1893 the management of the Topolobampo colonizing project was hopelessly splintered. On December 8, 1892, Owen had begun to publish a new journal in the United States, the *New City*, to counteract the infamies of the *Integral Co-operator*, which Hoffman was sending out from Enterprise, Kansas. In Owen's new journal optimistic reports from the colonies alternated with windy statements of principles and diatribes against Hoffman and Flürscheim. When Flürscheim described the Credit Foncier Company as bankrupt, for example, Owen's loyal cohort, John W. Lovell, denied this heatedly as company treasurer and accused Flürscheim of "a proposed form of brigandage by which all the stockholders and credit holders of the Credit Foncier Company were to be deprived of everything they had acquired by seven years of effort,

[63] Valadés, *Topolobampo*, pp. 59–60. Valadés adds: "The certainty is that Owen had not imposed any tendency on the colony. Who was going to impose tendencies in the midst of the chaos which followed the first months of work and organization!"

[64] Katscher, "Owen's Topolobampo Colony," pp. 171–172; Mosk, "Railroad to Utopia," p. 256 and note.

suffering and privation." W. A. McKenzie remarked bitterly: "This annex to the Credit Foncier [the K.S.I. Company], which was brought in to assist the parent company, has outgrown its parent, and, in a word, 'the tail wags the dog.' " [65] The only hope of success for the railroad and the colonies lay in unity, but hot words like these practically destroyed any chance for further co-operation.

In time affairs in Sinaloa naturally reflected the confusion and rancor of the home offices. During the first half of 1892 the ditch workers scraped away with their teams, and by midsummer the canal was completed. On the gala opening day, July 3, nine inches of water traveled the seven miles in ten hours. Less than two weeks later the company sold its rights at La Logia, and the colonists there made preparations to move to a new site near the irrigation canal at Los Mochis.[66] Some had high hopes for the new settlement, but others lost heart, and according to Valadés two hundred of them left the colonies during the latter half of the year. Those that stayed suffered a hard winter, for all the first year's crops at Los Mochis failed, excepting a little hay, because the colonists scattered too widely and cleared more land than they could care for.[67]

Evidently they needed more systematic direction and order, but during the following year the settlements became even

[65] *New City,* June 22, July 8, 1893, pp. 1–2, 7–8. By this time Schellhous had joined Owen's opponents (*ibid.,* Jan. 8, 1893, p. 6). In addition to denying the bankruptcy of the Credit Foncier Company, Lovell maintained that it held full title to the seven-mile irrigation ditch, because the ditch had been surveyed before the K.S.I. Company was really functioning (*ibid.,* Aug. 8, 1893, p. 4; Sept. 8, 1893).

[66] *Credit Foncier of Sinaloa,* July 1, 1892, p. 349; July 15, 1892, pp. 356–357; Aug. 1, 1892, p. 366.

[67] Even Owen lost heart at this time and stopped attending council meetings (Valadés, *Topolobampo,* pp. 61–62; *New City,* Dec. 8, 1892, p. 6). At this time a number of colonists were operating a logging camp on the Choix River (*ibid.,* Dec. 8, 1892, p. 12; Feb. 8, 1893, p. 9). According to a report in February the colony still contained 495 inhabitants (*ibid.,* Feb. 22, 1893, p. 6).

more decentralized. The colonists at Los Mochis split into two groups: those at the Engineer Farm, the Credit Foncier's officially sponsored tract, who lived communally along the lines of integral co-operation, and a number of individual farmers, euphemistically termed "voluntary co-operators," who lived on their own at "the Plat." During the summer they got into such a heated argument over water rights in the irrigation ditch that the governor of Sinaloa had to intervene and arbitrate the question. At about this time also Flürscheim instigated a revolt among Owen's settlers and led off a group of them to found a rival colony at Libertad.[68]

Clearly the end of the Utopian colonies as an organized experiment was in sight. For a time new settlers occasionally made the trip south to Sinaloa, and Owen's newspaper, the *New City*, continued to report cheerfully on activities in the colony, but between 1894 and 1898 most of the settlers at Los Mochis, Pacific City, and Libertad as well made their way back home, and in the latter year Owen admitted that his experiment had broken up. A few colonists remained as squatters at Los Mochis, holding scrip which gave them the right to use the irrigation canal, but even this deteriorated because of neglect. In 1901 the K.S.I. Company finally sold its rights at Los Mochis to the Sinaloa Sugar Company, an ordinary capitalistic enterprise controlled by B. F. Johnston. After considerable trouble with the colonists Johnston agreed to redeem their scrip at 10 or 12 per cent of its face value, but there is no evidence that he did anything more for the Credit Foncier Company or its representatives.[69]

[68] *New City*, April 22, 1893, pp. 7–8, May 8, 1893, p. 3, Aug. 8, 1893, p. 3; Katscher, "Owen's Topolobampo Colony," p. 172.

[69] Katscher, "Owen's Topolobampo Colony," p. 172; Louis Kaiser to Herbert H. D. Pierce, Mazatlán, Jan. 20, 1902, Kaiser to A. A. Adee, Mazatlán, April 5, 1902, State Dept., Consular Despatches, Mazatlán, VI. Johnston received from the Mexican government the right to use water from the irrigation ditch. He continued to have trouble with the colonists who remained in Sinaloa.

When the colonies broke up, the railroad project soon died. In 1894 and 1897 Owen negotiated new contracts with the Mexican government, but on January 2, 1899, the final contract was canceled. He seems to have retained some property and concessionary privileges in the vicinity of Topolobampo, however, for during the following year he arranged to transfer his remaining rights to Arthur E. Stilwell, a Kansas City promoter who wanted to have a try at building a transcontinental railroad.[70] After disposing of his holdings on the west coast, Owen wrote occasionally of starting up another co-operative project in Mexico or in the American South, but no one would listen to him, and he soon dropped out of sight.[71]

Contemporary opinion of Albert Kimsey Owen went the full gamut from eulogy to profanity. To his hymn-singing followers he was "our noble leader, Owen brave." When Edward and Marie Howland first met him, they were struck by his "exuberant health and spirits" and "the force of his magnetic eloquence." At the time of the first migrations one colonist described him on the basis of a week's acquaintance as "a man of indomitable spirit, of profound and comprehensive mind, of undoubted integrity, of great executive ability and deep earnestness and determination in the work in which he is engaged." [72] Anyone who could inspire, let alone deserve, such praise surely possessed some of the attributes of the promoter.

Unfortunately the hardships of colonial life and the internal squabbling brought out some less flattering portraits. After the first migrations and the Eaton-Hawkins affair, Alvin D. Brock

[70] México, Secretaría de comunicaciones y obras públicas, *Reseña histórica y estadística de los ferrocarriles de jurisdicción federal desde 1? de enero de 1895 hasta 31 de diciembre de 1899* (México, 1900), pp. 17, 45; Mosk, "Railroad to Utopia," p. 258; Clarence O. Senior, "The Kansas City, Mexico, and Orient Railroad," unpublished M.A. thesis, University of Kansas City, 1942, pp. 55–58.

[71] Katscher, "Owen's Topolobampo Colony," pp. 174–175.

[72] *Credit Foncier of Sinaloa*, Sept. 15, 1891, p. 199, July 1, 1891, p. 153; Owen, *Extracts from Newspapers*, p. 31.

called Owen "the modern Colonel Sellers" and his colony a "hell prison (rendered doubly torturesome by the presence of scores of ill-mannered and foul-tempered brutes in human form)." Naturally Hoffman and Flürscheim attacked him in later years on personal and ideological grounds, and Robert H. Cowdrey, another ex-member of the Credit Foncier Company, wrote that Owen was "a mere adventurer who makes a profit out of the necessities of others in order to enrich himself" and "a landowner who will drain them to the last drop of blood and then will laugh in his sleeve." [73]

Somewhere between the extremes of Sir Galahad and Simon Legree, Valadés pictures Owen a little more reasonably as an unusually warmhearted and optimistic humanitarian who desired well-being for all, but who was led astray by "a romantic style" and a certain "absence of direction." [74] Apparently he did not intentionally defraud Credit Foncier investors of their funds, but his imagination overreached itself, and his "joint-stock state" and transcontinental railroad project were too artificial and too ambitious to have much chance of success, even with unified support. As a result the investors in the Credit Foncier of Sinaloa lost their money, and even the holders of the K.S.I. securities can hardly have realized face value on them. Charges of embezzlement against Owen have not been proved, but most of the available information about the colony comes from the pen of Owen himself or his supporters, and without more objective evidence than this the question of his honesty cannot be definitively answered.

How accurately did Owen describe Mexico to his readers? In some respects he closely resembled most of the other promoters of this study. He exaggerated the total wealth of Mexico and its accessibility to a transcontinental railroad. He expressed

[73] The letter of Alvin D. Brock is from an article dated March 27, 1887, in the Los Angeles *Times*. The Cowdrey quotation appears in Katscher, "Owen's Topolobampo Colony," p. 173.
[74] Valadés, *Topolobampo*, p. 48.

the conventional admiration for Díaz and got along well with Mexican officials. Occasionally his co-operative principles and sympathy for the laboring classes aroused in him mild objections to the inequalities of Mexican society, and he criticized the country for depending too heavily on mineral wealth and for failing to provide full employment in a diversified system of industries.[75] Such flashes of insight appeared rarely in his writings, however, and he seldom applied the principles of integral co-operation specifically to Mexican society.

To what extent did Owen fail because of the peculiarities of the Mexican environment? In the case of the railroad project, undoubtedly the writings of John W. Foster, John Bigelow, and others who publicized Mexican instability and backwardness helped to dissuade some potential investors. Since the project never went beyond the planning stage for lack of capital, the Mexican environment did not have a chance to affect it directly, whether favorably or unfavorably.

On the other hand, in the case of the Topolobampo colonies, climate, soil fertility, lack of markets, and other environmental factors might seem to have been instrumental in the eventual failure. The case against the Mexican environment is considerably weakened by the subsequent history of the Sinaloa Sugar Company, which bought the Mochis lands in 1901. During the next fifteen years B. F. Johnston brought about 14,000 acres under cultivation here and at El Aguila nearby with the help of a large Mexican labor force, modern tractors, and extensive irrigation. By 1911 he was exporting $300,000 worth of crude sugar per year and about $400,000 of fresh vegetables, and one observer estimated his average annual profit as between $50 and $100 an acre.[76]

The soil was fertile enough, if it had water. Markets were

---

[75] Owen, *Integral Co-operation at Work*, I, 49–50.

[76] United States, *Consular Reports*, Feb. 5, 1912, p. 550. See also P. Harvey Middleton, *Industrial Mexico, 1919: Facts and Figures* (New York, 1919), pp. 159–160.

available, if transportation were improved. The climate was certainly no more hostile to the new settler than Texas in the summer and far milder than North Dakota in the winter. Topolobampo lay far enough from the population centers of Mexico to prevent serious clashes between cultures, at least for a time. Thus it must be concluded that environmental factors played a small part in the decline of the Utopian colonies. Owen failed largely because he could not reconcile Utopia with capitalistic promotion, because his executive abilities could not keep up with his imagination, and especially because he could not keep his followers from splintering. He failed in Mexico, but he would have failed just as surely in the American South or anywhere.

V

Ex-President: Ulysses S. Grant

THE United States does not always know what to do with its ex-presidents. Shorn of power almost overnight, some of them have found it hard to leave their ambitions behind in the White House. To be sure, most of them have followed Washington's example and sought decent obscurity in a comfortable retirement. A few have eased the shock of sudden desuetude with travel, banquets, and speeches in foreign countries, but others have insisted on returning to national politics. It is probably fortunate that not many try to capitalize their remaining influence in business ventures.

Perhaps our most restless ex-president was Ulysses S. Grant, who tried all these activities, one after another. After turning over the executive office to Hayes in March 1877, Grant, his wife and son, and a small group of friends embarked on a two-year voyage around the world. On his return to the United States certain loyal supporters started a boom to nominate him for a third presidential term, but the boom collapsed. Grant then lent his name to a number of business ventures—projects for a canal across Nicaragua and for a railroad in southern Mexico, a banking house in New York, and others. The name was potent enough to attract capital, but the man lacked financial experience and acumen, and Grant's business ventures ended disastrously with the failure of his son's banking house in 1884. Already suffering from a fatal cancer, the ex-president finally did what he should have done in 1877 or 1879: he retired from public activity and spent his remaining months writing memoirs of his Civil War experiences.

During the few years of his interest in Mexican railroads Grant brought to the promotional field a unique type of background and influence. Unlike his military colleague, General Rosecrans, he did not treat his project as a campaign in which opposition was to be swept aside in a frontal attack or cleverly enveloped and cut to pieces. He came to Mexico as a chief of state, temporarily out of office, whose good will Matías Romero found it worth while to cultivate and who could deal with Díaz and González on even terms. Certainly Grant did not use his background to blackmail Mexico, but his activities inevitably carried a quasi-official connotation largely denied to most other promoters.

Grant's contemporaries professed some doubts concerning his intentions in Mexico. Whitelaw Reid saw in them little but a desire for personal gain. As he told a friend, Grant was "exceedingly eager to make money," and, "dazed" by the magnitude of the Mexican ventures, he was "sure to be used in these schemes until he is only a squeezed orange." [1] Others suspected him of annexationism. Grant's fragmentary writings about Mexico, however, suggest that in the last years of his life he developed toward that country an ideology of economic imperialism closely similar to that of other promoters. In addition to a busi-

[1] Whitelaw Reid to Justin S. Morrill, May 18, 1883, Papers of Whitelaw Reid, Library of Congress. On the other hand, according to one biographer, Grant refused to accept any salary or stock as president of the Mexican Southern Railroad (Hamlin Garland, *Ulysses S. Grant: His Life and Character* [New York, 1898], p. 489). For a brief account of Grant's Mexican project see also Osgood Hardy, "Ulysses S. Grant, President of the Mexican Southern Railroad," *Pacific Historical Review*, XXIV (May 1955), 111–120.

ness venture for reasonable private gain, the Mexican Southern
Railroad was to be an avenue for the peaceful southward expansion of American trade and investment. In 1882 and 1883
Grant bound together his commercial policy and his quasi-official relations with Mexico by negotiating a treaty to remove
tariffs on certain American and Mexican products. Had this
reciprocal trade treaty worked, it would have given an outlet
into Mexico for American manufacturers and supplied his projected railroad with business. Appropriately enough, however,
it too was a failure.

I

Although Grant was so inarticulate that his early attitudes on
domestic and foreign affairs are ordinarily difficult to discover,
it is fairly easy to trace the evolution of his views on Mexico
from the time of his participation in the Mexican War. Despite
his excellent record as a lieutenant in Winfield Scott's invading
army, Grant regarded the war as unjustified aggression from beginning to end, and in later years he declared flatly, "I am always
ashamed of my country when I think of that invasion." Mexico
made a vivid impression upon him as a land of eternal spring, the
most beautiful place he had ever seen. And yet, as he wrote later,
"with a soil and climate scarcely equaled in the world she has
more poor and starving subjects who are willing and able to
work than any country in the world. The rich keep down the
poor with a hardness of heart that is incredible." [2]
Like American soldiers in Africa and Italy during World War
II he found outstretched hands wherever he went, and the

[2] Ulysses Simpson Grant, *Personal Memoirs of U. S. Grant* (New
York, 1885–1886), I, 53–56; John Russell Young, *Around the World with
General Grant: A Narrative of the Visit of General U. S. Grant, ex-
President of the United States, to Various Countries in Europe, Asia, and
Africa in 1877, 1878, 1879, to Which Are Added Certain Conversations
with General Grant on Questions Connected with American Politics and
History* (New York, 1879), II, 447–448; Lloyd Lewis, *Captain Sam Grant*
(Boston, 1950), pp. 210–214, 265, 276.

pathetic appeal of the common people to the occupying troops touched his sensitive nature. In later years he was to suggest partial remedies for the country's ills, but as a young soldier he could only follow orders. A group of wealthy Mexicans, seeking to persuade General Scott to resign his command, organize a government, and lead the country into the American Union, sounded out some of Scott's officers on the proposition, but Lieutenant Grant, contemptuous toward filibustering and homesick for his wife, refused even to listen to the offers. In 1848 he returned home, carrying with him a variety of indelible impressions.[3]

For the next fifteen years Grant had cares enough of his own without concerning himself with Mexico. If he welcomed or appreciated the War of Reform, there is no evidence of it, and he seems to have regarded the French Intervention and the accession of Maximilian as products of American secessionism. Not until 1864 did Mexico enter his active thinking again. In the autumn of that year President Juárez' minister to the United States, Matías Romero, happened to visit Grant's headquarters before Richmond at City Point. This visit was the beginning of a lifelong friendship between Grant and Romero. According to his aide, Adam Badeau, Grant did not generally like foreigners, but perhaps his sympathies for downtrodden Mexico made an exception in this case. As for Romero, he was impressed by Grant's simplicity, and he must have realized what Mexico had to gain from the sympathies of this rising military leader.[4]

During the last winter of the Civil War, Grant paid more attention to Mexican affairs and often predicted to his staff that they would have to fight the French and Imperialists. On

[3] Lewis, *Captain Sam Grant*, pp. 272, 282.

[4] Badeau, *Grant in Peace*, pp. 99, 348, 391–395; Matías Romero, *Speech of Señor Don Matías Romero, Mexican Minister at Washington: Read on the 65th Anniversary of the Birth of General Ulysses S. Grant Celebrated at the Metropolitan Methodist Church of the City of Washington on the 25th of April, 1887* (New York, 1887), pp. 2–4.

the evening of April 10, 1865, after writing to Sherman of Lee's surrender, he rose from his table in headquarters and declared, "Now for Mexico!" At once he hurried General Phil Sheridan off to the Rio Grande frontier, giving him to understand that he need not go out of his way to avoid provoking the Imperialist troops across the border. Later he instructed Sheridan to collect any captured ordnance in his command and place it where it could be easily turned over to Juarist forces. Years afterward Grant told a reporter that he had planned to give Sheridan a corps and send him across the border to join Juárez and sweep onward to Mexico City.

Soon after this Grant was urging the Johnson cabinet to send a military mission to Mexico under General John M. Schofield. The Juárez government went so far as to issue a special series of bonds totaling $30,000,000 to finance the expedition, but President Johnson decided to send Schofield on a mission to France and rely on Seward's diplomacy to get the French troops out of Mexico. In later life Grant clung to the conviction that his plan of quick, decisive action would have saved Maximilian's life, overthrown Napoleon III in 1866 or 1867, and even avoided the Franco-Prussian War.[5] About a year after overruling Grant's plans for intervention in Mexico, Johnson appointed him an honorary escort to the new minister to Mexico, Lewis Campbell, but by that time Grant had become involved in Republican politics and refused to leave the country. This was his only opportunity to play a direct role in Mexican affairs before his inauguration as president.[6]

According to Badeau, Grant came to the presidency with the intention of peacefully purchasing northern Mexico. Certainly if he had wanted to intervene in Mexico, any one of several border incidents would have furnished him a plausible excuse;

[5] Badeau, *Grant in Peace*, pp. 154–155, 180–181; Garland, *Ulysses S. Grant*, p. 314; Young, *Around the World with General Grant*, II, 163–165.

[6] Oberholtzer, *History of the United States*, I, 510–511, 514–515.

but a number of factors restrained his hand. In the first place, he wished above all to avoid another Mexican War. Secondly, in his appetite for American expansion he soon bit off more than he could chew by negotiating an annexation treaty with the Dominican Republic. Thirdly, his secretary of state was the cautious and unexcitable Hamilton Fish, instead of an expansionist like Oliver P. Morton or Zachariah Chandler. Even so, the border situation was a constant source of worry to both governments, and although Grant and Fish managed to avoid outright war, they could not solve in the slightest the basic dilemma.

Grant's remarks on border lawlessness and on the Free Zone in his messages to Congress offended some sensitive Mexicans, but on the whole the Juárez and Lerdo administrations accepted at face value his desire for friendship. During the campaign of 1872 an editorial in *El siglo diez y nueve* called him "simple, republican at heart, and generous in character" and a dependable friend of Mexico, although another editorial criticized his governmental ability. In later years a nationalistic Mexican historian conceded that the Grant administration "manifested the best and most friendly sentiments with respect to our country, and was able to resist entirely the powerful [annexationist] suggestions of the dominant spirit of the United States." [7]

Between the collapse of Grant's postwar proposals for military intervention in Mexico and the end of his presidency various enthusiasts sowed in his mind the seeds of future promotional interest in Mexico. Disliking Rosecrans, Grant would not have paid much attention to his optimistic reports, if, indeed, he ever saw them at all. In 1867, however, another Civil War general, James Longstreet, tried to secure the use of Grant's

[7] *El siglo diez y nueve,* July 15, 1872, pp. 1–2, Oct. 4, 1872, pp. 1–2; Cosmes, *Historia de Méjico,* XX, 632. When Grant's appointee as minister to Mexico, Thomas A. Nelson, replaced Rosecrans in 1869, there was a momentary annexationist scare until Nelson made clear the friendly intentions of the Grant administration (*ibid.,* pp. 629–632). There was another brief and equally groundless panic in 1876 (*Two Republics,* Jan. 12, 1876, p. 2; March 8, p. 2; May 10, p. 2).

magic name for the letterhead of a projected railroad from New Orleans to Mazatlán by way of Houston and Ringgold Barracks, Texas, but there is no evidence that Grant consented, and in any case the project got no further than good intentions.[8]

Grant was also acquainted with several of the other promoters discussed in this study. Edward Lee Plumb approached Grant diplomatically through Secretary of State Fish, to whom he wrote in 1872 and 1873, describing Mexico's "vast quantities of sugar and coffee" and predicting an annual trade of $200,000,000 between the United States and Mexico. By 1875, after a few more letters of this sort, Plumb was visiting Grant's summer home at Long Branch to lay his projects before the president.[9] In that same year Albert K. Owen presented to Grant his project for surveying a railroad route from Austin, Texas, to Topolobampo,[10] and, as will presently be seen, Grant was a personal friend of Alexander R. Shepherd during most of his presidency and afterward.

It is difficult to measure the influence of other promoters upon the taciturn president, but Grant did at least transplant a number of arguments from Plumb's letters to his own speeches on Mexico in 1880 and 1881. In any case, by 1876 he had clearly given up the idea of purchasing or otherwise acquiring Mexican territory, and the alternative policy of systematically encouraging international trade and communications by promotional projects may have lain dormant in his mind awaiting a stimulus to bring it out into the open.

II

If this is so, Grant's two-year tour around the world after his retirement from the presidency supplied the stimulus. His

[8] James Longstreet to Ulysses S. Grant, New Orleans, April 10, 1867, Chicago Historical Society Collection.

[9] Edward Lee Plumb to Hamilton Fish, Mexico City, Aug. 30, 1872, and New York, Aug. 15, 1873, Plumb to Sebastián Lerdo de Tejada, New York, Aug. 5, 1875, Plumb Collection.

[10] Valadés, *Topolobampo*, pp. 34–35.

enthusiastic reception in foreign capitals healed some of the wounds inflicted by his recent critics, and, even more important, the trip widened his horizons and removed some of his innate provincialism. It is true that he never learned to appreciate much of the rich European cultural heritage. In Switzerland, for example, he finally rebelled against the long succession of cathedrals and ruins and asked querulously, "Why should we waste our time on any more architecture?" But he could appreciate some massive works of nature and man, such as the Alps and the Pyramids, and he enjoyed meeting Disraeli, Bismarck, and other political figures who spoke his language.

Most important of all, he observed and remembered evidences of Europe's material progress. "Through his eyes the spirit of America looked at bridges, roads, railroads, mines, and found therein food for its patriotic admiration for American achievements." [11] The "incredible" scientific progress of the Japanese made a particularly deep impression on him, and during his month's visit there he began to formulate a new policy of American commercial expansion into such areas as the Far East and Mexico. His companion, Badeau, never overly impressed with Grant's originality of thought, believed that his tour made him for the first time "a profound thinker and an international statesman" and that "he was never so fit to be President as when his party rejected him." [12]

If Grant had any idea that his trip could be made in privacy, it was soon dispelled. The New York *Herald* sent a reporter, John Russell Young, to cover the tour, and his accounts of banquets, interviews, and flattering speeches refurbished the ex-president's reputation and provided a becoming contrast with the criticism of the Hayes administration. Consequently when

[11] William B. Hesseltine, *Ulysses S. Grant, Politician* (New York, 1935), p. 430; see also Badeau, *Grant in Peace*, pp. 305–307, 312–313, *et passim.*
[12] Badeau, *Grant in Peace*, pp. 320–321.

Grant landed at San Francisco in September 1879, the public received him not only as a returning hero but as a possible candidate for the Republican presidential nomination nine months hence. As he traveled eastward and then settled down in Philadelphia for another round of banquets, speeches, and interviews, the pro-Grant forces in the party realized that he had returned too soon. Accordingly in January 1880 his managers hustled him off to visit Cuba and Mexico with his wife, General and Mrs. Phil Sheridan, and other friends, so that he might increase his "availability" with new honors which could be reported to the American public.[13]

Their hopes were not disappointed. At Havana the Spanish authorities outdid themselves to match the European reception, and mid-February the Grant party left the island for a similar program of festivities in Mexico.[14] At Veracruz two of Grant's old friends, General Ignacio Mejía and Matías Romero, welcomed him with speeches, and on February 21 Romero, Minister John W. Foster, other dignitaries, and over twenty-five hundred soldiers escorted the party into Mexico City before a crowd of fifty thousand.

Then followed a succession of the parades, banquets, and tours which were to become the standard operating procedure of the Mexican government. On one evening a band serenaded the famous American with patriotic anthems and a potpourri of operatic selections which Grant, being tone deaf, could hardly have recognized. On another occasion the government decorated the Tivoli de San Cosme with pictures of Washington, Lincoln, Grant, and Juárez and held a gala banquet, at which General Sheridan, blushing to the tips of his ears, surprised everyone by delivering a "spiritual and ingenious" speech. Grant did not enjoy one of the festivities—a bullfight, which he left early in order to stop the slaughter. Doubtless his practical,

[13] Hesseltine, *Ulysses S. Grant*, pp. 431–436.
[14] New York *Tribune*, Jan. 25, 1880, p. 1; Feb. 17, p. 5; Feb. 20, p. 5.

materialistic mind appreciated trips to the great coffee plantations of Córdoba and to an excavation designed to drain the Valley of Mexico.[15]

The Mexican press welcomed the general with a burst of flattery that would have turned anyone's head. In a gesture of unusual felicity the Hayes administration chose this moment to withdraw an unpopular order of 1877 which had authorized American troops to cross the border freely, and Mexican journalists were in a mood to embrace the nearest American, especially if he were a military hero. *La libertad* published a long biography, referring briefly and without comment to Grant's activities in the Mexican War, but dwelling lovingly on each Civil War battle. *El republicano* deified the great triumvirate of the Civil War—John Brown, "the Hidalgo of the North," Lincoln, and Grant—and *La república* called Grant "the soldier of Humanity." [16]

Thus by sending Grant to Mexico his managers unintentionally encouraged a "hands-across-the-Rio-Grande" movement. The effects of his visit went beyond mere journalistic enthusiasm and political oratory, however. As already noted, at the beginning of 1880 Mexico was ripe for railroad building, but because of border lawlessness and the debt situation American and British capitalists were hesitant to commit themselves to long-term projects. When Grant reached Veracruz, American interests connected with the Denver and Rio Grande and Atchison, Topeka, and Santa Fe Railroads were dickering for the right to build lines from the Rio Grande to Mexico City, but the negotiations had reached an impasse. Frustrated on all sides, Matías Romero must have regarded his old friend as a *deus ex machina*.

[15] *Ibid.*, Feb. 21, 1880, p. 8; Feb. 22, 23, p. 1; Feb. 27, p. 5; Feb. 28, p. 1; March 5, p. 1; March 9, p. 5; March 14, p. 2. See also *El monitor republicano*, Feb. 25, 1880, p. 3; Feb. 29, p. 3.

[16] *La tribuna*, March 18, 1880, p. 3; *La libertad*, Feb. 22, 1880, p. 1; *El republicano*, Feb. 22, 1800, p. 1; *La república*, March 17, 1880, p. 1.

Romero and other progressive Mexicans lost no time in sounding their visitor concerning his future plans for Mexico. Bishop Eulogio G. Gillow, a member of Romero's clique, drew Grant out on the subject of "peaceful conquest" and was relieved to hear the general reply that the United States was already so large that the addition of more territory would lead to disunity and disaster.[17] Sheridan's speech at the San Cosme banquet and other utterances of the visitors confirmed the impression that they favored better communications and increased trade between the two countries as steps toward more prosperity, not toward annexation. Accordingly on March 10 Romero, Gillow, Minister of *Fomento* Vicente Riva Palacio, and others directed a letter to Grant, formally asking him to publicize among American capitalists the advantages of railroad building in Mexico. A week later Grant replied, declaring himself in full sympathy with the project and promising to give aid in every possible way, both as an American citizen and as a friend of Mexico.[18]

These assurances were all that Romero could have hoped for at the moment, and he had good reason to feel encouraged as Grant made his way out of the country, accompanied by his party and Minister Foster. When the ex-president reached Galveston in April, preparations were already under way for the Republican convention in June. Grant seems to have been optimistic about his chances, as he followed his managers' directions to make a dignified triumphal march up the length of the crucial state of Illinois to his home in Galena. But when the convention met, alas the opposing Blaine forces were too strong, and after a deadlock for thirty-five ballots they shifted to a "dark horse," James A. Garfield, and nominated him instead.

Grant's defeat not only ended his political career but compelled him to look about for some sort of gainful employment,

[17] Antonio G. Rivera, *Reminiscencias* (Los Angeles, 1915), Appendix, as quoted in Valadés, *El porfirismo: Nacimiento,* pp. 317–319.
[18] New York *Tribune,* April 2, 1880, p. 5.

for he wanted to continue living in his elegant New York City home, and, as he had told Badeau over six months earlier, he could not afford this without additional income. Therefore he accepted the titular presidency of a Nicaragua canal company at this point, and a little later he assumed similar positions in a New Mexico gold mining company and a company for the laying of a cable between the United States, Cuba, and Mexico.[19] It is not unreasonable to suppose that during 1880 Grant followed the activities of his friend, Alexander R. Shepherd, who had just organized a company to work the rich Batopilas silver mines in southwestern Chihuahua; if so, Mexico could not have been long out of his thoughts.[20] Obviously the stage was set for some sort of partnership between Grant and Romero, if the proper terms could be arranged.

In the early autumn of 1880 Romero received from the governor of the Mexican state of Oaxaca a concession to construct a railroad from Mexico City to Oaxaca (the state capital), with branches to both coasts, for a subsidy of about 7,000 pesos per kilometer.[21] As he admitted, he could have secured capital more easily for a line from Mexico City to the Rio Grande, but in September, Díaz had granted concessions to the Mexican Central Railroad and the Mexican National Railroad. Not wishing to compete with them, Romero accepted his Oaxaca concession and set out for the United States to look for capital. Landing at New Orleans in early October, he proceeded to New

[19] Hesseltine, *Ulysses S. Grant*, pp. 436–440, 444–445; Badeau, *Grant in Peace*, p. 318; Philip H. Morgan to James G. Blaine, Mexico City, July 30, 1881, no. 464, United States, *Foreign Relations*, 1881, p. 780. Grant declined an offer of money to lend his name to the Panama project (Oberholtzer, *History of the United States*, IV, 711).

[20] Newspaper clippings in the Shepherd Papers contain speculations concerning Shepherd's influence on Grant. See, for example, Washington *Capitol*, Dec. 5, 1881.

[21] Matías Romero, *Informe de Matías Romero al gobernador del estado de Oaxaca respecto de la compañía que organizó para construir el ferrocarril de Oaxaca y del traspaso que le hizo la concesión de 25 de agosto de 1880* (México, 1881), p. 3, and *Speech on the 65th Anniversary*, p. 11.

York by way of St. Louis and Chicago, much pleased at the widespread interest in his visit and project. After talking to Grant and other American friends in New York, Romero realized that he had arrived at exactly the right moment, for the two northern railroad concessions had aroused a flurry of interest in Mexican resources. Furthermore, Grant had anticipated his coming with a speech in Boston about trade opportunities in Mexico.[22]

Romero secured some sort of hearing from most of the American railroad men or companies with interests in the Southwest: General William J. Palmer of the Denver and Rio Grande and Thomas Nickerson of the Santa Fe, who already held Mexican concessions; General Grenville M. Dodge of the Texas and Pacific; and Collis P. Huntington of the Southern Pacific. In particular, he attracted the attention of Jay Gould, who was about to tilt with Huntington for control of western Texas. Foreseeing trouble ahead in his Southwestern campaign, Gould prepared to turn the new interest in Mexico to his own uses if possible and at the same time to bind ex-President Grant to him in a railroad-building alliance.[23]

On November 11, 1880, Romero entertained Grant and about twenty leading railroad men at a banquet in Delmonico's famous New York restaurant. Both he and the ex-president delivered speeches praising Mexico as a field for railroad investment and anticipating the day when the country could supply most American imports of tropical products. Since Huntington and Gould had already agreed in preliminary conversations that subsidies were not necessary if the other concession terms were liberal enough, the speakers were able to forestall embarrassing questions about the financial status of the Mexican government. In order to avoid ruinous competition for Mexican concessions

[22] Romero, *Informe al gobernador de Oaxaca*, pp. 7–16; New York *Tribune*, Oct. 14, 1880, p. 2.

[23] Romero, *Informe al gobernador de Oaxaca*, pp. 16–19; Chicago *Tribune*, Aug. 13, 1880, p. 5, Sept. 17, p. 8.

it was suggested that all interested parties pool their resources in one major effort, and before the banquet broke up, a committee was appointed to consider the subject further.[24]

This proposal to co-operate in Mexican railroad building died soon after birth. In subsequent committee meetings it was quickly apparent that Palmer and Nickerson, who already held Mexican concessions, were reluctant to hand them over to a general group, for the publicity resulting from the banquet at Delmonico's had created a brisk demand for their new securities. On the other hand, Gould, who had nothing to lose and everything to gain from co-operation in Mexico, presented a most disingenuous plan for a united effort with Grant as general arbiter over any disputes that might arise. Nickerson and the Mexican Central interests eventually expressed some willingness to co-operate, but Palmer insisted on carrying out his concession alone.[25] In view of the character of his would-be allies, it is difficult to quarrel with his decision.

Holding positive promises of help from the Gould group, Romero and Grant now proceeded to organize their company, in order to transfer the Oaxaca concession to it. Since New York had no general provision authorizing charters for companies operating abroad, Grant and Gould persuaded the state legislature to pass a special law for their Mexican railroad. Romero accompanied the general to Albany and received a special lesson in the fine art of lobbying, American style. On March 23, 1881, after the passage of the enabling act, the Mexican Southern Railroad Company was incorporated in New York City, with Grant as president, General Grenville M.

[24] New York *Tribune*, Nov. 12, 1880, p. 5.
[25] Romero, *Informe al gobernador de Oaxaca*, pp. 28–34. At various times the following men took part in the deliberations: Edward D. Adams, General Grenville M. Dodge, Charles F. Woerishoffer (representing General Palmer), Thomas Nickerson, Collis P. Huntington, Jay Gould, Henry G. Marquand, John S. Kennedy, J. H. Work, F. S. Bond, and J. B. Horison (New York *Tribune*, Nov. 28, 1880, p. 1, Dec. 24, p. 1; New York *Herald*, Dec. 24, 1880).

Dodge, a Gould representative, as vice-president, and Russell Sage as treasurer. In order to carry out the requirements of the Oaxaca charter, the incorporators subscribed one million pesos of the capital, and on March 26 Romero formally transferred his concession to the new company.

Two days later Romero and Grant set out for Mexico City, well satisfied with their progress. Their next step was to secure a formal concession from the national government, with a provision for higher maximum freight and passenger rates than the Oaxaca concession allowed. This was a *sine qua non* of the American railroad men; in fact, Grant had to agree to go to Mexico himself in order to secure enough support to incorporate the company.[26]

The Mexican newspapers received him somewhat less ecstatically than the year before, for his new partner, Romero, had the usual number of political enemies, and during the winter all kinds of rumors had circulated about Grant's "enormous speculation . . . which is said to be a political-financial combination of Macchiavellian devices." Some said that he was coming to Mexico to negotiate commercial and frontier treaties to benefit the Gould interests, and others were sure that the Americans were buying up bonds of the English debt in preparation for demanding Mexican territory.[27] On April 22 Grant dispelled most of these rumors with a speech at a banquet given him by the Oaxaca delegation in Congress. In the presence of Generals E. O. C. Ord and John B. Frisbie, who had often been accused of annexationism, Grant reiterated his basic interest in Mexican-American commerce and declared that annexation of Mexican territory would be impossible even if the Mexican people wished it.[28]

[26] Romero, *Informe al gobernador de Oaxaca*, pp. 40–53; New York *Tribune*, Feb. 17, 1881, p. 2.

[27] *La república*, March 10, 1881, pp. 1–2; *El siglo diez y nueve*, April 4, 1881, p. 1.

[28] *El monitor republicano*, April 26, 1881, p. 1; Romero, *Informe al gobernador de Oaxaca*, Appendix, pp. i–iv.

The Mexican Congress promptly took up the question of the Mexican Southern Railroad concession. This differed from most others in that no subsidy was granted, and the company argued that in return the government ought to relax most of the restrictions common to other concessions. The congressmen were in general agreement as to the value of the Mexican Southern project to the country, but some of them objected to details, such as the exclusion of governmental representatives from the board of directors. Others introduced amendments requiring the company to hire government inspectors and carry the mails free, but these were voted down. Congress also granted a substantial increase in the maximum rates and extended the railroad route to the Guatemalan border. The concession was finally approved at the end of May, and Grant left immediately for the United States.[29]

At the beginning of the following year the company secured further concessions for the construction of port works at Antón Lizardo on the Gulf of Mexico and for the survey and colonization of lands along its route. In his rosiest dreams Grant even included Central America in his plans, for on October 6, 1882, he induced President Justo Rufino Barrios of Guatemala, then visiting the United States, to grant him a concession for 250 miles of railroad.[30] This concession was a sheer waste of paper and ink, for, as events soon demonstrated, Grant could not carry out even his simplest plans in Mexico.

III

Although ex-President Grant did not write any publicity leaflets himself for the Mexican Southern Railroad project, his speeches, letters, and magazine articles between his return from

[29] México, *Diario de los debates, Cámara de diputados: Décima legislatura constitucional de la Unión* (México, 1880–1898), II, 777–878, especially 808–816, 839 ff., 856–857, 873–878; *El monitor republicano*, May 17, 1881, pp. 1–2, May 29, p. 3; *El hijo de trabajo*, May 29, 1881, p. 3.

[30] *Diario oficial*, Jan. 11, 17, 1882, p. 2; J. Fred Rippy, *Latin America and the Industrial Age* (New York, 1944), p. 134.

abroad in 1879 and his death in 1884 give a general idea of his thinking about American economic imperialism in Mexico. The basis of his "new policy" for Far Eastern and Mexican relations, to which Badeau referred after Grant's world tour, was a firm belief in the inevitable expansion of American economic power. "Stepping at once into the front rank among the powerful nations of the earth," he wrote, "the United States has entered, as it were spontaneously, upon a career of development almost unparalleled in the history of the world."

Where the Far East was concerned, he never had a chance to elaborate a plan of action, but one can surmise that its point of departure would have closely resembled the Open Door. In the Western Hemisphere, however, he grew more nationalistic, and he gave as an important reason for supporting the Nicaragua Canal Company against Ferdinand de Lesseps' project in Panama the fact that the former enterprise was purely American.[31] It is hardly necessary to add that he extended the protection of the Monroe Doctrine to Mexico. In 1865 he had champed at the bit in his eagerness to set out after Maximilian, and if in the 1880's he made few references to European threats, it was because no threats existed, and in view of the sensitivity of the Mexicans it was best to avoid remarks of a military nature. In an uninformed way he made a few tentative references to the ideological basis of the Monroe Doctrine—the protection and expansion of democracy. Badeau quoted him as saying, "Besides, we want to encourage republican government, and particularly on this continent."[32]

One part of Grant's international program was clear: he did not propose to convert his railroad project into a filibuster for Mexican territory or in any way agitate for the purchase of land. He told a group of mechanics in Boston:

[31] Ulysses S. Grant, "The Nicaragua Canal," *North American Review*, CXXXII (Feb. 1881), 108, 144.

[32] Badeau, *Grant in Peace*, p. 353; New York *Tribune*, Nov. 12, 1880, p. 5.

I did and said all I could [in Mexico] to allay their apprehensions of danger from the approach of the universal Yankee . . . [I told them] we were a people of homogeneous institutions from one end of the country to the other, and there was no political advantage accruing to any political party by the accession of territory in any particular direction . . . ; that, if we acquired territory, it would have to be with the consent of the people occupying that territory and our own consent. [Applause.]

Later in Mexico City he was still more emphatic:

I am sure that, even if it could be shown that all the people in Mexico were in favor of annexation of a portion of their territory to the United States, it would still be rejected. We want no more land. We do want to improve what we have, and we want to see our neighbors improve and grow so strong that the designs of any other country could not endanger them.[33]

Grant repeated these sentiments so often that he might have been accused of protesting too much, were it not that the sensitive Mexican nationalists needed constant reassuring.

Occasionally Grant carried this line of argument so far that one wonders why he was interested in Mexico at all. For example, he told Bishop Gillow that in Mexico "illiterate Indians without ambition predominate" and that whereas European immigrants to the United States could be easily absorbed the Mexican mixture of Spanish and Indian was so heterogeneous that "many years would elapse before those sixteen million inhabitants could mingle with American spirit and education." [34] Usually, however, he had much good to say about the Mexican people, and he told their prospective employers, the American railroad magnates, that those offshoots "of the old Aztec" were "wedded to their homes . . . peaceable, quiet, innocent, in- offensive, very religious and virtuous people, and they are will-

[33] New York *Tribune*, Oct. 14, 1880, p. 2; April 26, 1881, p. 5.
[34] Rivera, *Reminiscencias*, as quoted in Valadés, *El porfirismo: Naci- miento*, pp. 318–319.

ing to work and very industrious when they can see the wages coming in Saturday night." The fact that they would work for almost nothing was a great point in their favor too.[35]

As for the government of Mexico, Grant recognized some of its shortcomings, but he was optimistic about the future. According to his view of Mexican history, the Spanish and the Mexican Church had so stunted political growth that the effective history of the government must be dated from 1867. "They have had thirteen years really, of growth," he said "and considering that they have been impoverished by wars, foreign and domestic, I think they have done remarkably well." [36] He showed some concern about the outcome of the election of 1880, and when Díaz succeeded in transferring the presidency to González without a revolution, he breathed more easily. The following spring he met a group of American Protestant clergymen in Mexico, who had good reason to fear disorder, and told them that in the long run railroads would strengthen the government's hand in making life and property more secure.[37]

To Grant's way of thinking, the economic advantages of closer relations with Mexico outweighed any temporary disadvantages of political disorder and reinforced or at times even overshadowed the humanitarian and ideological advantages of such relations. Like the other promoters under discussion, he believed Mexico to be "on the eve of a great advance." Agriculture, mining, industries were all waiting for improved communications, as Romero had repeated so often. It would be to the advantage of the United States to take part in the work of development, Grant went on, if only because our foreign commerce could be directed into more profitable channels. Instead of buying coffee, sugar, and other tropical products from Cuba and Brazil, why not buy them from Mexico? Mexican coffee and sugar were grown by free men, not slaves, and instead of

[35] New York *Tribune*, Nov. 12, 1880, p. 5.   [36] *Ibid*.
[37] Grant to Romero, April 13, June 21, 1880, reprinted in New York *World*, Sept. 25, 1880; New York *Tribune*, May 2, 1881, p. 1.

requiring sterling exchange in payment Mexico would gladly accept American manufactures. In this manner the United States could greatly reduce its annual bill of $300,000,000 for sterling exchange and build up a Mexican trade totaling $200,000,000. With this argument Grant achieved the perfect synthesis of idealism and self-interest. As he jokingly remarked to his Boston mechanics, "We are not so particularly generous as to want to benefit our neighbors at our own expense. . . . But when we can benefit ourselves, and them, too, greatly, we are the most generous people in the world." [38]

In order to understand how the Mexican Southern Railroad project fitted into Grant's program for American-Mexican relations, it is necessary to turn away from his own writings to a publicity pamphlet of the company written by Robert B. Gorsuch, an American railroad engineer who had dabbled in Mexican projects since the 1850's. This pamphlet bore a strong family resemblance to the optimistic writings of Rosecrans, Plumb, and Owen. At the beginning it declared that when railroad connections were completed from the Rio Grande to Mexico City, they would still miss the richest section of Mexico —the South, which "possesses in a more marked degree than any other section the natural elements making it a specially promising field for railway enterprise." [39]

In support of this statement Gorsuch claimed for Oaxaca preeminence in almost every conceivable type of natural resources. It had a greater variety of climate than the rest of Mexico, and

[38] Grant to Elihu B. Washburne, Galveston, Texas, March 25, 1880, in [Ulysses S. Grant], *General Grant's Letters to a Friend, 1861–1880* (New York, 1897), pp. 106–107; New York *World*, Sept. 25, 1880; New York *Tribune*, Oct. 14, 1880, p. 2, Nov. 12, p. 5. The argument about free labor in Mexico is an exact repetition of one used by Plumb in a letter to Hamilton Fish, dated Aug. 30, 1872 (Plumb Collection).

[39] Romero, *Informe al gobernador de Oaxaca*, pp. 37–39; Robert B. Gorsuch, *The Mexican Southern Railway to Be Constructed, under a Charter from the Mexican Government, through the States of Vera Cruz and Oaxaca* (New York, 1881), p. 3.

its agricultural products were thus more numerous—coffee, sugar, cotton, tobacco, tropical fruits, rare woods, and a host of others. He paid special attention to coffee, quoting Minister Foster's opinion that Oaxacan coffee was "equal to the best known in any country" and repeated Romero's prediction that a skillfully managed coffee plantation would return 100 per cent on the original investment. In addition, Gorsuch claimed for Oaxaca undeveloped deposits of metals and petroleum. Cattle, fish, and game were also abundant, varying with the altitude. He even found an argument to exploit the Indian ruins at Mitla and Monte Albán: they were not only archaeological curiosities but also evidences of the large populations which the land had supported in the past and could support again.

Gorsuch concluded that what Oaxaca needed more than anything else was good transportation to exterior markets. Coffee exports from Veracruz had grown from 671 pesos in 1869 to over 1,500,000 pesos in 1879, thanks to the Mexican Railway. In order to increase these exports further and develop the other resources of Oaxaca, he announced that the Mexican Southern Company intended to develop deepwater ports at Antón Lizardo, southeast of Veracruz, and at Huatulco, a Pacific port not far above the Isthmus of Tehuantepec. Between these ports the company would construct an interoceanic railroad, with a branch north to connect with the Mexican Railway and another south to the Isthmus of Tehuantepec. Gorsuch's pamphlet was only a preliminary prospectus, and the route was later changed to a main north-south line from Mexico City through Oaxaca to the Isthmus of Tehuantepec, paralleling the Mexican Railway as far as Puebla. The coastal connections were thus reduced to mere branches.[40]

What was the exact position of Jay Gould in the Grant-Romero project? On June 7, 1881, one of his agents secured a

[40] Gorsuch, *Mexican Southern Railway*, pp. 3–19. Gorsuch estimated the cost of the main line and two branches as 15,150,000 pesos. For the later route see *Diario oficial*, Jan. 31, 1882, pp. 3–4.

concession for a line through eastern Mexico from Laredo via
Ciudad Victoria to Mexico City, with branches to Tampico and
Veracruz. This line was formally named the Mexican Oriental,
Interoceanic, and International Railroad Company, and on May
14, 1883, its concession was merged with that of the Oaxaca
project. This combined enterprise took the name Mexican
Southern Railway.[41] At the end of 1883 J. H. Work, the secretary of the consolidated company, declared that the new line
would form a part of the "Southwest system" of railroads in
the United States—that is, the Gould network. The southern
section of the line, from Mexico City to the Isthmus of Tehuantepec, would serve the prosperous cities of Puebla and Oaxaca
and regions producing coal, marble, sugar, cotton, coffee, and
many other items with the aid of "a perfect system of irrigation
and a climate unsurpassed in its uniform mildness." An accom-
panying map, dated 1884, showed a main line running from
Laredo to the Guatemalan border, with branches to San Luis
Potosí and Antón Lizardo and other connecting lines to Tampico and Veracruz.[42]

There is some doubt that Gould, Grant, and Romero were all
equally interested in every section of this sprawling 1,200-mile
railroad network. True, Grant's name was associated with both
parts of the project, but Romero seems to have concerned him-

---

[41] Chicago *Tribune*, Feb. 19, 1881, p. 3; New York *Tribune*, March
8, 1881, p. 1; Dublán and Lozano, *Legislación mexicana*, XIV, 808–820.
The text of the consolidated concession of May 14, 1883, embodying
references to earlier concessions, is contained in Nimmo, *Trade between
Mexico and the United States*, pp. 57–59.

[42] J. H. Work to Joseph Nimmo, New York, Dec. 18, 1883, in Nimmo,
Trade between Mexico and the United States, pp. 54–56. By 1884 Gould's
company had completed grading beyond Mier and laid about a mile of
track. Early in the year the contractors and the Milmo National Bank
of Laredo sued the company for money owed them. The company went
into receivership, and a Mexican court appraised its holdings (including
the concession from the government) at $455,000. See Warner P. Sutton
to William Hunter, Matamoros, April 30, 1884, State Dept., Consular
Despatches, Matamoros, XIX.

self mainly with the southern line, from Mexico City to Oaxaca and beyond, while the northern section to the Rio Grande was commonly spoken of as "Gould's line." The fact that Mexico's need for northern railroads was being rapidly satisfied by the construction of the Mexican Central (completed in 1884) and the Mexican National (completed in 1888), together with Gould's reputation for speculation, suggests that he may never have intended to construct the northern line at all but secured the Mexican concession only to strengthen his hand against his American rivals. There is no evidence of speculative intent in the activities of Grant and Romero for the southern route, and without some evidence one can only take their high-sounding proposals at something like face value.

IV

Perhaps the clearest indication that Grant's interest in Mexico went beyond mere short-term speculation was the role which he played in negotiating a reciprocal trade treaty between the United States and Mexico during 1882 and 1883. There was nothing new about the idea of such a treaty with Mexico. In 1831 the Jackson administration had negotiated a reciprocity treaty, only to discover that the prevailing high Mexican tariff largely dissipated any theoretical advantages of commercial equality. In 1857 and 1859 the two countries included reciprocal trade provisions in two unratified treaties, and successful reciprocity treaties with Canada and the Hawaiian Islands (in 1854 and 1875 respectively) publicized the idea of reciprocity before the American people.[43]

Thus it is not surprising that Americans interested in Mexican resources and railroads during the late 1870's began to call for a reciprocal trade agreement with Mexico. In 1876 a reciprocity

[43] Samuel Flagg Bemis, *A Diplomatic History of the United States* (3d ed.; New York, 1950), pp. 63–64, 79, 292–299, 301–302; Rippy, *United States and Mexico*, pp. 212–213, 224; Mexico, *Report on the Actual Condition of Mexico*, pp. 164–166.

bill was introduced into the House of Representatives, and an approving editorialist in the New York *World* pronounced Mexico "one of the very richest countries upon the globe in natural resources . . . [and] easily capable of supporting a population as dense as that of China." Yet, he added, we sell Mexico less than one-fourth of Mexico's imports, and we buy more from Mexico than we sell her. Obviously, he concluded, a trade treaty would benefit both sides. Unfortunately the Díaz revolution of 1876, the recognition impasse, border lawlessness, and the Free Zone killed the bill, and three years later another resolution looking in the same direction suffered the same fate.[44]

In spite of these failures, sentiment for close trade relations with Mexico was growing, as a result of the speeches of Díaz' personal agent, Manuel Zamacona, the writings of Matías Romero, and the efforts of American railroad men to secure Mexican concessions. After 1880 reciprocity sentiment spread more rapidly, as the Mexican Central and Mexican National Railroad companies began construction south of the Rio Grande, and Grant, Owen, and others issued optimistic propaganda for their own purposes. At the same time, as mentioned earlier, skeptics such as John W. Foster and John Bigelow expressed doubt that railroads could earn any profits in Mexico. The cold water which they threw on Mexican railroad projects naturally dampened reciprocity sentiment as well.

During the same years sentiment in favor of reciprocity was also growing south of the Rio Grande. At first many Mexican merchants argued that they already enjoyed profitable relations with European companies which would lose business and pay fewer import duties if the government signed any commercial treaties with the United States. They asked: "Would it be to

---

[44] United States, 44th Congress, 1st Session, *Congressional Record*, IV, 374, 3065; 45th Congress, 3d Session, *House Report 108* (Washington, 1879), *passim;* New York *World*, May 21, 1876. Volumes of the *Congressional Record* for 1878–1880 contain references to several other resolutions of this sort.

the benefit of Mexico to be materially and morally subjected by
. . . the United States?" [45] Friends of reciprocity replied that
an increase of peaceful trade with the United States would keep
the border quiet and forestall American annexationists. A leader
in this group was Matías Romero, who was willing to make
special concessions to American merchants in order to attract
capital for railroads and other improvements.[46]

Thus there existed strong sentiment in favor of reciprocity on
both sides of the border when James G. Blaine became Garfield's
secretary of state in March 1881. Observers expected him to cut
a dashing figure in foreign affairs, and the Chicago *Tribune*
called on him to negotiate a commercial treaty with Mexico as
the first step toward "a great American international commercial system." [47] Before he could do anything, his chief was as-
sassinated, and on December 18 Blaine relinquished the state
department to Frederick T. Frelinghuysen. Circumstances
obliged the new secretary to act quickly, for in November the
Mexican government had denounced the American-Mexican
commercial treaty of 1831. Congress received several resolutions
from a new commercial treaty and promptly appropriated
$20,000 for the expenses of a diplomatic commission.[48]

After securing the proper statements of willingness from
Mexico, Frelinghuysen appointed ex-President Grant and William H. Trescot to negotiate a new treaty, and Mexico completed the commission with Romero and Estanislao Cañedo. The
appointment of Romero as head of the delegation was irreproach-
able, for he had served twice as minister of *hacienda* and prob-

[45] Editorial from *La sociedad*, reprinted in *Two Republics*, Jan. 19,
1876, p. 4.

[46] *Ibid.*, Jan. 5, 1876, p. 3; New York *World*, Nov. 29, 1878; Mexico,
Report on the Actual Condition of Mexico, pp. 154–155, 168–170.

[47] Chicago *Tribune*, March 11, 1881, p. 4.

[48] Callahan, *American Foreign Policy in Mexican Relations*, pp. 420–
421. The situation was complicated by American intervention in a Mexi-
can-Guatemalan boundary controversy at the same time (*ibid.*, pp. 412–
417; Valadés, *El porfirismo: Nacimiento*, pp. 330–337).

ably knew the United States better than any other Mexican. On the other hand, the United States possessed abler experts in Mexican affairs than Grant—John W. Foster for one—and it seems clear that his personal popularity played a large part in his appointment. There is no evidence that he sought or expected the honor, but the odd coincidence that partners in a railroad enterprise were to negotiate a treaty which might favor that enterprise aroused a certain amount of hostile comment.[49]

Without much difficulty the four commissioners carried out their assignment and signed a commercial reciprocity convention on January 20, 1883. The core of this convention consisted of two lists of products which were to be admitted free from Mexico into the United States and vice versa. The United States placed twenty-eight categories of Mexican products on its free list, most of them farm or forest products of which the most important were coffee, fresh tropical fruits, henequen and ixtle fibers, uncured hides, the lower grades of sugar, and unmanufactured leaf tobacco. In return Mexico placed seventy-three categories of American products on its free list. Most of them were manufactured goods, including agricultural tools, steel rails, locomotives, steam engines, all kinds of tools for artisans, and wire. One important type of manufacture was conspicuously omitted—textiles. The Mexican free list also included minerals, such as coal, crude petroleum, quicksilver, and sulphur, as well as a few agricultural products.[50]

The publication of the Grant-Romero treaty raised a variety of protests in both the United States and Mexico, which delayed ratification for over a year. Some of the first objections were

[49] Badeau felt that Frelinghuysen appointed Grant in order to draw him closer to the Arthur administration (Badeau, *Grant in Peace*, pp. 351–352). Estanislao Cañedo, the second Mexican commissioner, was a close friend of Edward Lee Plumb and at one time his agent.

[50] William M. Malloy, ed., *Treaties, Conventions, International Acts, Protocols and Agreements between the United States of America and Other Powers, 1776–1909* (61st Congress, 2d Session, Senate Document 357; Washington, 1910), I, 1146–1152.

fantastic. The New York *Sun*, for example, declared that the real purpose of the treaty was to bankrupt Mexico and stop subsidy payments to American railroad companies, so that they would withdraw and sell their concessions to Gould and Huntington. Other writers, however, worked out a more plausible case. The New Orleans *Picayune* called the treaty a blow to Southern interests, since it removed all protection for local producers of sugar, hemp, tobacco, fruits, vegetables, and woods in order to benefit the Mexican Southern Railroad, which would haul these products to market. Others criticized the treaty for not ending the nuisance of the Free Zone.[51]

On the other hand, supporters of the treaty presented an effective case based upon the argument that the treaty, though limited and lopsided, was a step in the right direction—toward free trade. Joseph Nimmo, chief of the Bureau of Statistics, answered Southern farmers with the prediction that the treaty and the new international railroads would greatly increase trade between the South and Mexico. The Chicago *Tribune* printed a long interview with Grant, who reassured Louisiana that Mexican sugar would never be plentiful enough to distress American producers seriously. As for the dangers of annexing Mexican territory and people, the *Tribune* disposed of the possibility in brutal fashion: "Increased familiarity will certainly breed sufficient contempt for the 'greaser' population to ward off any closer association." Southerners remained unconvinced, and their Senators managed to prolong consideration of the treaty, but on March 11, 1884, the friends of the treaty finally secured its ratification by the narrow two-thirds vote of forty-one to twenty.[52]

Mexican journalists advanced similar arguments, accusing

[51] The New York *Sun* is quoted in the Chicago *Tribune*, Feb. 6, 1883, p. 4, and answered in *ibid.*, Feb. 27, 1883, p. 4. See also New Orleans *Picayune*, no date, as reprinted in *El monitor republicano*, March 13, 1883, p. 2.

[52] Chicago *Tribune*, Jan. 1, 1883, p. 4; Jan. 25, p. 3; Feb. 12, p. 3; Jan. 10, 1884, p. 4; Jan. 18, p. 4; Jan. 21, p. 1; March 12, p. 1.

Romero and Cañedo of an unpatriotic pro-American bias and declaring that Mexico would never profit from the treaty, either because she could not produce enough sugar and other products for export or because the Louisiana sugar producers would never allow the treaty to be ratified. Others went further and called it the *coup de grâce* of Mexican independence and industry, which would be ruined by American competition. The *Diario oficial* answered as many objections as possible, and when the treaty finally came to a vote in the Mexican Congress, the administration bloc quietly ratified it on May 17.[53]

The exchange of ratifications did not end the treaty battle, however, for the United States Senate had added to the treaty an amendment requiring congressional legislation to carry it into effect. The battle now shifted to the House of Representatives, and before the question was settled, both houses of Congress had their full say. Unfortunately for the treaty, the election of 1884 was now at hand, and the candidates, James G. Blaine and Grover Cleveland, had chosen the tariff as one of the principal issues of the campaign. In addition, as soon as the election was decided, the "lame duck" president, Chester A. Arthur, made a last-minute effort to force through Congress similar reciprocity treaties with Spain and the Dominican Republic. Consequently it became impossible to judge the Mexican reciprocity treaty alone and on its own merits.

It is unnecessary to follow the congressional debates in any detail. The outstanding speaker for the treaty was Abram S. Hewitt, the ranking Democratic member of the House Ways and Means Committee, who defended it with orthodox free-trade arguments as a step in the direction of a broader and more profitable foreign trade.[54] Senator Justin S. Morrill of Vermont, the

[53] *El monitor republicano*, Feb. 10, 1883, p. 2; *Diario oficial*, April 2, 1883, p. 2.
[54] For a discussion of Hewitt's general tariff policy see Allen Nevins, *Abram S. Hewitt: With Some Account of Peter Cooper* (New York, 1935), pp. 419 ff. The best example of Hewitt's arguments for the Mex-

high priest of protectionism, made the most effective case for the opposition in a speech which denounced reciprocity treaties in general as unconstitutional, money-wasting, and useless. Somewhat shortsightedly he declared: "The time is long past when nations can be enormously enriched by any excessive profits upon foreign trade." Turning to Mexico, Morrill recognized her "rare beauty" and varied resources but complained that because of her backward population reciprocity would amount to exchanging a Lexington or Morgan horse for a Mexican mustang and stump-tail mule. At the same time he argued that Mexican sugar production might increase beyond all expectations and flood the American market.[55]

Consistent or not, in the end the protectionists carried the day. Cleveland, the new president, favored low tariffs, but he would not put himself out to save treaties negotiated by his predecessor, and without his support Hewitt and the free traders did not have a chance of success. On July 22, 1886, the House approved a motion to pass over the Mexican reciprocity bill, by a vote of 162 to 51, and its supporters made no further effort to keep the issue alive. Most of the votes for reconsideration came from Southern Democrats, and representatives of the Northeast and Northwest overwhelmingly supported the motion.[56] Except for a handful of votes, the tally clearly suggests that protectionists were unwilling to risk a breach in their principle for possible trade with Mexico and that the South had come to favor reciprocity either out of loyalty to the Democratic party platform and to the free-trade tradition or out of hope for new markets in Mexico.

---

ican reciprocity treaty is in United States, 48th Congress, 1st Session, *House Report 1848* (Washington, 1884), *passim.*

[55] United States, 48th Congress, 2d Session, *Congressional Record,* XVI, pt. 1, 506–513.

[56] 49th Congress, 1st Session, *ibid.,* XVII, 7341. Mexican reactions to the congressional debate are found in México, Secretaría de fomento, *Reciprocidad comercial entre México y los Estados Unidos* (México, 1890).

V

When the House of Representatives finally decided not to carry out the reciprocity treaty with Mexico, the principal American negotiator was no longer on earth (he died in 1885) to witness the defeat. After signing his name to the treaty in January 1883, Grant left the ratification to others, surprised at the intensity of the opposition and pained to see that his personal influence made little difference in the debates. Meanwhile, he turned to his private business affairs. After the Mexican government approved the revised Mexican Southern Railroad concession in 1881, the company sent out three or four engineering commissions to make a preliminary survey of the route into Oaxaca, and local newspapers there continued to issue optimistic bulletins about the operations well into 1882. At the end of 1883 J. H. Work reported that most of the line had been surveyed and that some construction work was going on south of Laredo.

Soon, however, capital stopped flowing from the United States; a familiar anemia set in; and the hopeful citizens of Oaxaca, like those of Topolobampo and the towns along the Rosecrans and Plumb lines, had to content themselves with words while awaiting the appearance of roadbed and rails. In the United States, Grant too marked time, entertaining Porfirio Díaz during the latter's visit to New York in 1883 and issuing impressive predictions about the future of American-Mexican trade.[57]

In the end Grant ruined the chances of his Mexican project

[57] Badeau, *Grant in Peace*, p. 397; Francisco Meijueiro, *Memoria que el C. General Francisco Meijueiro, gobernador constitucional del estado libre y soberano de Oaxaca, presenta a la 11ª legislatura del mismo, el 17 de setiembre de 1881, sobre todos los ramos de la administración pública* (Oaxaca, 1881), p. 17; *Diario oficial*, Jan. 31, 1882, pp. 3–4; Manuel Martínez Gracida, *Efemeridades oaxaqueños, 1853–1892* (México, 1892), pp. 187, 189–190; J. H. Work to Joseph Nimmo, New York, Dec. 18, 1883, in Nimmo, *Trade between Mexico and the United States*, p. 54; Grenville M. Dodge, *Personal Recollections of President Abraham Lin-*

through his own recklessness and inexperience. During the spring of 1882 gossips in Mexico City reported that the ex-president had lost most of his money in the stock market. Although false at the time, the rumor soon became true. Since most of the honorary business positions which Grant had accepted in 1880 had brought him no income, in 1883 he invested all his liquid capital, about $100,000, in a banking firm founded by his son, Ulysses, Junior, and one Ferdinand Ward, a financial genius by reputation. Ward milked the unsuspecting Grants of all their own and borrowed money, and on the morning of May 6, 1884, Grant went down to his office to learn that the bank had failed, Ward had fled, and he himself was bankrupt.

Realizing for the first time, perhaps, how shallow was his knowledge of finance, the old man pulled himself together and began to sell off house, furniture, and trophies in order to raise funds. A magnanimous public showed complete sympathy, and offers of aid poured in from all sides. When Matías Romero learned of his friend's plight, he immediately called on him and left behind a check for $1,000, which Grant repaid as soon as he was able. The partnership of Grant and Romero was now dissolved, for the general's bankruptcy, combined with the business depression of 1884, ended all chances of securing capital for the Mexican Southern Railroad, and Grant settled down to pay off his debts by writing magazine articles on his experiences in the Civil War. But not for long: in October a physician diagnosed certain pains in his throat as an incurable cancer, and through the winter and spring Grant raced against death to complete two volumes of his memoirs, in order to leave his wife a steady income. The race was narrowly won, and on July 23, 1885, less than a month after the memoirs were finished, their author died.[58]

For a time after Grant's death the mourning nation forgot his recent blunders in the memory of his more remote military

coln, *Ulysses S. Grant, and General William T. Sherman* (Council Bluffs, Iowa, 1914), p. 96.

[58] *Diario oficial*, May 10, 1882, p. 1; Hesseltine, *Ulysses S. Grant*, pp. 445–452; Badeau, *Grant in Peace*, pp. 419–461.

glory and in the pathetic dignity of his end. Mexico had less to forget, for most of the literate public had only a dim idea of Grant's political and financial shortcomings, and as for his failure to build the Mexican Southern Railroad, they were willing to take the intent for the deed. Newspapers observed his death with obituaries and full accounts of his last moments, and on August 26 the governments of the Federal District and Mexico City held a massive memorial program attended by President Díaz, his cabinet, and the leaders of society. A band played funeral marches and elegies; various orators eulogized the American friend; and an army captain read a set of doggerel verses praising the "two illustrious generals," leaders of powerful nations, whose discussions started a parade of "bridges, rails, and [railroad] cars" across the Rio Grande.[59]

The simple chromo suggested by these verses gives a clue to Grant's real significance in American-Mexican economic relations. He came to Mexico in 1880 after four years of strained relations between the two countries, when American policies in Mexico had been so suspected, denounced, defended, and damned on both sides of the border that no Mexicans and perhaps few Americans could be sure of just what the United States was trying to do. During the confusion Grant was in Europe, safe from involvement. Thus when he visited Mexico, the Mexicans knew of him only that he had hated the Mexican War, that he had wanted to give aid against Maximilian, that he had kept the peace as president, and that Europe had acclaimed him as a military hero. He was glamorous; he was safe. At the same time in the United States he enjoyed an unmerited reputation for conservative economic wisdom, and his speeches and interviews lent much weight to the optimistic view of Mexico which Romero and his associates had worked so hard to circulate. It was a pity that he went bankrupt and dropped his railroad project, but he did not need to succeed. By 1884 he had made

[59] México, Ayuntamiento, *Corona funebre dedicada a la memoria del Gral. Ulises S. Grant* (México, 1885), *passim*.

his contribution to American-Mexican relations as a symbol of peaceful economic imperialism.

In view of the later history of the Mexican Southern Railroad it is hard to believe that Grant could have fulfilled his optimistic predictions even if he had not been halted by bankruptcy and death. In 1885 the Grant concession was declared void, and three years later the Mexican government transferred it with a handsome subsidy to H. Rudston Reed of the British firm of Reed and Campbell, which completed a narrow-gauge line from Mexico City to Oaxaca in 1892. In 1909 the National Railways of Mexico leased the Mexican Southern property. Somewhat later the chairman of the Mexican Southern board of directors reported that although dividends were paid regularly to all stockholders between 1897 and 1914 they received little or nothing before and after those dates.[60] With no support other than that of the fickle opportunist Gould, it is highly doubtful that Grant could have done even this well.

As an expansionist Grant was sometimes a little ahead of his age. His attempt to annex the Dominican Republic anticipated the Caribbean policy of McKinley by about thirty years, and American protectionists were not yet ready to permit the kind of "dollar diplomacy" exemplified by the Grant-Romero reciprocity treaty. In sponsoring the Mexican Southern Railroad, however, Grant was exactly abreast of his generation, and his enthusiastic speeches about Mexican resources and potential markets give an accurate picture of American promotional thought in the 1880's.

[60] *El monitor republicano,* June 2, 1885, p. 3. Another line, the Pan-American Railway, was completed to the Guatemalan border and later sold to the government. See Powell, *Railroads of Mexico,* pp. 146–147, 154; Gurza, *La política ferrocarrilera,* pp. 125–127; Mexican Southern Railway, Limited, *Proceedings at the Thirty-sixth Ordinary General Meeting of the Company Held at Winchester House, Old Broad Street, London, E.C., on Wednesday, the 3rd Day of December, 1924* [London, n.d.], pp. 4–5.

VI

City Boss: Alexander R. Shepherd

"PROMOTER" is necessarily a loose term. Sometimes promotional activities ended with the formation of a company and the sale of stock in Mexican railroads, mines, or lands. More often the promoter had to continue his search for development capital as long as his project lasted, and sometimes he had to direct operations in Mexico at the same time. Not all promoters, however, were effective administrators, and Albert K. Owen's colony at Topolobampo failed partly because he lacked this skill.

While the enthusiastic Utopian struggled with his irrigation ditches and his schismatic followers, another promoter was quietly building up a more worldly but equally ambitious mining colony across the mountains in southwest Chihuahua. In contrast to the theoretical reformer, Alexander R. Shepherd brought to his mining project an excellent practical background for administering a company and handling groups of men—machine politics. After making a private fortune in Washington city buildings, he entered the District of Columbia government and set out to renovate and beautify the shabby capital. The pragmatic, materialistic Grant admired Shepherd's energy and approved his plan, but District taxpayers screamed to the heavens when they learned of the great appropriations required and denounced him as a second "Boss" Tweed. A congressional investigation followed, and after months of name-calling and contradictory evidence Shepherd found himself out of office, his future prospects in Washington blackened by charges of corruption and dishonesty.

In a Mexican mining camp such charges counted for little. What mattered was that Shepherd knew how to get engineering projects in motion and had enough friends among sympathetic Republicans to secure capital for a new venture. Accordingly in 1880, after a preliminary reconnaissance, he set off with his family to mine silver in the remote Batopilas Valley back in the Sierra Madre of Chihuahua. Through years of constant labor and despite repeated setbacks, he cleared out old tunnels abandoned by the Spaniards, gained access to new, rich ore bodies, and installed an efficient, modern reducing plant. During the 1880's his companies declared several dividends, but from then until his death in 1902 development expenses swallowed up profits, and the project never enriched its supporters.

What did Shepherd do for Mexico at the same time? "He had found the region wild and peopled with ignorant peons," said one observer; "he left it well developed and with schools, hospitals, and all the other evidences of efficient leadership." [1] But in the Mexico of Porfirio Díaz efficient leadership often meant regimentation, and in Batopilas it required a paternalistic company rule of the sort which American labor was beginning to resent. Not for nothing did "Boss" Shepherd hold his nickname. Fortunately the boss wielded his powers with a light hand, so that Mexicans respected him and prospered under his system. In the long run Mexico needed—and would demand— more than Shepherd's paternalism, but under the circumstances of the day he had much to offer his adopted country.

[1] Marcosson, "Our Financial Stake in Mexico," p. 23.

I

Alexander Robey Shepherd was born in Washington, D.C., on January 31, 1835, the son of a native Marylander of some means. When he was ten years old, however, his father died, leaving a widow and seven children so poorly provided for that Mrs. Shepherd had to open a boardinghouse, and after only a few years of schooling young Alexander went to work at the age of fifteen as a carpenter's apprentice. In 1852 he entered the plumbing and gas-fitting firm of John W. Thompson, the leading contractor in the District, and seven years later he became a partner in the firm. By 1870 he was perhaps the best-known building contractor and real-estate promoter in the city, with a number of other financial interests and many political acquaintances.[2]

Contemporary descriptions of Shepherd always emphasize the impression of power and energy which he created wherever he went. He was a tall, handsome man, as strong as an ox, with a broad, stubborn face like a bronze statue of Martin Luther, a resonant voice, and a full, musical laugh. "When we was layin' the pavements," said a workman later, "we'd git on better an' do more work if the Boss would come and look after us for fifteen minutes than if the whole Board of Works stood over us all day." [3] Perhaps this was because Shepherd was not afraid to seize a mallet or a trowel himself when the work was being done wrongly.

Men such as Shepherd were designed for the reckless, demanding life of the frontier, but a combination of circumstances

[2] Biography of Alexander R. Shepherd, typescript, no author mentioned, in Shepherd Papers, pp. 1–2; William Tindall, *A Sketch of Alexander Robey Shepherd* (Washington, 1911), pp. 49–52; [Washington *Star*, Sept. 24, 1887]. Where newspaper references are given in brackets, they represent clippings in the Shepherd Papers gathered by a professional collecting service.

[3] [New York *World*, 1872]; [New Orleans *Times*, n.d.]; [Cincinnati *Enquirer*, n.d.]; [New York *Graphic*, n.d.].

made him seem, for a time, as much at home among the Grecian porticoes of Washington as in the forests of Oregon or California. When the Civil War ended, the national capital needed reconstruction almost as much as the South. Nearly all the streets were dirt except for a few cobbled or graveled roadways. Tiber Creek and Washington Canal, meandering through the center of town, were open sewers, and Slash Run Swamp sent out occasional waves of malaria over the northwestern suburbs. Chickens, geese, cows, and pigs roamed at large. Horace Greeley's New York *Tribune* reported in 1867: "Washington is the concrete of seediness. It is a poor relation of prosperous cities. It is out at the elbows, shabby at the toes, generally dingy and neglected, while the public buildings shine upon its poverty like pinchbeck jewelry." [4]

Public opinion of conditions in Washington reached its low point during the first year of the Grant administration, and in the autumn of 1869 a special convention of Westerners and Southerners at St. Louis suggested that the capital be moved to the Mississippi Valley.[5] Such a drastic remedy was obviously impracticable, but it frightened the residents of the District into action, and on February 21, 1871, they secured an act of Congress creating a territorial form of government for the District. Perhaps in order to bolster the city's sagging credit, Grant appointed Henry D. Cooke, brother of Jay Cooke, as governor of the District. Shepherd, who had been the moving force of the District citizens, became vice-chairman and *de facto* director of the all-important board of public works.[6]

---

[4] Tindall, *Sketch of Shepherd*, pp. 55–56; Wilhelmus Bogart Bryan, *A History of the National Capital* (New York, 1916), II, 489–496; New York *Tribune*, Feb. 25, 1867, as quoted in Hesseltine, *Ulysses S. Grant*, p. 292.

[5] [Washington *Star*, Sept. 24, 1887].

[6] In 1864 another committee, including Shepherd, had made similar recommendations and obtained a higher tax rate but without bringing about many concrete improvements (Bryan, *History of the National Capital*, II, 500–503, 568, 574–579, 592, 595). Three of the other four

In a report of June 1871 this board estimated its immediate expenditures for improvements at $6,578,397 and recommended a loan of $4,000,000 which, it thought, would make further property assessments unnecessary. The board, however, failed to take into consideration the energy and optimism of its vice-chairman. Signing contracts right and left with his old friends in the city's building trade and ordering around gangs of laborers like platoons and regiments, Shepherd attacked the public-works problem on all fronts at once. During the next three years, according to a report of his board, 207 miles of sidewalks were laid, 118 miles of streets paved, and over 600,000 feet of sewers installed.[7]

Once an improvement was decided on, the devil himself could not have stood in the way. For example, when opponents petitioned a judge for an injunction to prevent the demolition of the North Liberty Market House, "an unsightly and hideous group" of buildings, a friend of Shepherd took the judge for a drive in the country while gangs of men pulled down the eyesores. Similarly, one Sunday night after he had failed to persuade the Washington and Alexandria Railroad to change the grade of a track running past the Capitol, Shepherd coolly ripped out the rails and buried the old roadbed six feet deep.[8]

Such ruthless, impatient measures naturally created enemies. Undoubtedly some, as Shepherd charged, were simply old "Bourbons" who disliked change of any sort, but liberals regarded him as an incipient local dictator, and the North Liberty Market case in particular gave them an opportunity to cry out against infringement of individual liberties.[9] Others saw danger

members of the board of public works were old friends of Shepherd: Cooke, who had worked with him in the earlier citizens' movement; S. B. Brown, a government contractor; and James A. Magruder, an army engineer. See also Tindall, *Sketch of Shepherd*, pp. 53–55.

[7] Biography of Shepherd, typescript, pp. 5–7.

[8] *Ibid.*, pp. 7–8; [Washington *Star*, Sept. 24, 1887]; Bryan, *History of the National Capital*, II, 600–602.

[9] Biography of Shepherd, typescript p. 8. When the North Liberty

in the race question, for some of the new government's support
came from the large Negro population of the District. But these
complaints were dwarfed by the staggering cost of the new improvements, for Shepherd later told the congressional committee
that he had spent $18,872,565.76, and other estimates went as
high as $26,000,000 and $30,000,000.[10]

As District property owners gradually learned the truth, they
began to accuse Shepherd and Cooke of building up a huge
"ring" with the connivance of notorious hangers-on of the Grant
administration. Shepherd's freehanded methods of operation and
his careless bookkeeping undoubtedly gave substance to some
of these charges. Whatever the evidence of his records, there
seems no doubt that some made fortunes out of the city's beauti-
fication and others went bankrupt. As for Shepherd's political
acquaintances, he almost certainly made use of Orville E. Babcock, William J. Murtagh, and other unsavory "fixers" of
Grant's entourage, although his chief source of influence in that
quarter was probably his personal friendship with the president.[11]

After two years of charges and countercharges Shepherd de-

Market was demolished, a butcher who owned a stall in the market tried
to prevent the action and died in the wreckage of the building ([Wash-
ington] *Times* [Dec. 29], 1897, p. 1).

[10] Tindall, *Sketch of Shepherd*, pp. 58–59; United States, 43d Congress, 1st Session, *Senate Report 453* (Washington, 1874) I, vii.

[11] It is not surprising that observers could not agree as to the quality
and permanence of the work done under the Shepherd regime. Bryan
states that the sewer system, for example, was so well laid out that it required few important changes, but in 1887 the *Nation* reported that
miles of "asphalt" and treated wood pavements quickly went to pieces
(Bryan, *History of the National Capital*, II, 600–601; *Nation*, XLV
[July 21, 1887], 47). On Shepherd's political associations see Allen Nevins, *Hamilton Fish: The Inner History of the Grant Administration*
(New York, 1936), pp. 657–658, 723, 759, 820. Grant remained loyal to
Shepherd throughout, and in 1881 he declared that "if they had let
Shepherd alone, he would have made a magnificent investment for the
Government, and would have abated a terrible nuisance at the same
time" (newspaper clipping, dated Sept. 10, 1881, in Shepherd Papers).

manded a full congressional investigation of the charges against him, and on March 5, 1874, a committee of three Senators and five Representatives began to hear testimony on the finances of the District. In the course of nearly six weeks of hearings the committee collected over 2,400 pages of testimony and supporting documents. The anonymous writer of a biography of Shepherd preserved in the family papers conceded that "a more thorough and searching investigation never was had," but he complained that the committee suspended the regular rules of evidence and accepted all sorts of hearsay and secondhand statements. The Democrats on the committee, he added, were more interested in finding a "Republican Tweed" to offset the recent Tammany scandals than in getting at the truth, and although the Republicans held a majority on the committee, one of their members (J. M. Wilson, of Indiana) voted with the opposition more often than not, because of personal spleen against the Grant administration.[12]

In its final report to Congress the joint committee calculated the total tax burden on District property owners as nearly $21,000,000, exclusive of ordinary running expenses for the future, and censured the Cooke-Shepherd administration heavily for exceeding the legal debt limit. The report said much less about the quality of work done and nothing directly about Shepherd's honesty. In the end the committee denounced the territorial form of government as cumbersome, ill co-ordinated, and expensive, and it recommended the appointment of a temporary commission to manage the affairs of the District while permanent arrangements were made.[13]

Whatever the shortcomings of Shepherd's work in Washington, the congressional investigation left many questions unanswered and many accusations unproved. Probably a better investigation was impossible in a decade of financial troubles,

[12] Biography of Shepherd, typescript, pp. 10–25.
[13] United States, 43d Congress, 1st Session, *Senate Report 453*, I, i–xxix and especially xxix.

open scandals, and bitter party politics. But despite the committee's refusal to indict individuals and its silence on the subject of Shepherd's honesty, the real result of the investigation was a crushing judgment against him. His office was abolished and his government remodeled, and when Grant stubbornly appointed him commissioner in the new regime, the Senate tabled the appointment. What was harder to bear, the opposition newspapers assumed that their charges had been proved, and in the Grant administration's last unhappy years of scandal and exposure Shepherd was often linked with Babcock, Belknap, and others of the same sort. Opinions of "the boss" in Washington itself continued to be divided, but outside the District his detractors won an easy victory. Even today he regularly receives his quota of dishonorable mention in history textbooks as merely another of Grant's rogues.

II

For several years after Shepherd's fall from power he devoted his full attention to his construction business and his real-estate operations, but luck had deserted him, and he was soon in financial straits. His enemies gloated that he was only suffering the inevitable result of pyramiding his holdings on money borrowed during his days of public influence, but when he finally had to suspend operations in November 1876, his friends blamed the general hard times and bad investments and pointed out that his creditors not only granted him an extension of time but even kept him in control of his bankrupt businesses. For three years he worked to settle up his estate and support his family. During this time his only public activity was to direct a yellow-fever relief expedition from St. Louis to New Orleans. Even in charitable work he could not escape his reputation, for although he accompanied the expedition himself at some personal risk, opposition newspapers accused him of misusing the relief funds and called the whole affair a junket.[14]

[14] Chicago *Tribune*, Nov. 14, 1876, p. 3; Biography of Shepherd,

Casting about for some way to recoup his losses outside Washington, Shepherd conceived the idea of managing silver mines in Mexico, perhaps on the advice of a brother who was on the staff of the Denver *Tribune*. A descriptive passage in Baron von Humboldt's works drew his attention to the mineral district of Batopilas, an almost inaccessible river valley in the mountains of southwest Chihuahua. Despite their inconvenient location, the Batopilas mines lay closer to the American border than most major silver districts in Mexico, and historical accounts, though conflicting, placed their total production during the colonial period well above 100,000,000 pesos. In the nineteenth century the principal Batopilas mines had come under the control of a group of men including William G. Fargo of Wells, Fargo and Company. Their manager, J. R. Robinson, operated the mines on a small scale, but he was growing old and wanted to retire. Unable to find anyone to take his place, the American owners were looking for a purchaser.[15]

Once Shepherd's interest in Batopilas was aroused, nothing would satisfy him but a personal inspection of the area. Knowing little of mining techniques, he enlisted the aid of those who did, including a friend, Lyndon H. Stephens, and on June 29, 1879, his party left Washington for Mexico. They chose the long way around—via Panama to Mazatlán, then in a small schooner to Agiabampo, a sandspit on the Gulf of California. After riding on muleback for days in the broiling sun they arrived at Batopilas early in August. Here they stayed for a month, talking to old residents, few of whom spoke any English, and examining mines and production records.

Shepherd's immediate reaction was favorable. He wrote to his wife that the fine prospects of the mine had hitherto been wasted

---

typescript, pp. 25–28. The biographical account quotes a laudatory article in the St. Louis *Post*, Oct. 4, 1878. For an unfavorable account of the yellow-fever expedition see New York *Sun*, Feb. 2, 1879.

[15] *Consolidated Batopilas Silver Mining Company* [New York? 1879], *passim;* Denver *Republican*, April 9, 1899.

by poor management and primitive machinery. "The thing has paid so well with slight effort," he declared, "that the owners have been content to get out merely that which showed on the surface. . . . The managing people here have nice quarters and a good time. . . . An isolation of five years would be exile and banishment but I believe it would insure a fortune." Later he told a Washington reporter that Chihuahua contained more mineral wealth than the whole United States, that Mexicans were eager for American capital, and that their revolutions were "hardly as formidable as a fireman's riot in New York used to be." [16]

Having obtained enough information on which to act, Shepherd and his party returned home through dangerous, Indian-infested country, by way of El Paso and New Mexico. In New York he organized the Consolidated Batopilas Mining Company with a capital of $3,000,000 and purchased the property of Fargo and his associates, taking them into his board of directors. George W. Quintard of New York became president of the new company and Robinson a vice-president, residing in New York; Shepherd made himself vice-president and general manager of operations in Mexico. Among the largest stockholders were George M. Pullman, General Horace Porter, and George W. Blanchard.[17] The property which the new company controlled included "the Great Batopilas mine" (apparently the San Miguel group), several other important mines in the vicinity, surface rights to about nine hundred square miles of land, mort-

[16] Biography of Shepherd, typescript, p. 28; Alexander R. Shepherd to Mrs. Alexander R. Shepherd, Batopilas, Aug. 16, 1879, typescript in Shepherd Papers; Washington *Republican*, Sept. 27, 1879.

[17] J. D. Smith, president of the New York Stock Exchange, was treasurer, Lyndon H. Stevens secretary, and the board of directors included A. H. Barney, William G. Fargo, ex-Senator Jerome B. Chaffee, Henry Havemeyer, Andros B. Stone, and Benjamin P. Cheney (Biography of Shepherd, typescript, p. 29; *Economist* [Boston], Dec. 27, 1879). Porter was at this time vice-president of the Pullman Company, Blanchard vice-president of the Erie Railroad.

gages on several farms, a group of large buildings with some smelting machinery, and agencies in Chihuahua and other towns through which to send monthly shipments of silver to New York.

During the winter and early spring of 1880 Shepherd and his wife gathered supplies and put their affairs in order for an indefinite period of isolation and hard work in the mountains of Chihuahua. By the end of April all was ready, and on May 1 they set out for Mexico with their seven children, ranging from three to nineteen years old, four dogs, and so much baggage that they had to charter a private railroad car as far as San Antonio. Here they struck out across the hot Texas plains in an army ambulance, spending their nights in army forts or camping in tents. Since temperature and weather conditions were constantly changing, everyone had to be provided with warm coats, dusters, raincoats, flasks, and pistols each morning, but Shepherd usually managed to get them under way by eight o'clock. Upon reaching the Rio Grande, they crossed into Mexico without any difficulty, but by the time they entered the city of Chihuahua, Mrs. Shepherd and the children were so tired that Shepherd rented a large house for them to live in while he went on to Batopilas to prepare a permanent home and direct mining operations.

After a summer's rest Mrs. Shepherd and the children were strong enough for the last stage of their journey. They began by crossing a treeless waste "just like the Texas plains, only more so," but after a short halt at Carichic, a dusty adobe ranch, they started up the first foothills. From there on the trip was a long succession of discomforts and dangers: frequent rainstorms, narrow paths, steep cliffs above and below, chill in the mountains and in the valleys stupefying heat. The last day was the worst, and as the party, dressed in heavy flannels, descended the final slope toward the Batopilas River, Mrs. Shepherd nearly fainted from exhaustion. Just when it seemed that no one could go any farther, they caught sight of a white house on the other side of the river, and soon the hacienda of San Miguel came into view. No one had expected them to arrive so early, but a few mine workers spied them and clustered around to see the "gringos," and then Shepherd hurried out. When one of the girls saw her father wearing a beard, she leaped from her mule in fright, fell into the river, and had to be pulled out, while her mother and the rest of the party, hot, tired, and stiff, slowly dismounted and looked around the little settlement in curiosity. After nearly six months of travel, they had arrived.[18]

III

Even before his family's arrival Shepherd had begun to organize his new enterprise in preparation for what he hoped would be immensely profitable operations. With his customary energy he started out to expand his holdings. After rapid inspection of mines in the neighborhood he secured control of many promising areas by various agreements and formed ten companies in the United States to operate them, making himself manager of each one. The largest of those, the Descubridora Consolidated Silver Mining Company, controlled claims totaling 640,000 square meters in area and containing at least 120 distinct ore veins, of which one-third were very promising. It also held surface rights on 640 acres fronting on the Batopilas River, a splendid site for a mill.[19]

[18] This account of the Shepherd family's trip is based on several typescripts in the Shepherd Papers, especially a diary of Mrs. Shepherd, written in 1882, and a diary of one of the older girls. See also Washington *Post*, Aug. 30, 1880. The party arrived in Batopilas on October 21.

[19] Biography of Shepherd, typescript, p. 31; "Mexican Bonanzas," unidentified newspaper clipping (probably 1882), Shepherd Papers; Cleveland *Herald*, April 16, 1883; *Mining News*, Aug. 18, 1883; *Moody's Manual of Railroads and Corporation Securities* (New York, 1900–1924), 1911, p. 3592. The full list of those companies with their capitalization is as follows: Descubridora Consolidated Silver Mining Company ($3,000,000), Camuchin Consolidated Silver Mining Company ($1,000,-000), Peñasquito Silver Mining Company ($1,000,000), Santa María Silver Mining Company ($1,000,000), Valenzuela Consolidated Silver Min-

During the first six years of Shepherd's operations his various companies spent about $2,000,000 in the development of the existing mines. Sometimes a little digging paid off quickly: for example, after spending over 4,000 pesos on the Roncesvalles mine, he struck a deposit of black silver and ore which yielded 200,000 pesos. More often, however, the returns were slower, and he estimated that the average annual yield from 1880 to 1887 was only 600,000 pesos. Much of this money had to be used to buy new equipment, but in spite of these expenses the companies paid dividends totaling nearly $1,000,000 during this period.[20]

Even before the preliminary construction operations were finished, Shepherd was planning longer tunnels and a new reduction hacienda, but these, he realized, would require more capital and a guaranteed source of water power. In 1886 he secured permission to dam the Batopilas River, as part of a general development contract with the Mexican government. Dated April 12, the contract also gave Shepherd's companies the right to exploit all abandoned mines in an area of about sixty square miles, exempted them from import duties on machinery and all Federal taxes except the stamp tax, and granted them an annual rebate on other import duties. In return, Shepherd accepted Mexican status for his companies, deposited a bond of 25,000 pesos in the Banco Nacional, and agreed to keep at least fifty miners at work six months out of each year.[21]

---

ing Company ($1,000,000), Animas Silver Mining Company ($500,000), Consolidated Roncesvalles Silver Mining Company ($500,000), New Giral Silver Mining Company ($50,000), Charcas Syndicate, and Consolación Mining Company (no figures given for the last two). Shepherd also apparently controlled the nearby Ballinas mine himself.

[20] Unidentified newspaper clipping (probably 1882), Shepherd Papers; Cleveland *Herald*, April 16, 1883; Batopilas Mining Company, *Report*, 1902, p. 3.

[21] México, *Diario de los debates de la Cámara de disputados: Duodécima legislatura constitucional de la unión* (México, 1884–1887), IV, 508–511. He also agreed to smelt three-fourths of his ore in Mexico and not to mortgage his concession to a foreign government or admit a government as partner in any way.

Having settled his legal position in Mexico and secured a potential power supply, Shepherd decided in 1887 to appeal to American investors for more development capital, holding out to them the lure of a million dollars of dividends paid by the various companies since 1880. In order to make his operations more efficient and minimize the variation in rates of yield among the many mines, Shepherd also decided to consolidate his various corporations into one. He visited the United States, and here, on October 13, 1887, he incorporated the Batopilas Mining Company in New York, with an authorized capital of $9,000,000. This company exchanged $5,175,000 of its stock for that of six of the old companies and bought up the others outright.

No sooner was the united company formed, however, than Shepherd suffered a disappointment. He had based his hopes for development operations very largely on a bond issue of $1,000,000, but investors took up less than half of this, and in the end he received no more than $200,000 for his work—less than one-fourth of what he had expected. Unable to push construction at full speed, he invested nearly all his own savings in the enterprise, borrowed as much as he could on friends' security, and plowed all the proceeds from mining and smelting into development operations, postponing dividends until the work was done.[22] This procedure would take more time than he had planned, and he resigned himself to an indefinite residence in Mexico—an exile which continued for fifteen years, broken only by rare visits to the United States, until his death in 1902.

The Batopilas silver deposits were usually fissure veins, cracks in the rock which had become filled with minerals originally in solution and later solidified. Much of the silver appeared as pure native metal in crystals, plates, or tangled clumps of wire. Although the veteran miners of the district claimed to be able to anticipate rich finds by the appearance of the surrounding rock, the Batopilas deposits were highly unpredictable, and espe-

[22] *Engineering and Mining Journal*, XLIV (Oct. 1, 1887) 236; *Moody's Manual*, 1911, p. 3592; Batopilas Mining Company, *Report*, 1902, p. 4.

cially in the early years Shepherd seldom had a great deal of "ore in sight" at any given time. On one occasion during a trip to the United States he drew a bank draft for $90,000 on the mines and wired instructions to his foremen to cover it. Up to the last day when this could be done, no silver had been produced, and they were much worried when the mine superintendent reported nothing but three loads of low-grade rock. An hour later, however, he uncovered a bonanza which saved the day. It was so rich that he could not find enough rock in it to blast and had to call in the shop crew to carve it out with cold cutters.[23]

From the beginning Shepherd tried to minimize the uncertainties of mining by thoroughness and efficiency. In his search for rich deposits he not only opened new veins but also extended the existing shafts and tunnels, some of them dating back to Spanish days. Although he soon discovered, contrary to expectations, that old refuse heaps contained relatively little silver, he profited in other ways from Spanish mistakes. Former owners had been content to use the "tribute" or share system, dividing the ores with the miners, but Shepherd, realizing that this method merely gutted the mines of their best ore, paid his men fixed wages and insisted on systematic mining. He also discovered that most of the Spanish and early Mexican workings lay close to the surface, because miners had wrongly assumed that all deeper ores would be encased in hard rock. Determined to mine these deeper ores, he straightened existing shafts, sank new ones, and imported hoisting machinery to replace the primitive leather buckets in which generations of Indians had painfully carried up the ore on their backs.[24]

[23] Grant Shepherd, *The Silver Magnet* (New York, 1939), pp. 64, 254; Mark R. Lamb, "Stories of the Batopilas Mines, Chihuahua," *Engineering and Mining Journal*, LXXXV (April 4, 1908), 689–691.

[24] G. Shepherd, *Silver Magnet*, pp. 196–198; "He Is the Monte Cristo of Mexico," unidentified newspaper clipping (probably 1896), Shepherd Papers; interview with Walter M. Brodie, [*Two Republics*, n.d.]; *Consolidated Batopilas Silver Mining Company*, p. 7. For a description of

Shepherd was particularly interested in one deposit, the Roncesvalles vein, lying several miles west of the Batopilas River in almost inaccessible hills. During 1885 he began to run a tunnel from the river to this vein, nearly two miles long and wide enough for two narrow-gauge tracks inside it. At first, lacking water power, his laborers followed the old Mexican procedure of blasting away the rock, a few inches at a time, and during the first two years the tunnel advanced only 370 meters. Eventually Shepherd brought in steel hand drills which he taught the natives to operate in pairs, one of them striking at the rock with a sledge hammer and the other turning the drill and cooling it with a stream of water from his mouth. Still later Shepherd substituted power drills, and the work went much faster. The Porfirio Díaz Tunnel, as he tactfully named it, was the major excavating work of his regime. It was not completed until 1899, but even before it reached its goal, it had crossed many new deposits which were then explored with side tunnels. Shepherd also ran connections between the Díaz Tunnel and the upper workings of Todos Santos and other rich veins, so that their ores could be rolled down to the mule cars in the tunnel. By 1902 the workings in the Díaz Tunnel and the Todos Santos vein were supplying 96 per cent of all ore smelted.[25]

During the first years of operations Shepherd had at his disposal two main reduction plants, Hacienda San Miguel and a separate mill near the Descubridora mine, about two hours' journey away. Since the location of San Miguel was more convenient, Shepherd made it his home and the center of his operations. He spent about $500,000 for new machinery for the

---

pre-1880 mining methods see Walter M. Brodie, "Silver of Batopilas," *Explosives Engineer*, VI (June 1928), 217–220.

[25] Unidentified newspaper clipping (probably March 1899), Shepherd Papers; Denver *Republican*, April 9, 1899; United States, *Consular Reports*, no. 105 (May 1889), pp. 3–5; *Engineering and Mining Journal*, LXIX (April 14, 1900), 437; Batopilas Mining Company, *Report*, 1901, p. 7.

hacienda, much of it built to order and all of it brought painfully over the mountain trails on muleback. In 1902 San Miguel
had about ninety stamps (of which perhaps twenty-five were
reserved for high-grade ore), amalgamating pans, cyanide and
leaching plants, a machine shop, and a foundry at which the
company could make its own castings. The buildings at San
Miguel housed this equipment and also included the main offices, the manager's house, dormitories, a dining room, a swim-
ming tank for employees, and stables for the mules. Around all
these stood a high, solid stone wall as protection against floods
and robbers.

In the 1880's Shepherd began to build a second great reducing
plant, Hacienda San Antonio, near the mouth of the Díaz Tunnel and about half a mile north of Hacienda San Miguel. By
1902 he had spent over $500,000 on this plant, which then con-
tained seventy-five stamps, concentrating tables, an electric
plant, and air compressors for the mines. The power for this
equipment came from a 764-foot dam across the Batopilas River,
which (together with an aqueduct over a mile long) cost the
company $986,000. Some stockholders doubted the wisdom of
building a large dam at such great expense of time and money,
but it would be hard to overestimate its importance to company
operations. As in many Mexican mining areas, the natives of
Batopilas had long since exhausted the meager wood supply of
nearby hills, and during the 1880's each three-hundred-pound
load of wood cost about a peso, except during the rainy season
when it could not be obtained at all. After the completion of
the dam Shepherd was able to furnish his richest mines with
electric lights, to the natives' amazement, and the use of power-
driven machinery and compressed air greatly facilitated the
digging of tunnels. Even then he continued to supplement his
water power with gasoline-driven engines, especially in the dry
season.[26]

[26] Walter M. Brodie, "The Mines of the Batopilas Mining Company
at Batopilas, Chihuahua: Extracts from Reports . . . (October 1923),"
pp. 4–5, typescript in Shepherd Papers; United States, *Consular Reports,*

With so much capital tied up in equipment and improvements Shepherd had to squeeze every possible ounce of silver out of the oxides and sulphides from his mines, especially since well over 90 per cent of their yield was third-grade ore.[27] When he first came to Batopilas, he reduced most of his ores by the time-honored Mexican process, mixing the ores with chloride and sulphate salts to release minute particles of free silver and then collecting these in an amalgam with mercury. Since tests showed that amalgamation did not get full value from all ores, he soon introduced lixiviation (leaching) from California and Colorado, and he recovered small amounts of gold by the cyanide process.

In his search for efficiency Shepherd imposed a strict regimen on Indians and foreigners alike. Head miners assigned work in the mines; timekeepers and paymasters carefully computed each man's production and wages; and these accounts were further examined by the mine superintendent, the bookkeeper, and the general manager. The best ores were weighed at the mines, shipped to Hacienda San Miguel in leather bags under the care of a trusted employee, and reweighed. Wherever necessary during the reduction process another employee kept records of weights and assays, and Shepherd insisted that the weight of the refined silver agree with these records. The refined silver was cast into seventy-five-pound bars, assayed again, and stamped. These bars and the remaining silver ores then had to be verified by the government tax collectors and shipped to the Banco Minero in Chihuahua, later to be sent to the mint or smelter, whose returns were compared with the company's figures.[28]

---

no. 105 (May 1889), pp. 2–5; Biography of Shepherd, typescript, pp. 31–32; Batopilas Mining Company, *Report*, 1902, *passim.*

[27] For example, the report for 1902 (p. 5) showed the following amounts of ore treated at the haciendas: first grade, 1,326,203 lbs.; second grade, 749,679 lbs.; third grade, 36,975,520 lbs. This proportion is fairly typical, at least of the later years. Unfortunately the report does not break down the value of the resulting silver according to classes of ore.

[28] Denver *Tribune,* [July 14, 1883?], clipping in Shepherd Papers; Batopilas Mining Company, *Report*, 1902, pp. 14–15. Sulphide ores were

An everlasting source of trouble and expense was the problem of transportation from one company property to another and from Batopilas to the outside world. Internal transportation difficulties could be met by concentrating on the more accessible mines first, and as these yielded a surplus, Shepherd improved the paths through the hills to the more remote mines and even constructed a few roads. By 1889 he was building a narrow-gauge railroad between one outlying tunnel and a point overlooking Hacienda San Miguel, from which he strung a cable to carry the ore the rest of the way. For many years his men had to ford the Batopilas River, and sometimes floods virtually isolated one part of his properties from another, but eventually he built a bridge across the river near Hacienda San Antonio.[29]

The problem of communications with the outside world was never completely solved during Shepherd's lifetime. When he first arrived in Mexico, Batopilas was about as accessible from the Pacific coast as from the north, but by 1882 the Mexican Central Railroad was running from the border to Chihuahua city, 236 miles from the company's mines, and thenceforth Shepherd received most of his supplies and shipped out his silver along this route. The first 115 miles south of Chihuahua could be easily made into an excellent carriage road, but pack mules and saddle horses were necessary for the rest of the trip, and freight took twenty-four to twenty-eight days to go between Chihuahua and the mines, even in dry weather.

Unable to level the mountains, Shepherd encouraged American promoters to build railroads across southern Chihuahua and even became a director of Albert K. Owen's unsuccessful Topolobampo railroad company. In the mid-1890's he supposed for a while that the Mexican Central would run a branch westward from Chihuahua city, and Mrs. Shepherd wrote happily to her daughter, "Thank the Lord that any *real* railroad is think-

---

shipped as far away as Aurora, Ill., to be smelted (G. Shepherd, *Silver Magnet*, p. 168).

[29] United States, *Consular Reports*, no. 105 (May 1889), pp. 2–5.

ing of us"; but nothing came of the proposal. A year or so later Shepherd's good friend Enrique C. Creel took up the remains of Owen's project and, by extending his Chihuahua and Pacific Railroad to the west, reduced the length of Shepherd's stage-coach route to sixty-five miles. At the end of Shepherd's life, however, passenger travel between mines and railroad still re-quired five days on muleback and one day in a stagecoach, and freight charges for this distance were about one hundred pesos per ton. A few years later (see Chapter VIII), Arthur E. Stil-well took over the Creel line and extended it to a point about 105 miles from Batopilas.[30]

After the railroad arrived at Chihuahua, Shepherd organized his silver shipments as efficiently as the rest of his business. Regu-larly every thirty days a *conducta* of pack mules set out from Hacienda San Miguel across the mountains carrying about 80,000 or 100,000 pesos in silver bars, two bars to the mule. Every forty miles along the rugged trail the company maintained a way station with a resident attendant, corrals, barns full of hay and corn, and beds and food for the *conducta* drivers. At Carichic the bars were loaded on Concord stagecoaches, with fourteen mules hitched to each coach, and the procession set off at a gallop on the last leg of the journey to Chihuahua. Equipment, supplies, and visitors went into Batopilas along the same route. Even an upright piano did not baffle the resourceful Shepherd and his Indians: they tied stout poles along each side, and three relays of eight men, relieving each other every twenty minutes, carried it on foot 185 miles over the mountains.[31]

Although Shepherd's original company prospectus described how miners loaded silver bars in the open streets without fear of robbery, he had to be constantly vigilant against bandit raids,

[30] Cleveland *Herald*, April 13, 1882, unidentified newspaper clipping (probably May 1896), Mrs. Shepherd to Grace Shepherd, Batopilas, July 25, 1894, all in Shepherd Papers; G. Shepherd, *Silver Magnet*, pp. 203, 276.

[31] G. Shepherd, *Silver Magnet*, pp. 60-62, 91-101, 107-108.

especially during the González administration, and he always sent out his silver bars under heavy guard. Later his son boasted that before 1911 the company never lost a bar of silver or a peso of payroll money through robbery, but this was due as much to Shepherd's reputation for toughness as to the general condition of the country. In 1884, for example, a renegade Indian ambushed and shot an American employee in a vain effort to seize payroll money. Anxious to teach the whole countryside a lesson, Shepherd had the man tracked down, and he badgered the state government until it carried out the death sentence which a court had imposed. Stories of this sort protected the company's property almost as well as the armed guard.[32]

Although ruthless with bandits, Shepherd treated his foreign and native laborers fairly, according to the standard of the times, as long as they remained industrious and honest. Nearly all his mine superintendents and upper officials came from the United States, and as his family grew up, he appointed his sons and his sons-in-law to responsible positions, answering a charge of nepotism with the curt statement that no one else would work for such low wages. From time to time other foreigners were listed on his payrolls: Negroes from the American South, a few disappointed colonists from Topolobampo, Italian stonemasons, German mechanics, and others. Many of these proved unsatisfactory, whether because of excess drinking, abuse of Indians, or other reasons. The fastidious Mrs. Shepherd could predict the demoralization of Americans—she called them "white men"—"as soon as they settle down to be one with the natives." [33]

Shepherd's greatest labor problem was that of getting the

[32] *Consolidated Batopilas Silver Mining Company*, p. 19; G. Shepherd, *Silver Magnet*, chap. iv, especially pp. 260–261; [Washington] *Star*, July 13, 1895, p. 7.

[33] G. Shepherd, *Silver Magnet*, pp. 70, 74, 111, 207, 242, 273, *et passim*; Mrs. Shepherd to John [Young], Batopilas, March 17, 1889, Mrs. Shepherd to Alexander R. Shepherd, Jr., Batopilas, no date (probably 1888), Shepherd Papers.

most possible work out of the ignorant, easygoing Indians who made up the great majority of his miners. Usually he paid them regular wages, in order to hold more control over their work, but occasionally he reverted to the share system in special cases. According to an American consular report of 1889, he paid unskilled labor about 1.25 pesos per day and ordinary miners two or three pesos per day, employing as many as a thousand men at a time, although the payrolls shrank during the rainy season (about June to November). The report added that general wages in the Batopilas district had risen from under a peso to two or three pesos as a result of the standards set by the company.[34]

Shepherd's wages compare favorably with those in other Mexican mining districts. Near the Gulf of California in the 1860's miners received as little as six pesos per month (plus a small allowance of corn), and even after 1900 ordinary miners in Chihuahua and Guanajuato received an average of about a peso and seventy-five centavos per day respectively.[35] In most of these places American laborers were paid up to $3.50, gold—six times as much as Mexicans doing similar work. Although figures are not available for Shepherd's American laborers, it is not likely that he maintained such a disproportionate wage scale, for he held a high opinion of the diligence, endurance, and obedience of Mexican labor as long as it was properly directed. The natives for their part regarded him with enormous respect as *el patrón grande*, even though they often had trouble understanding his peculiar pronunciation of Spanish. According to Grant Shepherd, "a renegade labor-union cast-off" came to Batopilas in 1898 and tried to organize the men, but after staying away from work for a few days they all returned. The

[34] United States, *Consular Reports*, no. 105 (May 1889), pp. 2–5.

[35] Cyprien Combier, *Voyage au Golfe de Californie* (Paris, 1864), pp. 213–214; United States, *Consular Reports*, Feb. 3, 1911, p. 457; Percy F. Martin, *Mexico's Treasure-House (Guanajuato): An Illustrated and Descriptive Account of the Mines and Their Operations in 1906* (New York, 1906), pp. 61 ff.

chief of police told them to ask the organizer if he could dupli-
cate Shepherd's benefits, especially in the way of medical attention and liberal advances on wages, and he soon left.[36]

Proper direction and efficient management were indeed the
bywords of Shepherd's labor policy, as of virtually his whole
enterprise. Since the Indians had little sense of property and
regarded the ore as belonging to God, it was necessary to search
each one as he emerged from the mines. The natives wore only
breechclouts and sandals in the steamy depths (where the tem-
peratures sometimes rose to 135 degrees), but they often hid
chunks of rich ore in their shoe soles, in cigarettes, and in their
drills, and sometimes a surgical operation was necessary to remove silver from their bodies. The Indians were as careless with
their own property as with that of other people, and after repeated cases of squandering and beggary Shepherd set up a
"company store," undercutting the prices of native retailers and
allowing an ingenious type of credit to the miners. Under this
system the first half of the week's pay bought groceries for the
miner's family, and only the second half was paid out to him in
cash on Saturday night.[37]

In the matters of health and accidents Shepherd was no less
attentive to the welfare of his laborers, partly out of humanitarian concern and partly for the practical reasons of avoiding
lawsuits and labor shortages. Explosions, cave-ins, and other
mine disasters cropped up with depressing regularity in the
company records, despite the superintendent's orders that smoking be limited to safe areas, that caps and blasting powder be
kept separately, and that one native take full charge of all blasting operations, to guard against badly timed charges. Mexican

[36] Denver *Tribune*, Aug. 8, 1883; G. Shepherd, *Silver Magnet*, pp. 218,
240.

[37] "Governor Shepherd as a Miner," unidentified newspaper clipping
(probably 1880 or 1881), Shepherd Papers; G. Shepherd, *Silver Magnet*,
pp. 218–221, 246–247.

law required the company to maintain a hospital for its workers, and by the 1890's this hospital usually held twenty or thirty patients all the time, most of them blast victims or suffering from pneumonia because their bodies could not stand the cold winter weather after a day's work in the hot mines. In an ordinary year the company physicians made up four or five thousand prescriptions without charge, and by forcibly vaccinating the reluctant Indians (with the aid of the police) they virtually rid the Batopilas area of smallpox.[38]

Because of Batopilas' isolated location, far from the most populous sections of Mexico, and because of the high degree of efficiency which Shepherd required for his operations, he soon found himself the ruler of a tight little community. This power understandably awakened the envy of some upper-class Mexicans in the area. In the early 1880's, for example, the wealthy Valenzuela family challenged his claim to the mine of that name and threatened suit. On September 16, 1882, their lawyer, Jesús L. Ulloa, delivered a fiery Independence Day address in Shepherd's presence against the company and against all Americans. Unable to understand all of the speech, Shepherd secured a complete translation and then withdrew from the rest of the day's festivities. At once, however, the local committee on arrangements called on him with an apology for the insult and canceled Ulloa's invitation to the banquet of the following day. Later, under threat of arrest by the state government, Ulloa himself apologized. After considerable argument over the Valenzuela claim, Shepherd finally bought out the family in 1884 and ended the suit.[39]

Díaz felt such respect and confidence in Shepherd that he

[38] L. H. Stevens to W. H. Hoffman, Batopilas, May 12 [no year], Shepherd Papers; G. Shepherd, *Silver Magnet*, chap. xx, especially pp. 261–262; [Washington] *Star*, July 13, 1895, p. 7.

[39] "Mother's Diary," entries for Sept. 1, 20, 1882, March 16, 1884, typescript in Shepherd Papers; [Denver] *Tribune*, [Aug. 3], 1883.

never objected to the latter's semiautonomous position within Mexico, and in the middle of the Valenzuela difficulties Shepherd told a newspaper reporter that except for a few annoying customs regulations he had found the state authorities of Chihuahua and Sinoloa always fair and pleasant to deal with. In later years he cultivated the friendship of the powerful Terrazas family, and the Chihuahua *Científico*, Enrique C. Creel, was his loyal supporter. The local *jefe político* of Batopilas sometimes envied Shepherd's influence over the Indians but rendered him many useful services, by throwing drunks and marauders into the local jail and by helping to prevent the stealing of valuable ores. Sometimes the boss and the *jefe* pooled their forces against bandits from the outside. On one occasion, to be sure, a resentful *jefe* threw one of the Shepherd boys into jail after a dispute over fighting cocks, but a message to the state governor straightened matters out.[40]

An excellent example of the powers which Shepherd wielded with official approval was his system for paying the miners' weekly wages. At first the men demanded silver coins, but currency was both expensive and dangerous to bring in from the Chihuahua mint. For a while the company cast small silver bars worth thirty, fifty, and one hundred pesos for the payrolls, but these soon proved cumbersome. Local merchants refused to accept Chihuahua banknotes, and at their suggestion Shepherd secured permission from the government to issue his own paper bills. These circulated freely in Batopilas, and the company redeemed them in silver currency on demand, deducting about 8 per cent for transporting the coin. In the mid-1890's the expansion of Mexico's banking system considerably loosened the country's currency, and at the request of the government Shepherd called in his scrip and burned it at a public ceremony.[41]

[40] [Denver] *Tribune*, Aug. 8, 1883; G. Shepherd, *Silver Magnet*, pp. 37–39, 212–217.

[41] Washington *Weekly Star*, April 23, 1886; unidentified newspaper clipping, [May 1896?], "Mother's Diary," *passim*, Shepherd Papers.

IV

For over twenty years Shepherd and his family made their home in this little self-centered domain. His earlier reputation made him fair game for newspapers in the United States, and they soon began to create a myth about a new Monte Cristo, living in luxury among fabulous silver mines. One journalist described his "fortress" surrounded by thirty-five-foot walls and manned by a corps of retainers living their entire lives within the walls. Another estimated the annual yield of the mines at $5,000,000 and declared that "several of the rooms in the castle are silverplated, floors, walls and ceilings." After Shepherd's death a writer in the New York *Tribune* estimated his wealth at $15,000,000 or $20,000,000 and described a palatial home inside the towering walls: a dinner table as heavily loaded as that of a Fifth Avenue hotel, a cellar full of wines, a great refrigerating plant, the latest newspapers on the drawing-room tables, a telegraph ticker to the outside world, furniture of silver and gold, a piano, and in the corners rare Aztec relics.[42]

The Shepherd family must have smiled to read these wide-eyed stories, for half of the details were pure invention. In reality, as the first company report after Shepherd's death pointed out, perhaps no company stockholder in the United States lived on such a simple scale as the Shepherds. Within the hacienda walls (which were built mostly before Shepherd's time) the family occupied a one-story adobe building, little different from any Mexican upper-class home. When Mrs. Shepherd and the children returned from the United States in 1884, they were delighted to find that the rooms had been white-washed and a bathroom with steam pipes installed. Eventually they acquired a few other comforts not common to the area, such as an ice machine and a piano, and Shepherd built a second small house in the mountains as a retreat in hot weather.

[42] Unidentified newspaper clippings, [New York *Tribune*, Sept. 21, 1902], Shepherd Papers.

Throughout their long residence in Mexico the family and the American colony followed a daily routine of hard labor, siestas, and simple, homemade amusements. After working through the morning and taking a siesta at noon, Mrs. Shepherd and the children held school in the late afternoon, and sometimes Shepherd himself and some of the other American residents took part in the lessons. In the evening everyone relaxed unless there was some emergency in the mines, the men playing cards and the women reading and sewing. On Sunday morning Shepherd took pride in presiding over the impromptu morning worship and led the singing with gusto. The isolated, confining life of the exiles frayed everyone's nerves at one time or another, but it also made the Shepherds a close-knit family, and after the children had grown up and married, they often brought their wives and husbands for long visits at Batopilas.[43]

Shepherd and his family were, of course, personages of much glamor to the common people of Batopilas, who watched and talked about nearly everything they did in public. One of the daughters described a shopping trip to the little town as a sample of this attention. After finding an unwilling escort, usually one of the Shepherd boys, the sisters would scramble on their horses, cautiously ford the river, and ride down to the plaza, where stood the houses and stores of the *gente fina*, the merchants of Batopilas. At one of these they might dismount, having heard that the store had recently received a shipment of new merchandise:

The two young bachelor merchant-princes were throwing themselves into their coats, and from behind the counter greeted us ceremoniously, individually, with the same formula observed in formal social calls, handshakings, inquiries into personal and family health,

[43] "Mother's Diary," p. 49 (entry of March 16, 1884), sketch and description of the mountain house, unidentified newspaper clipping, Mrs. Shepherd to daughters, Batopilas, Dec. 9, 1888, all in Shepherd Papers; G. Shepherd, *Silver Magnet, passim.*

state of the weather, whatever local news we might be supposed to share, etc.

By this time we were seated on stools at the counter and the merchant-princes, reinforced by their clerks, were taking down from long wall-shelves bolts of dress [stuffs], cambric, hamburg edging, coarse laces, all of their very best. One expressed admiration, never criticism, nor did one ask for what one did not see; . . . goods were purchased with expressions of appreciation for the privilege of buying them. Meantime in the patio of the merchant-princes in rear of the store, flowers had been gathered and a bouquet for each shopping-guest arranged, to be presented by the merchant-princes when the ceremony approached for the final rites. Handshaking was repeated, messages of remembrance and esteem for absent members of the family were exchanged for thanks for courtesies received. . . .

We rode on through the town, greeting friends and acquaintances in windows and doors, for everyone knew by this time that La Familia was at the stores, and no one missed voluntarily a glimpse of the Señoritas on their prancing horses.[44]

In such an isolated community a great variety of nuisances and dangers surrounded the family, and the eternal threat of serious illness worried Mrs. Shepherd, especially while her children were still young. During the early years they were often ill from the heat and the unfamiliar food, and occasionally it became necessary to take them and some of the men into the mountains for weeks at a time. It is not surprising that the family sometimes despaired of escaping from Mexico, and one of the boys wrote later that "these blooming old mines . . . look as if they had all decided to keep us in this God forsaken country for a long time to come." [45]

In 1882 and again in 1885 Mrs. Shepherd and the children

[44] "Shopping in Batopilas," typescript, Shepherd Papers.

[45] Frank Shepherd to sisters, [Batopilas], July 7, 1896, Mrs. Shepherd to Grace Shepherd, Batopilas, July 13, 1897 (also many other references in similar letters), "Mother's Diary," pp. 25–26, 44–49, 56–58, all in Shepherd Papers.

returned to Washington for long visits, but Shepherd himself had to stay in his mines, even though two of his daughters were married during the second trip north. Finally in 1887 he became dangerously ill from erysipelas and blood poisoning, after his horse had shied in a tunnel and his scalp had been torn open against a point of rock. When he had partially recovered, he set out for the United States, both in order to complete his convalescence and to carry out the consolidation of his companies. Although he had hoped to slip into Washington unnoticed, the newspapers fanned up the embers of the old dispute over the territorial government of the District. Not to be outdone, his friends and supporters formed a reception committee, and on October 6 about a hundred thousand people turned out to watch a great parade and review in his honor, with fireworks spelling out "Welcome" and the Marine Band playing "Home Sweet Home." [46]

Shepherd did not completely regain his health in the United States, and after contracting malaria, apparently on the return trip, he spent much of the following year taking quinine and trying to throw off the fever. Mrs. Shepherd and the children continued to travel back and forth between Batopilas and Washington, but after 1890 Shepherd spent five solid years at the mines, pushing work on the Díaz Tunnel and trying to increase the silver output. In the summer of 1895 operations were running so smoothly that he left the mines in charge of his sons and sons-in-law and set out for the United States. Once again the city of Washington turned out to welcome the now-legendary boss, and at a public reception in the Willard Hotel about seven thousand people crowded up to shake hands with him. [47]

[46] Typescript account of Shepherd's injury, "Mother's Diary," pp. 59–61, Shepherd Papers; [Boston *Herald*, July 19, 1887]; [Washington *Star*, July 16, 1887]; [Washington *Post*, July 18, 1887]; [Washington *Critic*, Oct. 7, 1887]; [New York] *Sun*, Oct. 6, 1887; *Nation*, XLV (July 21, 1887), 46–47; [Buffalo *Courier*, Oct. 16, 1887].

[47] Letter of Mrs. Shepherd (typescript), Nov. 1888, Shepherd Papers; [New York *Tribune*, July 18, 1895]; [Washington *Post*, Nov. 8, 1895].

After his return to Mexico, Shepherd left more and more of the operations to his children, being too old to scramble about the underground tunnels as before. In 1896 he and Mrs. Shepherd visited Mexico City to confer with Díaz and his officials, and he made a side trip by himself to Oaxaca to examine other properties there. It was well, however, that he did not take on any new responsibilities, for late in the following year he suffered a slight stroke. Shepherd soon recovered and insisted on remaining in Batopilas, but five years later he was stricken with appendicitis, and before the company physician could move him to a hospital, he died, on September 12, 1902, at the age of sixty-seven. As a last gesture of respect to *el patrón grande*, five teams of eight workmen volunteered to carry his casket on their shoulders over the mountain trails to Carichic.[48]

V

Six months before his death Shepherd summarized his accomplishments in a report to the company's stockholders. After twenty-two years of his management the company held property valued at 11,306,434.57 pesos which had yielded silver and gold to the amount of 13,863,304.84 pesos. This property included about forty-three miles of tunnels, mines, and workings; 70,575 acres of ranch lands; two reduction plants, the best in Mexico and equal to all but a few in the United States, capable of treating 3,000,000 pesos of ore annually; and several large-scale public works, such as the dam and bridge across the Batopilas River. At the time of his report the company employed about 900 men, and under his management the population of Batopilas

[48] Mrs. Shepherd to Grace Shepherd, Mexico City, June 4, 13, 1896, Mrs. Shepherd to Isabel Shepherd, Mexico City, June 14, 1896, Shepherd Papers; G. Shepherd, *Silver Magnet*, pp. 250–253. The Shepherd Papers contain many clippings about Shepherd's illness in 1897. On his death and later the elaborate funeral in Washington, May 4, 1903, see Tindall, *Sketch of Shepherd*, pp. 52–53, and Batopilas Mining Company, *Report*, 1902, p. 3. For Mrs. Shepherd's obituary see [Washington *Star*, March 11, 1930].

had grown from about 300 to about 4,000. All of this, he boasted, he had accomplished with a working capital of less than $400,000—the proceeds from the 1887 bond issue and from a few other minor sources.[49]

How had the finances of the Batopilas Mining Company fared during this period of construction? As already brought out, the original companies paid dividends totaling almost $1,000,000 before the consolidation in 1887, but from that time until Shepherd's death in 1902 the stockholders received nothing. During these long, lean years they, like the taxpayers of Washington, criticized him for plowing all profits into improvements, purchasing equipment and constructing works which, they thought, the company could not yet afford. What they failed to appreciate was that Shepherd was building for the future rather than for the present, basing his plans upon the fundamental assumption that American capital was in Mexico to stay.

Under slightly more favorable conditions he might have been able to carry on his full improvement program and issue modest dividends at the same time, for from 1880 to 1902 his annual silver production never fell below 300,000 pesos and rose several times above 1,000,000 pesos.[50] It was unfortunate that just at the critical moment, when it seemed as if a dividend could be declared, Shepherd's active mind conceived the idea of a new improvement, or some unforeseen calamity—a cave-in or a flood —wiped out the margin of profit. In 1882, for example, a sudden cloudburst sent a wall of water raging down the Batopilas Valley and in a few moments undid the work of many weeks.

Even in peaceful years the irregular decline in the world price of silver and the rising exchange rate often forced Shepherd to revise his expectations. During the 1880's the decline did not greatly disturb him, for he was mainly engaged in paying off debts in Mexico, but when he began to export large

[49] Batopilas Mining Company, *Report*, 1901, pp. 5–6.
[50] Brodie, "Mines of Batopilas," p. 7.

amounts of silver to the United States for equipment and to meet obligations there, he was forced to consider the world silver problem. Cleveland's gold policy and the defeat of Bryan in 1896 were heavy disappointments. If the United States had adopted bimetallism in the 1890's, the lot of Shepherd's investors would surely have improved, for in 1893 and 1894 the Batopilas mines produced unusually large yields of silver. Even in the midst of a depression, with silver prices falling, these increased yields enabled the company to pay off most of its debts for previous improvements, but after that time Shepherd found no new, large bonanzas, and the company had to begin borrowing again at a high rate of interest.[51]

When Shepherd died, some observers expected the company to go to pieces and cease operations, but his old friend Lyndon H. Stevens stepped into his shoes as general manager, and later one of Shepherd's sons and a son-in-law filled this position. During the next decade some of Shepherd's expectations for his company began to come true, for according to a report of Walter M. Brodie, its total net profits between 1901 and 1910 were 1,712,764.33 pesos.[52] During this period the company added to the capacity of Hacienda San Antonio and continued work on the aerial tramway from San Miguel mine to San Antonio, but undertook no new major construction projects. As a result, when increased mining yields coincided with general world prosperity and the stabilization of Mexican currency in 1905 and 1906, the company was in a position to pay off all of its old debts for construction work. When the outstanding bonds

[51] "Mother's Diary," pp. 30–33, Mrs. Shepherd to Grace Shepherd, Batopilas, Nov. 11, 1896, Shepherd Papers; Washington *Star*, Oct. 30, 1893; *Engineering and Mining Journal*, LXIX (April 14, 1900), 437.

[52] Brodie, "Mines of Batopilas," *passim*. Stevens was general manager from 1902 to 1908, Alexander R. Shepherd, Jr., from 1908 to 1910. The original president of the company, George W. Quintard, died in 1903, and Stevens served as president from 1908 to 1910. See various issues of Batopilas Mining Company, *Report*. Walter M. Brodie directed company affairs during much of the decade after 1910.

of the original 1887 issue matured during the following year, the company retired $32,000 at once and extended the remaining $366,500 for ten years, to be retired one-tenth at a time. Best of all, on December 31, 1907, the Batopilas Mining Company declared its first dividend, amounting to $55,870.37.[53]

This event was the high spot in the financial history of the company, for although it recovered quickly from the world-wide depression of 1907, its prosperous operations could not long survive the fall of Díaz. In 1909 the company founded a British subsidiary to exploit certain leased lands and attract new capital, but the sudden death of Stevens, then president of the company, during a business trip to London in 1910, and disturbances in northern Mexico during the following year prevented further expansion and produced a net deficit in the accounts. Despite frequent interruptions during the civil wars of the Huerta period the company earned a net profit in 1913 and 1914, but in the latter year most of the American employees left Mexico, and production declined to a trickle. The total value of silver produced between 1911 and 1920 was less than one-fourth of the figure for the preceding decade.

After the company reopened its mines in 1919, it found no new ore bodies. In 1925 the bondholders tried in vain to sell the mines, and when most stockholders refused to pay further assessments on their holdings, a small group of the principal share-owners organized a leasing company to operate the mines on a royalty basis. After about a year they gave up even this effort.[54]

[53] Batopilas Mining Company, *Report*, 1903, pp. 11, 21; letter to stockholders, New York, April 10, 1905 (published in place of an annual report), pp. 3–5; *Report*, 1906, pp. 3–4, 15, 1907, pp. 4–7.

[54] *Ibid.*, 1909, pp. 4–5, 15; 1910, pp. 4–5, 11; 1911, pp. 5–6; 1912, pp. 4–5; 1913–1914, *passim*. According to Brodie ("Mines of Batopilas," p. 7) the value of the total production in each decade of operations from 1880 to 1920 was:

1880–1890	5,147,741.86 pesos
1891–1900	7,202,730.14
1901–1910	11,187,733.47
1911–1920	2,554,939.13

VI

Although Shepherd left behind fewer promotional writings and prospectuses than some of the promoters already described, his letters and interviews with newspaper reporters followed the same general lines of argument as the earlier publicity campaigns. During his first years in Chihuahua many American newspapers spread the rumor that promoters had greatly exaggerated the wealth of Mexican silver mines and that Shepherd had nearly exhausted the deposits at Batopilas. A number of these appeared just before he visited the United States to consolidate his companies in 1887, and since he was incapacitated by his scalp wound, he commissioned his brother, W. F. Shepherd, to issue a full statement about the returns and the condition of his mines. A month later he issued a statement of his own, denouncing those malcontents who did not have "that particular kind of energy and determination necessary to make a mining enterprise a success" and who "expected to get a return from a mining venture just as quickly as from a lottery." Mining failures in Mexico, he insisted, were not due to poverty of ore but to superficial and careless work.[55]

Through the long years of hard work and no dividends Shepherd held to this opinion, and as he saw the effects of the American gold policy on his own fortunes, he attempted to convince his hearers that Mexico was reaping great profits from the silver standard. In 1896 he listed the new industries in Chihuahua encouraged by the high rate of exchange: an iron foundry and machine shop, textile mills making cheap clothing, a canning

---

On the later history of the company see Bernstein, "Mexican Mining Industry," I, 330; *Marvyn Scudder Manual of Extinct or Obsolete Companies,* III (New York, 1930), 175–176; *Robert D. Fisher Manual of Valuable and Worthless Securities,* VI (New York, 1938), 95.

[55] Pittsburg *Chronicle Telegram,* Sept. 23, 1885; San Francisco *Chronicle,* Sept. 24, 1885; [Denver *Tribune Republican,* Dec. 14, 1886]; [San Francisco *Call,* May 21, 1887]; [New York *World,* May 27, 1887]; [Omaha *World,* June 15, 1887]; [Milwaukee *Tribune,* July 19, 1887].

factory, a brewery, and ore smelters. He predicted that with cheap labor and a silver currency Mexico would make its people the richest in the world.[56] Isolated in Batopilas, where his benevolent paternalism was markedly raising the general standard of living, he could not have been expected to appreciate the unequal effects of the silver inflation on other parts of the Mexican economy.

Shepherd's opinion of the Mexican government was also that of the majority of the American promoters. Although he admitted the corruption of the González administration and called his advisers "thoroughly bad men," he had little but praise for the restored Díaz government after 1884. Díaz, he said admiringly, had many of Grant's qualities—"the same undemonstrative manner, and the suggestion of reserve power," and even something in his bearing and walk. In 1895 he called Díaz the greatest man in North America because he had made property "twenty times safer in Mexico than it is in the United States." He added, with the ruthless impulse of a man accustomed to giving orders: "Under our abominable system here [in the United States], if a gang of men rob a train they are entitled to a fair trial and the chances are they will buy their way out. Down there, if a train is robbed the culprits are shot at once, and a trial given them afterwards." [57] Too many other Americans in Mexico preferred order to liberty.

Shepherd frequently advertised his confidence in the stability and friendliness of the Mexican government. As early as 1883, in the midst of his troubles with the Valenciana family, he was attributing anti-American sentiment in Mexico to "demagogues and sensationalists who will strive to foment unpleasant feelings

[56] [Bowling Green (Ohio) *Weekly Democrat*, May 22, 1896]; unidentified newspaper clipping (probably 1896), Shepherd Papers.

[57] [*National Republican*, July 20, 1887]; [*Mexican Herald*, May 13, 1896]; [New York *Tribune*, July 18, 1895]. In 1938 Shepherd's son Grant echoed this view of Díaz: he "gave the Mexican nation an era of order and good government far above anything that we can approach now" (G. Shepherd, *Silver Magnet*, p. 260).

on the subject for the purpose of achieving some local notoriety. . . . The masses as well as the principal men . . . are favorable to American immigration, and want to see and feel the benefits of American enterprise and industry." Three years later he criticized a committee of the American House of Representatives for its unwarranted statements about Mexican insecurity in the debates over the Grant-Romero reciprocity treaty and declared: "The 'person and property of an American pursuing the peaceful avocations of industry and commerce' are as secure in Mexico as in any part of the United States"—more so than in Chicago during the Haymarket Riot or in Geronimo's haunts in the Southwest.[58]

Just as the Mexican government suited Shepherd, so also the American boss suited Díaz. Both his optimistic statements and his efficient administration of the run-down Batopilas mines so impressed Don Porfirio that in 1896 he told an American reporter that he "had at least two American friends in whom he could place at all times the fullest and most unquestioning reliance" —Shepherd and Collis P. Huntington of the Southern Pacific and Mexican International Railroads. Foreign Minister Enrique C. Creel, who was also northern Mexico's principal spokesman among the *Científicos,* praised Shepherd's "broad gauge" and called his mining concession "the largest and strongest title . . . that was ever granted to anybody in Mexico." Creel tried to persuade President McKinley to appoint him minister to Mexico, declaring that he was regarded as the most influential American resident in the country.[59]

Like Grant and the other subjects of this book, Shepherd looked for the economic regeneration of Mexico in railroads, mines, and industry. Nevertheless, as he and his family must have realized, economic efficiency was not enough to solve

[58] Denver *Tribune,* Aug. 8, 1883; [New York *World,* July 2, 1886].
[59] [Washington *Star,* no date, about 1896 and June 1897]; Sue Shepherd (Mrs. Walter M. Brodie) to Mrs. Shepherd, May 18, [1897?], Shepherd Papers.

Mexico's grievous social problems. Perhaps social benefits for all lay at the end of the road along which Shepherd and the others were guiding Mexico, but would such a government as that of Díaz ever reach the goal? Could Díaz divide the benefits fairly and at the same time maintain peace and security intact? Shepherd must have thought so, since he was willing to postpone dividends for twenty years in order to dig the tunnels, build the dam, and install the electric power equipment which a permanent industry would require.

VII

Cowboy: William C. Greene

SINCE American promoters often regarded Mexico as an extension of the Western frontier, it is not surprising that some of them carried south of the border the grandiose designs, the drawling braggadocio, and the slapdash energy of the Wild West. One of the most influential and colorful of the Western "big-time operators" in Mexico was William C. Greene, a rancher and Indian fighter who chanced on some of the richest copper deposits in Mexico, the Cananea mines, at a time in the late 1890's when the world needed copper. Relying on his native talent for bluff and none too careful about his business methods, Greene attracted Eastern capital, threw together smelters and concentrators, and within five years had created one of the largest copper-producing companies in the world. By 1906 he ruled a veritable empire in northern Sonora and Chihuahua: the busy mining town of Cananea, miles of underground shafts and tunnels, buildings full of refining machinery, and ranches, mining claims, and timberlands stretching for scores of miles back into the lonely Sierra Madre.

In his flush days Greene seemed the very epitome of beneficent American capital modernizing an undeveloped land. "The advent of Colonel Greene," wrote one admirer, "is the greatest thing that has happened for Chihuahua since the building of the Mexican Central." [1] Under his paternal direction, added another, "the frightened and poverty-stricken peons, afraid to own property other than [their] *serapes* and *sombreros* . . . are replaced by self-reliant men with money in the bank and an assurance for their future." [2]

Greene's fall was even faster than his rise. First of all a strike and riot among his Mexican laborers discredited him before the world, and the intervention of a volunteer American police force nearly precipitated a diplomatic crisis. Then at the end of 1906 a group of rival financiers allied with the Amalgamated Copper Company bought up control of Greene's organization and revealed that he had built up the great corporate empire on glib promises, publicity, and devious bookkeeping. The new owners possessed the technical skill and ability which Greene had lacked, and after a complete reorganization the Cananea mines and smelters became an important part of the Anaconda Copper Company, one of the new twentieth-century giants.

I

The life of William Cornell Greene is a mixture of facts, rumors, and unverifiable anecdotes. Most authorities agree that he was born in New York state during 1851.[3] In any case, his mother's family were New Yorkers, and he spent his childhood in the small town of Chappaqua. After several years in a country

[1] *Anglo-Colorado Mining and Milling Guide*, VIII (Jan. 28, 1905), 4.

[2] *Engineering and Mining Journal*, LXXXII (Oct. 6, 1906), 623.

[3] Leading obituaries mention Chappaqua, N.Y. Marvin D. Bernstein favors Hornellsville, N.Y., in "Colonel William C. Greene and the Cananea Copper Bubble," *Bulletin of the Business Historical Society*, XXVI (Dec. 1952), 179. Another source states that Greene was born at Duck Creek, Wis., on Aug. 26, 1853: *Press Reference Library (Western Editions): Notables of the West, Being the Portraits and Biographies of the Progressive Men of the West Who Have Helped in the Development and History Making of This Wonderful Country*, I (New York, 1913), 205.

school, he left home for the West about 1868 or 1870, and for years he drifted from one job to another, laying track for the Northern Pacific Railroad and working as a government contractor in Kansas and Colorado. In 1877 the reputation of Arizona's mines drew him to that territory, and he worked for a time as a miner during the boom days of Tombstone. Elsewhere in Arizona and probably in Sonora he prospected for mines and led a body of men in the everlasting Apache wars. The Indian fighting gained him only a lifelong nickname, "Colonel Bill," and whatever his mines produced he quickly gambled away. Late in the 1880's he was reduced to hauling firewood into Prescott on muleback, but about 1890 he "got a provident streak," bought a ranch near the Mexican border on the San Pedro River, married, and prepared to settle down.[4]

From contemporary accounts and pictures "Colonel Bill" was big-boned, with a round, fleshy face, curly hair, and a heavy mustache. He had an expansive personality and a hot temper and, like his better-known contemporary, John W. ("Bet-a-Million") Gates, would gamble on almost anything. On one occasion, for example, he is said to have walked into Edward H. Harriman's office for a business interview, brandishing a certified check for a million dollars. Knowing his reputation, Harriman blandly offered to match him for the check but was taken aback when Greene, without a moment's hesitation, slapped a half dollar on the desk and cried, "Heads or tails?" "Bill," sighed Harriman, "I think you are fool enough to do it."[5]

Another instance of Greene's impetuosity is the story of his unpunished murder. Some years after he settled on his ranch

[4] *Press Reference Library*, I, 205; *Dictionary of American Biography* (New York, 1928–1944), VII, 577; Ira B. Joralemon, *Romantic Copper: Its Lure and Its Lore* (New York, 1934), pp. 136–137; James H. McClintock, *Arizona, Prehistoric—Aboriginal—Pioneer—Modern: The Nation's Youngest Commonwealth within a Land of Ancient Culture* (Chicago, 1916), II, 603; Chicago *Tribune*, Aug. 6, 1911, p. 4.

[5] Marcosson, "Our Financial Stake in Mexico," p. 24.

in southern Arizona, he attempted to irrigate his lands by building a flimsy mud-and-brush dam across the San Pedro River. One day a flash flood washed away the dam and drowned Greene's little daughter who had been playing downstream. Mad with grief, he remembered his quarrels over water rights with a neighbor, jumped to the conclusion that he had dynamited the dam, and shot him down in cold blood. For no good reason except sympathy and friendship Sheriff Scott White and a jury freed Greene, who later rewarded his benefactors with jobs in his various companies.[6]

Soon after buying his San Pedro ranch Greene became interested in the mineral deposits of Sonora, perhaps twenty or thirty miles to the south. This border area, named Cananea (Canaan) by Spanish friars, had yielded considerable gold and silver in the eighteenth century. Its copper deposits were also well known, partly because they were usually found under a vivid type of iron-stained outcropping which could be seen for miles. These veins belonged to a much larger copper zone several hundred miles along in Arizona and Sonora which the negotiators of the Gadsden Purchase had neatly but unwittingly bisected in 1853. On the American side Bisbee, Douglas, and Prescott were becoming flourishing mining camps in the 1890's, but Sonora lagged behind, at first because of Apache Indian raids and later for lack of development capital.

After Indians and bankruptcy had frustrated the efforts of several Mexican miners in the early nineteenth century, the Cananea mines came into the possession of General Ignacio Pesqueira, governor of Sonora. During the 1880's several individuals and companies, mostly American, tried their luck at Cananea and failed for various reasons. At some time during the mid-1890's Greene heard more or less inflated stories about the wealth of the Cananea mines, examined the outcroppings himself, and learned that Pesqueira's widow still controlled most

[6] McClintock, *Arizona*, II, 603.

of them. In 1898 he secured from her for 47,000 pesos an option on the Cobre Grande group of mines.[7]

Greene arrived in Sonora at a most propitious time. In the first place, the Indian troubles had rapidly subsided after the capture of Geronimo in the late 1880's, so that life and property were now as safe as in most American mining areas. Then, too, the building of custom smelters in the 1890's had stimulated mining throughout northern Mexico, and in the decade following 1898 the introduction of electric power and the MacArthur-Forrest cyanide process for extracting gold were to encourage miners still further. Most important of all, the Mexican copper industry was on the verge of great expansion, in order to supply the new demands created by the rise of electricity in the United States and Europe. World copper prices rose to new heights, until in 1907 Percy F. Martin was to call copper the safest and most surely profitable of Mexican mining industries.[8]

Greene, realizing the opportunities which lay before him, began to talk grandly of making Cananea a second Butte, Montana, and he called in friends to help him secure capital and begin operations. One of them, Jim Kirk, reputedly the best miner in Tombstone, went to work as a foreman at Bisbee to supply the informal partnership with a little cash, while a second crony, Ed Massey, recruited a few Indians to begin reconnaissance operations at Cananea, hoping to cajole them into accepting promises instead of wages until Greene could find more money. At first the three planned to sell the mines outright to the highest bidder, and Greene dashed off a tempting prospectus. Early in

[7] Sylvester Mowry, *Arizona and Sonora: The Geography, History, and Resources of the Silver Region of North America* (New York, 1871), pp. 103–104; S. F. Emmons, "The Cananea Mining District of Sonora, Mexico," *Economic Geology*, V (June 1910), 315–317; Joralemon, *Romantic Copper*, p. 143.

[8] James W. Malcolmson, "Mining and Smelting in Mexico," *Mining World*, Sept. 15, 1906, pp. 303–304; Percy F. Martin, *Mexico of the Twentieth Century* (London, 1907), II, 311–312.

1899 he organized the Cobre Grande Copper Company as an Arizona corporation, turned over to it his option on the Pesqueira mines, and sold a controlling block of its stock to George Mitchell, a prominent smelter operator of Jerome, Arizona, and J. H. Costello, a Philadelphia capitalist.

Trouble appeared at once. The company built a small smelter at Cananea but could not produce enough copper to pay operating expenses, and further expansion was impossible because the backers had not paid for their stock. Greene determined to take back his mines and start again. Whether by accident or not he had neglected to register the Cobre Grande Company in Mexico, and in October 1899 he secured a court order from friendly officials at Arizpe, Sonora, dispossessing Mitchell and Costello. Greene then seized the mines by force and transferred them, together with the new smelter and a supply of extracted ore, to a Mexican corporation, the Cananea Consolidated Copper Company, which he had organized on September 30. He eventually agreed to buy up most of the Cobre Grande stock, but some dissatisfied minority stockholders who resented his highhanded actions kept the Arizona courts busy for years with fruitless litigation.[9]

On September 15, 1899, shortly before repossessing the Cobre Grande mining properties, Greene secured the incorporation of another company under the laws of West Virginia. This was the Greene Consolidated Copper Company, a holding company capitalized at $5,000,000, which acquired all stock of Cananea Consolidated, the Mexican operating company, and issued stock of its own for the American market. During the autumn Greene borrowed a few thousand dollars on the strength of Cananea's increasing production and went East to sell this stock. After

---

[9] Varying accounts are given in Joralemon, *Romantic Copper*, pp. 143–146, and McClintock, *Arizona*, II, 603–604. See also Bernstein, "Greene and the Cananea Bubble," pp. 180–182. The case of the leading Cobre Grande litigant was not finally settled in Greene's favor until 1910 (*ibid.*, p. 197).

much free spending in New York he established his reputation as "Colonel Greene, the copper magnate," although according to one story he was down to his last hundred dollars at one point and managed to save himself only because of a lucky evening in Canfield's gambling house.

Greene aimed some of his most persuasive arguments at H. H. Rogers and other members of the Standard Oil clique who were just then organizing the Amalgamated Copper Company. At first they merely laughed at him, but eventually he managed to convince one of Rogers' associates that the Cananea mines had a future. This man was Thomas W. Lawson, a stormy petrel of the Boston Stock Exchange who deserted his fellow speculators and financiers a few years later to write a series of muckraking articles and a book about Wall Street, *Frenzied Finance*. Lawson agreed to furnish development capital by honoring Greene's drafts to the amount of $1,000,000 in return for an option to buy a controlling block of shares in Greene Consolidated at $3.33 a share (one-third of par value). Greene is said to have celebrated his success by repudiating another stock-selling agreement which he had made shortly before with one James Shirley.[10]

Delighted with his success, Greene returned to Cananea and expanded his plant with the aid of the new capital, little suspecting that Lawson was to treat him to a taste of his own duplicity. After he had cashed drafts amounting to $135,000, Lawson suddenly refused to honor any more, and his lawyer informed Greene that he must repay the earlier notes within three months or lose control of his company. But Greene had already established contacts with John W. Gates, Edwin Hawley, and H. E. Huntington, who now came to his rescue, and since he had not yet delivered the promised stock to Lawson, he set up luxurious New York offices and distributed it to the general public. By 1902 the company had issued 600,000 shares of stock, and in

[10] New York *Tribune*, Aug. 6, 1911, p. 7; Joralemon, *Romantic Copper*, p. 147; *Engineering and Mining Journal*, LXXI (March 30, 1901), 414.

November of that year the stockholders voted to issue 120,000 additional shares, which were to be sold for twice the amount of par value. As a journalist wrote of him after his death, "Greene had a way with him that took in Wall Street, and, what was more, he had a command of language that enabled him to prepare literature that took with small investors outside." [11]

Although he broadened the shareholding base of his companies' operations, Greene never managed to shake himself free from the machinations of Lawson, Rogers, Gates, Hawley, and other Eastern financial magnates who had come to realize what a prize he had in his mines. In the autumn of 1903, for example, the Gates-Hawley group tried to take advantage of Greene's rising debts and falling ore values to depress Greene Consolidated stock to a ruinous level and force him to sell out. A mining expert published a report for them to the effect that the Cananea mines were about to peter out, and Greene's securities fell from $32 to less than $10 per share. According to one story, he covered his immediate needs by forcing one of his associates at the point of a six-shooter to return over a million dollars' worth of stock held on option. Fortunately for him the highly reputable Phelps Dodge Copper Company had recently bought twenty thousand shares of Greene Consolidated stock, and when he announced this to his minor shareholders, they stood by him and kept their stock. A few months later his miners discovered $100,000,000 worth of copper ore.[12]

In the bull market which followed the re-election of Theodore Roosevelt in November 1904 Greene "made a killing" by buying thousand of his own shares on margin. He lost his gains, however, in the "Lawson panic" which followed, for the Boston speculator had published a series of muckraking articles on

[11] New York *Times*, Aug. 6, 1911, p. 9; New York *Tribune*, Aug. 6, 1911, p. 7; Joralemon, *Romantic Copper*, pp. 148–149; *Engineering and Mining Journal*, LXXIV (Nov. 15, 1902), 663.

[12] Joralemon, *Romantic Copper*, pp. 151–152; New York *Tribune*, Aug. 6, 1911, p. 7.

"Frenzied Finance" in a popular magazine during the latter half of the year, and these produced a considerable public outcry against Wall Street and a fall in the market. At the same time Lawson began to "raid" Greene Consolidated and forced down its stock by starting the old rumors that the Cananea ore deposits were nearly exhausted.

Although Greene was not mentioned in the articles on "Frenzied Finance," he answered Lawson's accusations in a half-page advertisement in the New York *Tribune*, calling him "a parasite upon honest labor" who had long been "the leading advocate, votary and exponent" of the very system he attacked and offering to visit Lawson at his office in Boston and denounce him to his face. New Yorkers, knowing Greene's wild reputation, shivered excitedly, and the newspapers carefully followed the feud. Greene did indeed go to Boston a few days later. Lawson came to meet him at his hotel, and the two shut themselves up for a conference, while bystanders gaped and the Boston police stationed themselves around the hotel. To everyone's disappointment, nothing happened. After seven hours the two emerged quietly, and Greene left for the railroad station. As he stepped into his carriage, a shot rang out, but it was only a photographer's flash apparatus.[13]

II

While Greene swaggered and bluffed his way along Wall Street and State Street, his copper companies were expanding their possessions and production in Sonora at a rate which surprised even the bonanza miners of Arizona. Before long Greene had added to his original companies a network of others for building railroads, mining gold and silver, lumbering, and ranching.

The Greene Consolidated Copper Company and its operating

[13] New York *Tribune*, Dec. 13, 1904, p. 15, Dec. 17, pp. 1–2, Aug. 6, 1911, p. 7; New York *Times*, Aug. 6, 1911, p. 9. Joralemon gives a more dramatic account (*Romantic Copper*, p. 153).

subsidiary, the Cananea Consolidated Copper Company, were the
most important of his creations. Between 1899 and 1906 the
two companies acquired property valued at about $12,000,000.
This included 10,412 acres of partly developed copper mines
and claims located in and around the townsite of La Cananea,
about twenty miles south of the American border, plus about
486,000 acres of timber and grazing lands which the company
leased to others. The Mexican government confirmed most
of these holdings in a concession of March 23, 1904. The
company's first major mine was the Cobre Grande, which
Pesqueira had opened, but Kirk and Massey soon discovered
others, such as the Veta Grande, with two large ore bodies,
the Capote and the Oversight.

The ore deposits, a bewildering variety of oxides, carbonates,
and sulphides, appeared in parallel limestone outcrops. They
were often "of monstrous size"—Capote alone was estimated
in 1906 to contain 40,000,000 tons—but the copper content
seldom ran above 4 per cent. As in the case of the Batopilas
silver ores, it could not always be predicted where they would
occur. In 1904, for example, Massey discovered the large, rich
ore body which later bore his name at a point which a mining
expert had previously called a "zone of impoverishment." Under
these conditions the rate of output was constantly changing,
but by 1906 it had increased to about 3,000 tons of ore a day
from all the mines together.

As ore production increased, Greene had to build more and
more smelters and other refining machinery. When he arrived
at Cananea in 1898, he found the simple earlier smelters broken
down and overgrown with weeds, with much of their machinery
stolen. The first hundred-ton smelter which Mitchell built for
the Cobre Grande Company in 1899 was adequate only for
the richest ore, and rising expenses and Greene's extravagance
soon made necessary a much larger output. In December 1900
the first of a new series of smelting furnaces was "blown in,"
and by the middle of 1902 Greene had six of them in operation.

During the next four years he added two more and boasted that one of these was the largest reverberatory furnace in the world.[14]

In Greene's enterprises, however, it was never wise to judge by size alone. This was especially true of his machinery, which was all too often ill-designed for its work. To illustrate, the furnaces could not be fired with coke, as originally intended, because of its expense. And when Arthur S. Dwight became manager of the smelter, he found the furnaces clogged with flue dust from the excessively soft ore. Thus they almost never worked at peak efficiency. After Greene began to mine poorer grades of ore, his engineers discovered that much of it was siliceous and needed concentrating before it could be smelted. Greene promptly built a six-hundred-ton concentrator, but as he had previously seen only silver and gold concentrators at Tombstone, his new plant was not well suited to copper and wasted about as much ore as it concentrated. "This mill is an excellent example of 'how not to do it,'" declared one engineer.[15]

In this case Greene soon realized his error and hired Dr. Louis D. Ricketts to build him a new concentrator. At first sight Ricketts' appearance usually did not inspire much confidence, for his clothes were so worn out and dirty that conductors are said to have thrown him off trains as a tramp and even the Mexicans called him *Mal Cinto* (Badly Cinched), but he had a doctor's degree from Princeton and a reputation as one of the ablest mining engineers in the Southwest. He spent $250,000 on the new concentrating mill, and operations at Cananea practically closed down during the last half of 1903 while he built it, but after its completion it was probably the

[14] *The Copper Handbook*, VI (Houghton, Mich., 1906), 537–545; Bernstein, "Greene and the Cananea Bubble," pp. 181, 183, 186–187.
[15] Bernstein, "Greene and the Cananea Bubble," pp. 185–186; Joralemon, *Romantic Copper*, p. 150; *Engineering and Mining Journal*, LXXXVI (Sept. 26, 1903), 463–464.

best and most efficient part of the plant. Greene offered Ricketts a permanent job with the company, but the engineer thought its financial structure too flimsy and declined.[16]

By 1902 the Greene Consolidated Copper Company had a smelting and concentrating plant with a daily capacity of over 4,000 tons of ore, the largest in Mexico. In addition it had an electric plant of 700 horsepower and pumps and nine miles of aqueducts to bring in water from the mountains for smelting and other needs. It also maintained about thirty miles of wagon roads, twenty-five miles of trails, and eleven miles of narrow-gauge railroad and owned most of the buildings in La Cananea —five office buildings, houses for foremen and laborers, a restaurant, stores, a fifty-bed hospital, a clubhouse, and so forth. It owned and operated such disparate enterprises as the Banco de Cananea, a brickyard, a telephone system of 150 phones, and two sawmills.[17] Before Greene had finished his work, a Mexican could easily live his entire life under the aegis of two paternal institutions, the Greene Consolidated Copper Company and the Roman Catholic Church.

Not content with the microcosmic world of his own company, the energetic promoter soon associated with it a long list of affiliates and subsidiaries. The most important of these for the copper industry was the Cananea, Yaqui River, and Pacific Railroad, which connected Cananea with the outside world. Apparently the line was originally intended to extend from the border south along the Yaqui Valley, but Greene completed only a thirty-eight-mile stretch from Cananea to Naco, Arizona, in order to ship out his concentrates and matte (nearly pure copper) on American lines. In 1903 Greene sold the line to Edward H. Harriman of the Southern Pacific, who joined it with the Sonora Railway to the west and used the two as the nucleus of his long Southern Pacific of Mexico line. In the

[16] Joralemon, *Romantic Copper*, pp. 150–151; *Press Reference Library*, I, 27.

[17] *Copper Handbook*, VI (1906), 537–545.

sale contract Greene's company received special freight rates to Naco for twenty-five years.[18]

Perhaps Greene's most ambitious enterprise was the Greene Gold-Silver Company, incorporated during 1902 in West Virginia with a capital eventually raised to $25,000,000. Greene sometimes sold its stock with the impression that it had a direct connection with his flourishing copper mines at Cananea, but this was not true. He had formed the company to operate old abandoned silver and gold mines which Mexicans had eagerly sold him over an area of two or three million acres in Sonora and Chihuahua. According to his publicity, those mines had yielded at least $120,000,000 in the past, and concessions contained eleven different reduction plants, but the properties were scattered all over northwestern Mexico, some of them in almost inaccessible places, such at the Mulatos mines in the isolated Sahuaripa district of Sonora. Greene put Massey in charge of operations, and crews of workers began to hack out mountain roads and lay the foundations for cyanide plants. He described the properties as having "almost indefinite possibilities," but few subscribers realized how much work and planning would be needed to realize these possibilities.[19]

After he had laid the basis of his economic empire in mining projects, Greene proceeded to found other companies to exploit the agricultural products of the area. Hoping to supply his mines with lumber and timbers instead of importing them from Puget Sound at $30,000 a month, he organized the Sierra Madre Land and Lumber Company and secured for it large timber concessions along the east slopes of the mountains in Chihuahua. In order to reach these inaccessible forests, as well as some of the Greene Gold-Silver Company mines, he then

---

[18] *Mining World*, Sept. 15, 1906, pp. 313–316.

[19] *Copper Handbook*, VI (1906), 545–547; Francisco Trentini, *El florecimiento de México* (*The Prosperity of Mexico*) (México, 1906), II, 232–236; New York *Times*, Aug. 6, 1911, p. 9; *Engineering and Mining Journal*, LXXXI (April 14, 1906), 731; *Anglo-American and Mexican Mining Guide*, XII (Jan. 30, 1909), 9.

bought up the Rio Grande, Sierra Madre, and Pacific Railroad, a partly built project which some optimistic Americans had hoped to extend from El Paso to the Gulf of California. In the Cananea area he purchased the Turkey Trot Ranch, the best in Sonora, covering several thousand square miles and so well irrigated that his fine herds of Herefords could survive the driest season. North of the border, in Arizona, he formed what he called the Casa Grande Irrigation District to build an earth dam across the Gila River and irrigate $50,000,000 worth of land. And he added to his original little ranch in the San Pedro Valley and stocked it with blooded cattle.[20]

Thus whenever "Colonel Bill" found the hotels and gambling houses of New York monotonous or the rivalry of his Wall Street associates distressing, he could recharge the batteries of his ego in a domain of wide-open Western country where his word was law:

It was a principality, and Bill was its feudal lord. His vacqueros [*sic*] and their families filled half a dozen villages. When he had a trip of inspection over the railroad that ran through his range for a hundred miles, the Mexican foremen rode in from all parts of the ranch to pay their respects to the great "Meester Greene" who sat in state in the palatial "Verde" to receive them. They pretty nearly worshipped him. Bill never forgot to ask about their wives and children, and when the "Verde" was set out on a siding for a few hours, he wasn't too proud to invite them to sit down with him and eat a banquet such as they had never dreamed of. . . . No man ever knew better how to get along with the Mexicans. Dozens of them would have cheerfully committed murder for him if he said the word.[21]

[20] Joralemon, *Romantic Copper*, pp. 155–158; United States, *Consular Reports*, no. 292 (Jan. 1905), p. 123. Others of Greene's companies were the Greene Consolidated Realty Company, the Greene-Kirk Gold and Silver Company, the Greene Consolidated Coal Company, the Greene Consolidated Gold Company, the Guaynopita Copper Company, the Balvanera Mining Company, the Belen Mining Company, the International Ore Treating Company, and the Santa Brigida Gold Company (*Press Reference Library*, I, 205).

[21] Joralemon, *Romantic Copper*, pp. 158–159.

At least this was the reputation which the redoubtable Greene inspired.

In a similar manner the production and dividend records of the Greene Consolidated Copper Company from 1900 to 1902 seemed to indicate to the casual observer great prosperity based upon solid foundations and prudent management. During the first two years of operations Kirk and Massey found enough high-grade ore in the Capote and Oversight mines to supply the smelters directly, and in the year ending July 31, 1901, the company produced 28,826,000 pounds of refined copper. After this time the quality of ore declined, except for a short period after the discovery of the Massey ore body, but the installation of concentrators helped to compensate for the decline. As a result, although the average ore yield in 1905 was only 3.84 per cent, the company produced over 60,000,000 pounds of refined copper in that year—the highest production in Mexico. By this time it had issued dividends totaling $2,812,000 to over five thousand shareholders. Copper prices in the United States were higher than they had ever been, and Greene's directors laid plans to increase the company capitalization to $10,000,000.[22]

Thus at the beginning of 1906 Greene's Cananea empire presented a picture of prosperity and paternalistic benevolence. Underneath the surface, however, all was not well, for the great corporate structure rested on jerry-built foundations. Greene's operations were shot through with waste and in-efficiency which resulted in high producing costs, and these, together with attacks on his companies by outside rivals, caused one crisis after another which had to be camouflaged.

During the first two years of production refined copper cost the company twenty-five cents a pound, although Greene was smelting only the best ores. In 1902 and 1903 the gradual exhaustion of these best ores coincided with a temporary decline

[22] Bernstein, "Greene and the Cananea Bubble," p. 183; *Engineering and Mining Journal*, LXXX (Aug. 26, Oct. 14, 1906), 376, 713.

in the price of copper and the Gates-Hawley raid on Greene's stock. W. H. Weed and some other mining experts contradicted the spreading rumors that the Cananea deposits were nearly "played out," and Greene preserved outward appearances by issuing more stock and adding H. E. Huntington, Bernard Baruch, and other prominent men to his board of directors. The board voted to withhold dividends for the time being, instituted rigid economies, and prevailed upon Greene to appoint several mining experts as directors and officials. As already noted, the company then hired Dr. Ricketts to build a new concentrating plant and virtually ceased operations until it was completed. In 1904 and 1905 the efficient management of Arthur S. Dwight reduced operating costs to about eleven cents a pound, but this was high in comparison with American mines, and much of the machinery was still inefficient and ill-suited to Greene's needs.[23]

The openhanded colonel was even more extravagant in directing his other enterprises. All of them were overstaffed with his cronies. The Sierra Madre Land and Lumber Company tried to operate an expensive standard-gauge railroad to El Paso instead of a short line of narrow gauge, and it built great sawmills full of the latest machinery. The company brought in as draft animals big Percheron horses, which soon died of overwork in the high altitudes, "and an army of five-dollar-a-day Michigan teamsters and lumberjacks ate their heads off at the palatial company boarding house. . . . Mine timbers might about as well have been made of pure silver." In a similar manner the Greene Gold-Silver Company ran up debts and spent the investors' money without having much to show for it but half-finished, widely scattered excavations and hopes. Greene even tried to drill for oil in Sonora, but when after several

[23] Bernstein "Greene and the Cananea Bubble," pp. 183–185; *Engineering and Mining Journal*, LXXV (March 14, 1903), 415–416, LXXVI (Oct. 24, Dec. 31, 1903), 638, 1000–1004, LXXVIII (Dec. 8, 1904), 898–899, LXXIX (Feb. 2, 1905), 250; *Copper Handbook*, VI (1906), 545.

failures he asked Ricketts where he should drill next, the doctor replied dryly, "In Pennsylvania." [24]

Under the circumstances it is not surprising that most of Greene's companies issued no dividends. The wonder is that in spite of its inefficiency the Greene Consolidated Copper Company managed to declare dividends of $2,812,000 between 1900 and 1903 on a total capital (in 1905) of $8,640,000. The explanation seems to be that Greene paid many of them out of later receipts from sales of stock—one of the oldest tricks in the portfolio of the shady promoter. As an observer commented later: "It all lies in the bookkeeping, and a clever accountant can 'prove' anything desired, by going over the figures of the Greene Consolidated Copper Co." Greene kept his books so badly that none of his figures was really reliable. It later appeared that the company had never produced copper so cheaply as it claimed, and it is doubtful whether Greene ever knew exactly what his copper cost him.[25]

From time to time, especially during the crisis of 1903, Greene's critics called for reliable financial reports and statistics, in particular concerning ore reserves, instead of the grandiose statements with which he furnished them.[26] The prosperity of 1904 and 1905 silenced many of them, however, and as late as 1906 the prudent, watchful Horace J. Stevens, editor of the usually reliable *Copper Handbook*, defended Greene against what he called deliberate efforts to wreck his organization by barefaced lying. Greene and his officials, being only human, had made mistakes, he conceded, but their enemies had forced them to the expedient of issuing premature dividends, and "the

[24] Joralemon, *Romantic Copper*, p. 156; T. A. Rickard, *Interviews with Mining Engineers* (San Francisco, 1922), p. 455, as cited in Bernstein, "Greene and the Cananea Bubble," p. 188.

[25] *Copper Handbook*, VIII (1908), 757.

[26] *Engineering and Mining Journal*, LXXV (March 28, 1903), 469; LXXVIII (Dec. 15, 22, 1904), 938, 981–982.

present capable management" was speedily correcting all errors.[27] Stevens was soon to acknowledge his error, for during 1906 a series of catastrophes shook the Cananea companies to their foundations and dislodged their redoubtable founder and president.

III

The first serious misfortune to descend upon Greene and his Cananea empire was a strike at his mines and smelter in June 1906. During most of the nineteenth century Mexico had been regarded as an employer's paradise, for Mexican labor, scattered and rigidly controlled, had little opportunity or active desire to organize unions or strike for higher wages. After 1880, however, conditions began to change. Gradually the railroads broke down the barriers of physical isolation, and after several false starts railroad workers united in 1904 to form the Confederation of Railway Societies of the Mexican Republic, the prototype of nearly all later Mexican railroad unions. Meanwhile scattered strikes broke out from time to time in other industries, and a great variety of small-scale craft organizations sprang up among the semiskilled workers of the Federal District and a few other urban areas.

At first Díaz and his officials paid little attention to Mexican labor organizations, except to put down their occasional strikes, but after 1900 more radical tendencies began to appear. In that year an anarchist group in Mexico City, led by Ricardo and Enrique Flores Magón, began to publish a newspaper, *Regeneración*, and soon they had organized a chain of clubs. They aimed their first blows at the Church and the conservatives, but before long they were attacking Díaz himself. The police destroyed their printing press and imprisoned a few, but the Flores Magón brothers managed to escape to the United States, and in 1905 they re-established their newspaper at St. Louis and organized a unit of what they called the Mexican Liberal

[27] *Copper Handbook*, VI (1906), 545

Party. From their new headquarters the brothers and their cohorts flooded northern Mexico with propaganda denouncing capitalism, the Roman Catholic Church, and the Mexican government.[28]

Respectable upper-class Americans deplored the violent publications of the Mexican exiles, but one group of American laborers aided their work, probably unintentionally. This group was the Western Federation of Miners, the largest American mining union of the early twentieth century. Founded in 1893 at Butte, Montana, the Federation sought to organize laborers in camps all over the Far West, and it naturally canvassed the copper mines of southern Arizona for grievances. To the St. Louis junta, the notorious "boss rule" of Sonora made that state useful as a "horrible example" of Díaz' dictatorship. American mining interests and Greene himself seem to have laid the principal blame for the Cananea strike upon the Western Federation of Miners, but there is no doubt that the St. Louis junta played an equal or perhaps more important part in bringing about the events of June 1906.[29]

From the beginning of their operations Greene's enterprises attracted the attention of labor organizers and propagandists. In 1906 he employed about 5,500 men. Greene undoubtedly believed that they had no cause for complaint, for his wage scale was well above the average in Mexican mines, so that landowners sometimes accused him of stealing their laborers away from them. In addition, his companies rented reasonably clean and dry houses to the miners and supplied them with

[28] Marjorie Ruth Clark, *Organized Labor in Mexico* (Chapel Hill, N.C., 1934), pp. 5–9; Ricardo Flores Magón, *Land and Liberty: Mexico's Battle for Economic Freedom and Its Relation to Labor's World-wide Struggle* (Los Angeles, [1913?]), *passim;* Cosío Villegas, *Historia moderna de México,* IV, 298–316.

[29] *Encyclopedia of the Social Sciences* (New York, 1930–1935), X, 506; Eduardo W. Villa, *Compendio de historia del estado de Sonora* (México, 1937), pp. 456–457; *Engineering and Mining Journal,* LXXXI (June 9, 1906), 1099–1100; *Anglo-American and Mexican Mining Guide,* IX (July 28, 1906), 103.

hospital facilities and a brick clubhouse. A number of laborers
even kept savings accounts at the Banco de Cananea. Governor
Izabal remarked after the strike: "Rather than mine operators,
they look like persons of the middle class." [30]

As usual, wage rates were the principal bone of contention.
Like most other mine operators in Mexico, Greene paid higher
wages to American employees than to Mexicans doing the same
work. At first he tried to offset this differential by assessing
his Americans heavily for hospital fees and rent and by hiring
them only for short terms. But after his reputation for stinginess
spread across the border, only the poorest class of Americans
would work for him, and in the spring of 1903 a group of them,
probably organized by the Western Federation of Miners, struck
for more money. Thereupon a detachment of Mexican *rurales*
(police) escorted them into Arizona as undesirable aliens. [31]

In 1906 Greene's differential wage scale still existed—3 or
3.50 pesos a day to Mexican labor and about $5, gold, to
Americans. Company officials protested that Mexican labor
could never be relied on and that an American would receive
only $1.50 or $2 for work which might take a Mexican a day
to complete. [32] Nevertheless the unequal wages and the snobbish-
ness of Americans toward "the greasers" rankled in the minds
of Greene's Mexican miners, especially after they talked with
friends who had visited across the border. Early in 1906 a
few mineworkers and others founded a club at Cananea which
soon associated itself with the St. Louis junta, and in April,

[30] Bernstein, "Mexican Mining Industry," I, 551–570, and "Greene
and the Cananea Bubble," p. 190; Report of Governor Rafael Izabal to
the Minister of *Gobernación*, Hermosillo, Sonora, June 19, 1906, in
Diario oficial, June 28, 1906, p. 804 (hereafter cited as Izabal, Report).

[31] *Engineering and Mining Journal*, LXXV (March 14, 1903), 416;
LXXVI (Sept. 26, 1903), 466.

[32] Greene employed more men than Bisbee and other comparable
American camps, but the lean ore of his mines was one reason (*ibid.*,
LXXXII [Oct. 6, 1906], 627).

Enrique Bermúdez set up a newspaper to attack Díaz and Greene indiscriminately.[33] Throughout the first half of the year the tension increased, and company officials unobtrusively strengthened their police system and waited to see what would happen. Outwardly, however, life at Cananea followed its quiet routine, and on May 31, less than twenty hours before the riot began, a Mexican baseball team crossed the border peacefully and played "the best game seen in Bisbee in years."[34]

On the afternoon of the baseball game little groups of miners were already excitedly discussing a strike. The company had recently announced a new pay raise for American laborers, and agitators had been working upon the Mexicans to demand a similar raise for themselves. At some time during the evening a miner friendly to Greene warned him that socialist agitators and representatives of the Western Federation of Miners were planning an uprising for the next morning. Greene was a little incredulous but nevertheless stationed special police forces. During the night the shift at the Oversight mine laid down their tools and went on strike, and on the following morning, June 1, the workers at Capote and Veta Grande mines, the smelter, and the concentrator followed suit.[35] A delegation of workers presented to Greene and the company a list of demands focused directly on conditions in the mines: a basic wage of five pesos a day, reduction of working hours from nine to eight, limitation of Americans to one-fourth of the force in any

[33] Bernstein, "Greene and the Cananea Bubble," p. 190; Herbert O. Brayer, "The Cananea Incident," *New Mexico Historical Review*, XIII (Oct. 1938), 390–391. This account is based primarily upon Arizona newspapers. Cosío Villegas states that two protest groups were founded in Cananea during 1906: the Unión Liberal Humanidad, led by Manuel M. Diéguez, and the Club Liberal Cananea, led by Lázaro Gutiérrez de Lara (*Historia moderna de México*, IV, 316–317).

[34] On the other hand, a few days earlier a Mexican policeman had killed an American saloonkeeper "without cause or provocation" (Brayer, "Cananea Incident," pp. 389, 391).

[35] *Ibid.*, pp. 392–395.

given division, promotions for Mexicans, and certain specific personnel changes.[36]

Nothing in these demands indicated that the movement was anything more than an ordinary strike, but at the same time handbills appeared everywhere, calling on the miners to overthrow "a Government which is composed of ambitious persons who criminally contemplate oppressing the people." The writers of the handbills had done their utmost to start a "race war" by linking Díaz with the hated Americans, and at the end they exhorted: "CURSE the thought that a Mexican is worth less than a Yankee; that a negro or a Chinaman is to be compared to a Mexican. That this is a fact is the result of the very bad government which gives the advantage to the adventurers rather than to the true owners of this unfortunate land." [37]

Whether the ordinary miners understood the larger issues posed by the handbills, they knew the meaning of "five pesos a day" and "eight-hour shifts." During the morning they milled around in Ronquillo, the Mexican section of town, while their committee negotiated with the management (and lowered its demands to four pesos). At one point Greene spoke to the crowd himself in fluent Spanish. He told them that he sympathized with their demands, having once been an ordinary miner himself, that the company was already paying the highest wages of any mining outfit in Mexico, and that he would treat

[36] This version of the demands is that of Leon Díaz Cárdenas (Bernstein, "Greene and the Cananea Bubble," p. 190). Governor Izabal enclosed with his formal report a milder version, in which the miners' committee complained that the Oversight mine was about to be leased under contract and asked only for Mexican foremen, a wage raise of one peso, and an eight-hour day (Izabal, Report, p. 805). Cosío Villegas attributes the authorship of the petition to Esteban B. Calderón, secretary of the Unión Liberal Humanidad (*Historia moderna de México*, IV, 317).

[37] The full text is given in Brayer, "Cananea Incident," pp. 392–393. For a Spanish version see Izabal, Report, p. 808. Izabal blamed the handbills on the Unión Liberal Humanidad, but Calderón denied that his group was responsible (Cosío Villegas, *Historia moderna de México*, IV, 317).

them fairly, as he always had in the past. It seemed apparent that he was not going to grant the demands, but the Mexicans did not know just what to do about it, and some of them drifted away to their homes. Probably the agitators and leaders went to work on them again, for in midafternoon an ill-organized crowd began to move slowly up into "the Mesa," as the American section of Cananea was called, toward the company's lumberyard, offices, and construction depots, looking for new recruits among the workers there. Before them they carried red banners reading "Five pesos, eight hours." [38]

At the lumberyard the violence which everyone felt in the air very soon precipitated murder. Someone had phoned ahead to warn the yard manager, George Metcalf, and when he saw the crowd of strikers approaching, he closed the gate and stood in front of it, rifle in hand, while from the inside others, at his orders, showered the strikers with stones and brickbats and turned a fire hose upon them. Maddened by the resistance, the strikers swarmed over Metcalf, clubbing and stabbing him to death with rocks and the sharp points of miners' candlesticks. His brother Will rushed to his rescue but was shot down before he had gone a dozen steps. Apparently there was firing on both sides, and three of the mob were killed before the others could force their way into the lumberyard and set it on fire.[39] There is no reason to believe that most of the mob intended this

[38] Brayer, "Cananea Incident," pp. 392–393; Izabal, Report, p. 802; Albert W. Brickwood to Secretary of State, Nogales, Sonora, June 22, 1906, U.S. Department of State, Consular Despatches, Nogales, IV (hereafter cited as Brickwood, Despatch, with date).

[39] There is considerable disagreement concerning this incident. The above account is based on the story of an eyewitness (Brayer, "Cananea Incident," pp. 396–397). An account by a refugee suggests that both Metcalfs were shot down (Chicago *Tribune*, June 3, 1906, p. 1). On the other hand, Governor Izabal (who arrived later) stated that George Metcalf stood behind the gate and shot two strikers as the crowd tried to enter. When the gate gave way, both brothers ran to a shed, and one continued firing. The crowd set fire to the shed, forced the Metcalfs out, and then killed them (Izabal, Report, p. 802).

violence in advance, but the shedding of blood committed them beyond recall, and they pressed on excitedly toward the plaza, which held the church, Greene's house, and several hotels.

Observers do not agree on exactly what happened next. Either on the plaza or in two cars on the street leading to it Greene and his general manager, Arthur S. Dwight, backed up by a group of armed Americans, tried to remonstrate with the strikers, but, incited by one of their leaders who was waving a red flag, the crowd shouted him down. Some of the more excitable Americans opened fire, and a fusillade followed, in which the flag-waver was riddled, two other Mexicans killed, and at least fifteen wounded. The poorly armed Mexicans scurried back toward their homes in Ronquillo, but as the mob broke up, some of them looted stores for arms and ammunition. During the evening small bands of strikers and the inadequate Cananea police, reinforced by American residents, fired back and forth at each other, and a few Mexicans were captured. The strikers damaged no more company property, but all kinds of inflated rumors spread among the Americans, who were especially afraid that the Mexicans would cut the railroad line to the outside world. Women and children were bundled into automobiles and hastily assembled at Greene's house, where a cordon of American men remained on guard through the night. Some of the families left during the evening on a special train for the border.[40]

Late in the afternoon, when rumors were spreading and no one knew whether the Mexicans would launch a concerted attack, Greene phoned to the manager of the Copper Queen Company at Bisbee, Arizona, for aid. The manager referred him to Captain Thomas Rynning of the Arizona Rangers, who later

[40] Brayer, "Cananea Incident," pp. 397–398. Izabal gave a slightly different account (Report, p. 802). Vice-Consul Brickwood heard and reported that a Mexican in the crowd tried to wrest a gun from an American and that other Mexicans fired first (Brickwood, Despatch, June 22, 1906).

said that Greene told him: "Hell is popping here, and every
American's life is in danger." [41] Meanwhile the Mexican authorities at Cananea and probably Greene also wired south to
the state governor, Rafael Izabal, at Hermosillo. Izabal started
north by train that evening with a special escort of about
twenty *rurales,* and he ordered the nearest local body of soldiers
at Arizpe, as well as *rurales* and fiscal guards at Magdalena, to
set out at once for Cananea. The most alarming messages to
leave Cananea on June 1, however, came from the American
consular agent, William J. Galbraith, who became panicky and
wired to Secretary of State Elihu Root for immediate aid,
saying that American citizens were being murdered and property
dynamited. He sent a similar telegram to the commander of
American troops at Fort Huachucha, Arizona (see Maps 5
and 6).[42]

As soon as the first reports of violence reached Bisbee, the
local marshal issued a call for two hundred armed volunteers.
Perhaps two thousand people gathered in the plaza at the
center of town to wait for bulletins, and the mayor prudently
ordered the saloons closed. When the volunteers had assembled,
a rag-tag-and-bobtail group carrying all kinds of weapons,
Rynning calmed them down and told them that they would not
set out at once, because Governor Izabal had asked him not
to cross the border before his arrival from Hermosillo. The
volunteers waited all evening, champing at the bit; and when
a trainload of refugees arrived from Cananea at eleven o'clock
with wild stories of murders and terror, a group of fifteen
young bloods, led by the local Y.M.C.A. physical director, shook
off Rynning's instructions, saddled their horses, and dashed off
toward the border at Naco. Here they got into a fight with

[41] Told by Rynning to Herbert O. Brayer (Brayer, "Cananea Incident," pp. 398-399).

[42] Villa, *Compendio de historia,* p. 460; Brickwood, Despatch, June 22,
1906. Most of the text of Galbraith's telegrams is given in the Chicago
Tribune, June 3, 1906, p. 2.

Mexican border guards, and the pride of the "Y" was shot in the arm. None of them crossed the border.

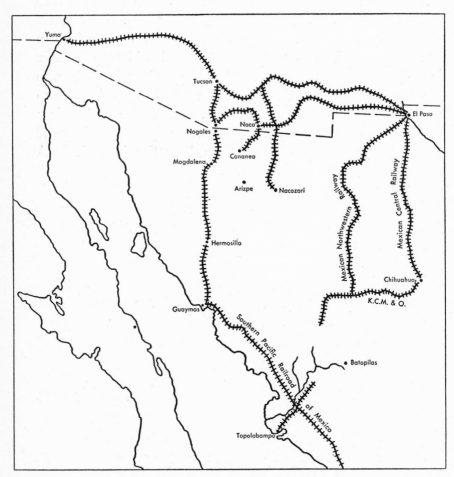

Map 5. Northwestern railroads about 1910

Just before midnight 270 volunteers left Bisbee by train for Naco. They arrived there at about one o'clock and spent the rest of the night waiting for Governor Izabal, their impatience whetted by another phone call from Greene, who reported sporadic firing in Cananea and urged them to hurry. Rynning, aware that his position as ranger captain and deputy marshal of the United States forbade his entering Mexico with troops, wired to the territorial governor for special permission. The governor refused and warned Americans to stay at home, but his telegram was delayed, and Rynning did not receive it in time.

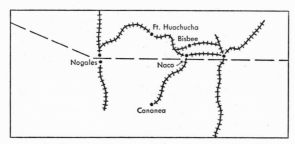

Map 6. Scene of the Cananea strike, 1906

Meanwhile Izabal, the governor of Sonora, had his problems too. It was impossible to reach Cananea from Hermosillo by train without crossing American soil, and as he was traveling northward, the Federal government at Mexico City instructed him under no circumstances to take any troops into the United States, lest he create a precedent for Americans. Consequently Izabal had to send his police guard overland from Imuris to Cananea, while he and his political henchman, Military Governor Luis Torres, went on to Nogales and changed to an American train for the short trip to Naco. American Vice-Consul Albert W. Brickwood joined them at Nogales, and the three arrived at Naco at seven thirty on the morning of June 2.

Here the Mexican governor faced a difficult dilemma. He dared not allow American troops to cross the border on his own authority, but from all accounts the disorder at Cananea seemed to require immediate action, and neither his own police guard nor the local detachment of *rurales* under Colonel Emilio Kosterlitsky could reach there for some hours. The troops from Arizpe would need three days to march north. Rynning suggested that if the Americans crossed the border as individuals, their action would not constitute a formal invasion, and Izabal, relieved, consented to the hairsplitting. The ranger captain lined up his men on the border and explained the problem to them, whereupon they obligingly ambled across the line "like a bunch of sheep" and offered their services to Izabal as soldiers. Torres swore them into the Mexican army, and Rynning accepted a captaincy in the Sonora militia, agreeing in the name of his men that they would all obey Izabal's orders. Having twisted the laws of both countries almost beyond recognition, officials and volunteers climbed aboard the train for the beleaguered mining camp, where they arrived in midmorning.[43]

When the relief train pulled into Cananea, Greene was waiting at the station with three automobiles, and perhaps half the town stood about, silently watching. Vice-Consul Brickwood noticed everywhere a "constrained state of mind" and a "feeling bordering on race hatred," and of course the American residents were very glad to see the reinforcements. Greene and the Mexican officials quickly reconnoitered the concentrating plant and the nearest mines, while the cars full of American volunteers were pulled up on sidings in front of the general offices and the volunteers themselves were marched up to the smelters.

In the square facing the principal company buildings Izabal prepared to address a crowd of perhaps three thousand, and various American residents (but not the volunteers) stationed themselves all around as guards, with rifles in hand ready for trouble. The governor scolded the Mexicans for killing and looting, but various young men interrupted him with questions about wages and his words had little effect. Greene then repeated his soothing remarks of the day before, adding that the company could not afford to pay its Mexican miners five pesos a day.

[43] This account is based almost entirely on Brayer, "Cananea Incident," pp. 399–404. Brayer obtained his facts directly from Rynning and from contemporary newspaper accounts, usually written by eyewitnesses. Many details are confirmed by Brickwood's shorter account (Brickwood, Despatches, June 23, 30, 1906). For Izabal's actions see Izabal, Report, p. 803.

Some of his audience muttered the obvious reply—"Why, then, raise American wages?" Before they could make much of this point, however, a sudden movement in the crowd alarmed the American guards, and they raised their rifles. "The crowd scampered like rats, but fortunately not a single shot was fired at this time," and Greene, Izabal, and the others retired into the office of the chief of police for a conference.[44] Cananea had narrowly escaped a massacre.

While Izabal and Greene addressed the crowd, the volunteers from Bisbee, under the command of Rynning and several other rangers who had accompanied them, marched back and forth several times between smelter and town as a display of strength and then returned to their railroad cars. Here they remained throughout the afternoon as a reserve in case of united mob action, but Brickwood, other American observers, and Izabal agreed that they never fired a shot or took any part in the action, however much they may have wished to do so. This does not mean that Cananea passed a peaceful afternoon. Shortly after lunchtime Izabal's personal escort of *rurales* arrived from Nogales, and from three o'clock until sundown these and various groups of American residents exchanged shots with Mexicans almost continuously. A group of American cowboys, for example, took up a position on a railroad trestle and poured bullets into the valley below. During this shooting three American bystanders were killed, as well as an unestablished number of Mexicans, and many were wounded.[45]

[44] Editor W. B. Kelley of the Bisbee *Daily Review* was in the crowd, and it is his account that has here been used (Brayer, "Cananea Incident," pp. 405–407). Izabal reported that he talked to four groups of miners, accompanied by Greene, and mentioned hearing shouts against the Americans, but he omitted the details given here (Izabal, Report, p. 803). According to one account of Izabal's speech he justified the differential wage rate by citing the interesting precedent of American and Mexican brothels, which, he said, were accustomed to charge five pesos and three pesos respectively (Cosío Villegas, *Historia moderna de México*, IV, 320).

[45] Brayer, "Cananea Incident," pp. 407–408; Brickwood, Despatch,

At about seven o'clock in the evening fifty or seventy-five *rurales* arrived in Cananea from Magdalena under the leadership of the notorious Colonel Emilio Kosterlitsky, a professional soldier of Polish birth who had migrated to Mexico by way of the United States and who enjoyed a wide reputation for toughness and ruthless application of the "law of flight." [46] "Almost as if by magic the firing ceased," wrote an observer, and Izabal, Torres, and Kosterlitsky issued an order establishing martial law. Greene and the Mexican officers, together with about thirty *rurales*, patrolled the American section of the town, warning eveyone they met to go home to bed. Izabal dismissed the Bisbee volunteers, but because of engine trouble their train remained in town until ten o'clock, and they did not arrive at their homes before the early hours of the morning.

Little happened at Cananea during the night, and when further Mexican reinforcements arrived next day, June 3, it was clear that the riot had ended and that the strike would fail. By midday more than fifteen hundred Mexican troops were encamped around Cananea, and a few workers had returned to their jobs. The following morning General Torres told the others that they could choose between mining at the old wages and entering the army to fight Indians. Most of the miners preferred Greene to the Yaquis, and within ten days mines, smelter, and concentrating plant were operating at full blast.[47]

There is considerable disagreement as to the punishment inflicted upon the Mexican community by Torres and Kosterlitsky, beyond the threat of army service. John K. Turner, who

June 22, 1906. Izabal declared that both Americans and Mexicans were drunk and that his *rurales* had to keep American employees from joining the fight (Izabal, Report, p. 803).

[46] McClintock, *Arizona*, II, 605.

[47] Brayer, "Cananea Incident," pp. 408–409, 413–414; Brickwood, Despatch, June 30, 1906. The company suffered no damage but the burned lumberyard. At Izabal's suggestion Greene replaced two or three foremen about whom the strikers had complained (Izabal, Report, p. 804).

witnessed none of the events of the strike, described an orgy of killings—miners shot at the edge of newly dug graves, hanged, impressed into the army, and shut up in penal colonies. León Díaz Cárdenas declared that after the troops arrived fifteen men who had been imprisoned early in the riot were taken out and shot, but that Vice-President Corral in Mexico City vetoed further killings for fear of scandal. It seems clear that the officials arrested everyone connected with the radical movements around Cananea on whom they could lay their hands.[48] The casualties in the actual fighting were four or six Americans dead, including the Metcalf brothers, and eighteen Mexicans, according to the most conservative estimates, but Herbert O. Brayer thinks that about thirty Mexicans may have lost their lives during the riot.[49]

Although the Cananea strike lasted only a brief weekend, both Mexico and the United States felt its effects for months afterward. For one thing, news of the violence set in motion the ponderous machinery of diplomacy. Galbraith's alarmist telegrams to Washington about murder and dynamiting threw the State and War Departments into confusion, and Secretary Root naturally instructed Ambassador David E. Thompson to ask Díaz how the United States might help to snuff out the riot. On being assured that Mexico had the situation under control, Root inquired more pointedly whether Mexico would welcome the assistance of American troops. Since this was exactly what Díaz did not want, he held a flurried conference with Thompson and suggested that the Mexican government would be glad to have American troops patrol their own side of the border to keep fugitives from escaping.

[48] Turner, *Barbarous Mexico*, pp. 218–219; Bernstein, "Greene and the Cananea Bubble," p. 192. Others, including Diéguez and Calderón, were imprisoned in San Juan de Ulúa (Cosío Villegas, *Historia moderna de México*, IV, 320).

[49] Brickwood listed only four Americans killed, Brayer six (Brickwood, Despatch, June 22, 1906; Brayer, "Cananea Incident," pp. 414–415).

By this time soldiers of the regular American army were in position on the border ready to intervene at a word. One of the telegrams sent by Galbraith had alerted the post commander at Fort Huachucha, who sent a detachment of cavalry to Naco. Galbraith continued to call for troops, but the War Department sent unequivocal orders to the detachment: "Absolutely and under no conditions are you to cross the line until further instructions." Since Izabal and Torres soon had Cananea under control, the American cavalry returned to Fort Huachucha on June 5.[50]

Although the two countries managed to avoid an outright intervention, the Cananea incident aroused suspicions which were slow to die away. On June 3 newspapers reported that the Western Federation of Miners had passed a resolution greeting the Mexican strikers and urging them to continue their class struggle. Not long afterward Mexican authorities and company officials claimed to have evidence that about three hundred American miners had secretly encouraged the Mexicans to strike, and the rumor spread that arrests would soon be made. Whether or not the report was true, about three hundred American miners left work in northern Sonora and returned to the United States during the next few days.[51]

On the American side of the line the Cananea strike started a whole series of alarming rumors. On July 12 newspapers quoted a dismissed employee of the Mexican Central Railroad who declared that a secret society of Mexican laborers had warned all Americans to leave Mexico by September 4 under threat of death, and another report, emanating from El Paso,

[50] Brayer, "Cananea Incident," pp. 410–413; Chicago *Tribune*, June 3, 1906, p. 2; Callahan, *American Foreign Policy in Mexican Relations*, pp. 522–523. There was widespread Mexican criticism of Izabal, and he was actually tried on a charge of permitting an American "invasion," but the court acquitted him (Cosío Villegas, *Historia moderna de México*, IV, 320–321).

[51] Chicago *Tribune*, June 3, 1906, p. 2; Brayer, "Cananea Incident," p. 414.

predicted a gigantic anti-American demonstration on the Mexican Independence Day, September 16, by the League of Mexican Railroad Employees. Made nervous by these rumors, Ambassador Thompson telegraphed directly to thirty-one American consular offices in Mexico for reports on anti-American sentiments. The replies ran the gamut between reassurance and alarm, but their general tone did not seem to threaten immediate danger, and when September 16 passed without a general uprising, the ambassador's ruffled feathers settled back into place.[52]

As rumors of danger to Americans in Mexico began to spread northward in the summer of 1906, persons and companies with interests there hastily damped the waves of alarm with soothing statements about the Mexican temperament. A week after the strike the *Engineering and Mining Journal* declared that the Cananea strike was "so entirely foreign to the Mexican character that it is the natural inference that the troubles were stirred up by anarchistic agitators, possibly incited, with the assistance of *mescal*, by the Western Federation of [Miners]," and it concluded with the pious hope that Mexico would not catch the infection of labor troubles from the United States. In October, Edward M. Conley called the labor scare a "summer sensation" created by journalists and declared: "There is no more danger of an 'uprising' of Mexicans against foreigners than there is danger of an uprising of Americans in New York against the foreign horde." But, he added, because of the great size of American investments in Mexico, perhaps American employers there ought to liberalize their attitude toward labor in order to show that "they have the interests of the country and its citizens at heart, as well as their own personal gain." [53]

[52] Callahan, *American Foreign Policy in Mexican Relations*, pp. 523–527.
[53] *Engineering and Mining Journal*, LXXXI (June 9, 1906), 1099–1100; Edward M. Conley, "The Anti-foreign Uprisings in Mexico," *World Today*, XI (Oct. 1906), 1059–1062.

If this advice could ever have solved the problems of American capitalists in Mexico, that time had already passed in 1906, for the discontent and hatred which produced the Cananea riot speedily gathered momentum. Mexican labor may have given confused and largely ineffectual support to the Madero revolution, but the Flores Magón brothers certainly helped to weaken Díaz in Sonora, and the state remained a center of discontent throughout the violent decade after 1910. Here and all over Mexico the peons of farm and mine gradually pulled themselves into something like cohesive movements, and the Constitution of 1917 amply recognized their needs and desires.

The triumphant Mexican labor movement of the 1920's and 1930's gave the strikers of 1906 a place in the official hagiography as "the seedbed of Revolution in the North." The mine union local at Cananea still bears the name "El Gran Sindicato Obrero 'Martires de 1906,'" for, as the state historian of Sonora put it thirty-one years later, despite the "semi-negative results" of the strike the little nucleus of workers at Cananea were "the advance guard of the armed struggle of 1910." [54]

IV

For a few months after the end of the Cananea strike Greene's companies continued production, their officials seemingly concerned only to make up for lost time. Inside, however, another crisis was developing. Whether because the strike had damaged the public confidence in Greene or because the securities market was becoming saturated just prior to the Panic of 1907, Wall Street and investors in general stopped buying Greene's securities. Creditors of the companies and of Greene himself— for he had run up large personal debts through his extravagance —began to press for payment. Hampered by inefficient ma-

[54] Clark, *Organized Labor in Mexico, passim;* Bernstein, "Greene and the Cananea Bubble," p. 192; Villa, *Compendio de historia,* p. 457. In 1936, thirty years after the strike, the surviving laborers were gathered together at Cananea and photographed (*ibid.,* p. 460).

chinery and too much overhead, the operating company could not produce enough copper to earn the required income. Somewhere, somehow, the improvident colonel would have to find new capital.

Greene's rivals had been waiting for just such an occasion as this. As early as 1903 rumors had circulated that agents of the Amalgamated Copper Company were buying up Greene Consolidated stock, and for a while the financial world expected almost daily the announcement that Greene had sold out to Rockefeller and the Standard Oil "crowd." [55] H. H. Rogers of Amalgamated Copper probably laid plans at this time to take over the Cananea empire, and during the next two years his agents acquired a few holdings, such as the America, a small mine on the edge of Greene's Cananea properties. On August 6, 1906, they incorporated the Cananea Central Copper company in Minnesota, capitalized generously at $10,000,000 and operating through Mexican subsidiaries, the Cananea-Duluth Copper Company and the Cananea Development Company. As one writer has put it, Cananea Central had plenty of capital but very little copper ore, whereas Greene found himself in just the opposite predicament.[56]

During the summer of 1906 miners and financiers passed around the rumor of a "deal" between the colonel and Thomas F. Cole of Duluth, a member of the Amalgamated group, and in December, Greene announced to his stockholders that Greene Consolidated would merge its properties with those of Cananea Central Copper Company, instead of trying to secure capital by issuing more of its own securities. On December 26 a new holding company was incorporated in Minnesota, the Greene Cananea Copper Company, capitalized at $60,000,000. Most of this amount was to be used to buy up the stock of Greene

[55] *Engineering and Mining Journal*, LXXV (March 14, 1903), 416; LXXVI (Aug. 15, 1903), 254.
[56] Joralemon, *Romantic Copper*, p. 163; *Moody's Manual*, 1911, pp. 3671–3672; *Copper Handbook*, VI (1906), 330.

Consolidated and Cananea Central at an exchange ratio favorable to the investors. Greene became a director of the new company, but everyone understood that he had lost most of his power, for Cole was the president of the company, and another important figure in it was John D. Ryan, who was later to become president of Amalgamated Copper after Rogers' death in 1909 and convert it into the great Anaconda Copper Company. Cole and Ryan brought Dr. Ricketts with them to hold a permanent position as general manager.[57]

As the dust settled in 1907, the world realized how completely Greene had been forced to sell out to his rivals. Cole and Ryan saw to it that their representatives were elected to the board of directors of Greene Consolidated at the annual meeting on February 14, 1907, and Greene lost his position in both organizations.[58] Greene Consolidated became only a "footbridge" between Cananea Consolidated, which owned the property under Mexican law, and Greene Cananea, which determined policy. Those shareholders who had not exchanged their holdings for the new stock now saw their property melting away before their eyes. Assets which, they had long assumed, belonged to their company, such as large blocks of shares in Greene Gold-Silver and other companies, now appeared in the possession of others. Even in the absence of clear proof it would appear that Greene, heavily in debt, juggled assets from one company to another without any clear authorization or record. The unfortunate shareholders tried to find out what was happening at a special meeting of Greene Consolidated in October 1907, but the chairman simply referred all questions to the other two companies, which were not represented at the meeting, and the investors learned nothing.

Probably no one will ever untangle the bookkeeping, for as

[57] *Anglo-American and Mexican Mining Guide*, IX (Aug. 31, 1906), 125; *Engineering and Mining Journal*, LXXXII (Dec. 22, 1906), 1183, 1192; *Copper Handbook*, VIII (1908), 746–755; *Dictionary of American Biography*, XVI, 262–263.

[58] New York *Times*, Feb. 15, 1907, p. 14; *Engineering and Mining Journal*, LXXIII (Feb. 23, 1907), 405.

Horace Stevens of the *Copper Handbook* put it, "the relations of the Cananea Consolidated, Greene Consolidated and Greene Cananea are so intricate and obscure that nobody but the principals can say exactly who is who, what is what, or which is which." His advice to the unfortunate shareholders was simple: Get out. Stevens admitted that they had been defrauded, but since their deceivers could not possibly make restitution, he concluded that they would do far better to accept the dilution of their holdings and hope for better management in the Greene Cananea Company.[59] Most of the investors followed this advice, for by March 1908 Greene Cananea had acquired 925,038 out of the 1,000,000 shares which Greene Consolidated had issued. After years of existence on paper the latter company was dissolved in 1917.[60]

When Greene had lost control of his principal money earners, the Cananea copper mines, his other enterprises quickly collapsed. The Greene Gold-Silver Company offered 100,000 shares of stock for sale in 1907, but few of these were taken up. As time went on, evidence leaked out to suggest that although the company's listed liabilities of $3,035,338 were real enough the assets which appeared on the balance sheet were mostly mythical. According to the *Copper Handbook*, the company bought nothing outright which could be secured on a part payment. "In consequence . . . at the first financial push, [it] fell to pieces like a house of cards." Late in 1908 the company went into receivership, but when the receiver looked for tangible assets at company headquarters, he found only $1.48 cash in the bank and some old office furniture. On February 12, 1909, the company's largest mining concession in Chihuahua and Sonora, covering nearly three million acres, expired, and in the following month the receiver placed the company in bankruptcy.[61]

As for the Sierra Madre Land and Lumber Company, Ricketts

[59] *Copper Handbook*, VIII (1908), 755–757.

[60] *Ibid.*, VIII (1908), 746, X (1910–1911), 907, 909; *Mines Handbook*, XIII (1918), 1682.

[61] *Copper Handbook*, VIII (1908), 757–760; *Engineering and Mining*

cut the ground out from under it by canceling its twenty-year contract for supply timbers to the Cananea mines as soon as he took over their management. Greene shortly sold this company and the Rio Grande, Sierre Madre, and Pacific Railroad to F. S. Pearson, a Canadian capitalist. On February 17, 1909, Pearson and Enrique C. Creel incorporated the Mexican Transportation Company, Limited (later renamed the Mexican Northwestern Railway), in Canada to acquire and operate several short lines in northern Mexico. Greene's Casa Grande irrigation scheme collapsed after a cloudburst washed out his dam on the Gila River.[62]

Meanwhile under the new organization the position of the Cananea companies began to improve. For a time the Greene Cananea Copper Company stood at the top of a pyramid of subsidiaries almost as complicated as Greene's financial empire, but eventually some of these were liquidated as unnecessary. As for the actual operations at Cananea, Ricketts took charge of them early in 1907. After he had made a tour of inspection in March, he declared that the mines were underdeveloped and needed a general reorganization and that the smelter was "an impossible structure" which would have to be completely rebuilt. Actually Charles F. Shelby had begun to overhaul the smelter under Greene's management, and Ricketts apparently let him finish the task while he went to work on other parts of the plant. Statistics showed the effect of Ricketts' work immediately, for in one year preceding September 1907 the cost of mining and mine construction dropped 37 per cent, and during 1907 mining and beneficiating costs together were 20 per cent less than during 1906.[63]

Ricketts had hoped to increase production too, but in the

Journal, LXXXVI (Nov. 7, 1908), 913, 929, LXXXVII (Feb. 27, March 20, 1909), 480, 628.

[62] Joralemon, *Romantic Copper,* p. 164; *Moody's Manual,* 1911, pp. 632–633; H. V. Poor, *Manual of Railroads,* 1910, p. 1851; *Moody's Magazine,* VIII (Oct. 1909), 11.

[63] *Copper Handbook,* XI (1912–1913), 413–414, 1369; *Engineering and*

United States the Panic of 1907 contracted markets and supplies of capital, while in Mexico rising costs of fuel and supplies and congestion on the railroads produced a general depression in the mining industry. In October 1907 he decided to shut down operations temporarily, and, remembering the labor troubles of 1906, he took pains to call in troops as the men were laid off, five hundred at a time. During the next year he took advantage of the occasion to install new furnaces, conveying devices, and other machinery, so that when work was resumed on July 11, 1908, the plant operated more efficiently than ever. In the middle of 1910 several mines, including the America, were closed again in order to decrease production, but at least two of these were reopened in 1911. In 1910 Greene Cananea's production amounted to 45,771,925 pounds of copper (as compared with over 60,000,-000 pounds under Greene's management in 1905), and at the beginning of 1911 the company declared its first dividend, amounting to twenty-five cents per share.[64]

During the revolutionary period the Cananea mines suffered much less damage and interruption of operations than most other Mexican mining companies. This was largely due to their fortunate location near the American border, although the circumspect neutrality of company officials also helped to keep them out of trouble. During 1914 and 1915 the Cananea mines operated only about half of the time, and from June to December of 1917 they were closed. After 1917 there was no interruption of operations. Production fell to 16,333,081 pounds in 1915 but rose again as far as 52,694,731 pounds in 1918. During the 1920's the mines continued to yield low-grade ore, and from 1922 to 1932 Green Cananea produced 388,909,021 pounds of

Mining Journal, LXXXIII (Jan. 5, 1907), 43, LXXXV (April 11, 1908), 754–755; Bernstein, "Greene and the Cananea Bubble," p. 194.

[64] *Mineral Industry,* XVII (1908), 225, XIX (1910), 176–177, XX (1911), 206; *Engineering and Mining Journal,* LXXXVI (July 25, 1908), 188, LXXXVII (Jan. 9, 1909), 58–59, XCIII (Jan. 27, 1912), 240; *Moody's Manual,* 1911, p. 3672. Figures for Greene Cananea's output from 1908 to 1920 are given in *Mines Handbook,* XV (1922), 1916.

copper—with a yearly average well under that of Greene's best year. The great difference between the two types of management, however, is shown in the cost of production, which never fell much below eleven cents a pound under the colonel, but which the Anaconda management eventually reduced to about four cents.[65]

Long before this Greene had left the scenes of his ill-starred labors. Early in 1907 there were rumors that he intended to start a new mining project somewhat west of Cananea, but his personal debts swallowed up the Greene Cananea securities which he had received in the merger, and the Panic of 1907 cost him what remained of his fortune. He spent his last days ranching in northern Sonora, where the company permitted him to keep some of his cattle lands. In the summer of 1911 runaway horses threw him from his carriage, and he fractured his collarbone and two ribs. Pneumonia set in, and too late his wife summoned help from El Paso. Doctors and nurses, carrying tanks of oxygen, made a record-breaking trip from El Paso to Naco on a special night train and drove across sixty miles of desert in automobiles, but in vain. On August 5 Greene died, his riches gone, his policies discredited, and his name a synonym for extravagance and waste.[66]

In 1906, when Greene still seemed infallible, a writer declared that he would do for northern Mexico what Cecil Rhodes had done for South Africa.[67] Aside from political activities, Greene and Rhodes had much in common. Both were typical of a hard-handed nineteenth-century imperialism which wrested profits from the barren soil and the downtrodden native, occasionally for the benefit of both. However much one may admire their energy and resourcefulness, which created empires where buz-

[65] Bernstein, "Mexican Mining Industry," II, 1017–1024.
[66] *Engineering and Mining Journal*, LXXXIII (June 1, 1907), 1043; *Dictionary of American Biography*, VII, 577–578; New York *Times*, Aug. 6, 1911, p. 9.
[67] Trentini, *Prosperity of Mexico*, II, 239.

zard and cactus had previously held sway, one cannot always admire their methods. This is perhaps especially true in Greene's case, since he ended his life in failure. His eventual collapse highlighted his shortcomings all the more vividly and demonstrated some of the inherent weaknesses of promoting: its reliance on promises and appearances, its thirst for quick results, and its impatience with methodical, orderly progress.

VIII

Railroad Tycoon: Arthur E. Stilwell

MORE than any other man described in this book Arthur E. Stilwell was a born promoter. Rosecrans, Grant, and Greene did not enter business until middle age. Plumb, Owen, and Shepherd showed the instincts of promoters at an early age, but during part of their careers they allowed themselves to be diverted into diplomacy, Utopian crusades, and politics. Stilwell was a business promoter first, last, and always. He became a traveling salesman before he was nineteen years old, and thereafter, if one may judge from his own accounts, he spent his happiest moments sitting at a desk across from some company president or banker, trying to sell him something—first stationery, then insurance, and finally stocks and bonds.

The greatest promotional ventures in Stilwell's life were railroad systems centering in or leading to Kansas City, where he lived during most of his active years. The city was becoming a railroad center when he first arrived there in 1879, but it had not yet managed to capitalize its strategic location at the gateway of the American Southwest. Stilwell encircled it with a belt line to improve its position as a railroad junction point and then built a trunk line directly south to the Gulf of Mexico at Port Arthur,

Texas, in order to relieve the Kansas City area from dependence on Eastern railroads. Forced from control of this railroad in 1900, he then proposed to make the city an entrepôt of Oriental trade by following Owen's railroad route to the Mexican Pacific port of Topolobampo (see Map 3). Ten years later this project seemed on the verge of success, and a St. Louis newspaper declared of Stilwell: "He is the Collis P. Huntington and the Edward H. Harriman of the present day. . . . To the middle Southwest he is what James J. Hill is to the great Northwest." [1] In 1912, however, the Kansas City, Mexico, and Orient Railway went into receivership, and he left railroading for good.

Stilwell laid claim to an attribute which many promoters have seemed to possess at one time or another—second sight. Specifically he declared that at irregular intervals spirits appeared to him in dreams, once, when he was fifteen, to reveal his future wife to him, and from time to time thereafter to suggest new business projects or lines of action. When a hurricane destroyed Galveston shortly after he had built a protected Gulf terminus for his railroad at Port Arthur, he gave due credit to his spirit friends.[2] Alas, they could not protect him against earthly rivals, and he blamed Edward H. Harriman, John W. Gates, and other "cannibals of finance" when his Gulf railroad went into receivership and he lost control. Later he declared: "Had I worked as faithfully for England or her Colonists as I had for my country, in place of 25 years of persecution, I would now be in the House of Lords." [3] Similarly, when his Mexican project collapsed, he blamed the Madero revolution (of which his spirits had failed to warn him) and the ensuing confusion and property destruction. One may reasonably doubt whether this was the only explanation of his failure.

In later years Stillwell's spirits continued to visit him, with

[1] St. Louis *Globe-Democrat*, Dec. 18, 1910, pt. 4, p. 5.
[2] Arthur E. Stilwell and James R. Crowell, "I Had a Hunch," *Saturday Evening Post*, CC (Jan. 14, 1928), 77–78.
[3] Stilwell, *Forty Years of Business Life*, p. 31.

predictions of World War I and of the Russian revolutions of 1917 and advice as to how man might live to be 140 years old. The predictions were accurate enough, but something went wrong with the advice, for Stilwell died in 1928 at the age of only 68.

I

Arthur E. Stilwell was born on October 21, 1859, at Rochester, New York, into a prosperous family of Anglo-Dutch stock. His grandfather, Hamblin Stilwell, was a minor capitalist of upper New York state who had helped to build the Erie Canal and the New York Central Railroad and had been one of the founders of the Western Union Telegraph Company. At the age of fourteen Arthur ran away from home with $70 of savings and worked in a St. Louis hotel for several months, but his father soon lost most of his money in oil speculations, and the boy returned home to set himself up in a small printing shop. Characteristically, he had to hire someone to teach him the trade.[4]

Restive at the restricted life and limited possibilities in the East during the depression years of the 1870's, Stilwell drifted from one job to another, always on the lookout for new ways of making money. For a while he was the most promising salesman of the Travelers Insurance Company, of Hartford, Connecticut. In the mid-1880's he settled in Kansas City and founded the Real Estate Trust Company to build cheap houses and sell them to laborers on an installment plan not unlike a life insurance policy, promising to cancel all remaining payments on the death of the purchaser. As Stilwell told reporters with his usual

---

[4] Stilwell's autobiography, "I Had a Hunch" (written jointly with James R. Crowell) appears in the following issues of the *Saturday Evening Post:* Dec. 3, 1927, pp. 3 ff.; Dec. 17, pp. 24 ff.; Dec. 31, pp. 24 ff.; Jan. 14, 1928, pp. 31 ff.; Jan. 28, pp. 26 ff.; Feb. 4, pp. 38 ff. Somewhat briefer accounts of his early life occur in Stilwell, *Forty Years of Business Life,* cited in the preceding note, and Arthur E. Stilwell, *Cannibals of Finance: Fifteen Years' Contest with the Money Trust* (Chicago, 1912).

eye for publicity: "You can live in your endowment policy and raise chickens in its back yard." [5] With persistence and luck he persuaded A. J. Drexel, E. T. Stotesbury, and other prominent Philadelphia capitalists to invest $300,000 in this company, and within six months he had declared a dividend of 6 per cent. Soon he was making plans to finance buildings and stockyards all over the Middle West.

As Stilwell surveyed his new domain, however, he quickly realized that almost unique developmental opportunities lay at his very feet in Kansas City, potentially a major railroad center and distribution point, which as yet contained only one grain elevator and wholly inadequate storage and transfer facilities of any kind. Late in 1886 he took up an unused concession for a belt-line railroad around the city, set out for Philadelphia, and before he stepped off the train had drawn up all the necessary papers to issue $1,000,000 of 6 per cent railroad bonds and $2,000,000 of common stock. Once again his Philadelphia friends subscribed handsomely, and he had no trouble selling the remaining bonds in Kansas City. By similarly prompt action he managed to buy up 160 acres of neglected bottom lands along the Missouri River, before anyone else realized how the railroad would increase their value. Between 1887 and 1891 Stilwell's company completed the Kansas City Belt Line and connected it with the major transcontinental systems passing through the city.

Long before the belt line's completion Stilwell had been thinking about his plans for an even more ambitious railroad which would connect Kansas City with the Gulf of Mexico and break the Eastern monopoly on the transportation of Western grain for export. Fearing that premature announcement of his plans might injure his belt-line company, he started with a short southward extension to coal fields at Hume, Missouri, and then to the Joplin lead mines. Finally on January 26, 1893, he organized

[5] Darrell Garwood, *Crossroads of America: The Story of Kansas City* (New York, 1948), pp. 132–133.

the Kansas City, Pittsburg, and Gulf Railroad, with a charter to build through Fort Smith, Arkansas, and Shreveport, Louisiana, to the Gulf of Mexico, and his plan stood completely revealed.[6]

For a few months Stilwell managed to secure enough capital for his Gulf project from his customary local and Eastern sources, but they were soon dried up by the Panic of 1893. In his search for capital during the next four years his "hunches" led him first to financiers in the Netherlands and later to George M. Pullman, the railroad-car magnate, who had once been a protégé of Stilwell's grandfather. Aided by their stock purchases and loans, the Gulf railroad made steady progress toward its goal, and, indeed, during the first year of the depression it accounted for fully one-third of all new American railroad construction. As the track drew near the Gulf, Stilwell abandoned his original plan to make Galveston his terminal and decided to build a new city on Lake Sabine, to be called Port Arthur in his honor. The through railroad from Kansas City to Port Arthur was opened with great ceremony on September 11, 1897, and about a year later the company finished a ship canal from Lake Sabine to the Gulf.

Undoubtedly, as Stilwell's many autobiographical writings maintained, the Gulf railroad did much to develop southern Missouri, Arkansas, Louisana, and eastern Texas, for Stilwell quickly associated his company with colonization, mining, lumbering, and public utilities projects and subscribed in his own name to several humanitarian enterprises, such as a night school and free library in Kansas City.[7] Other evidence, however, somewhat tarnishes the luster of his self-publicity. He boasted

[6] Rose McMaster, "Origin and Development of the Kansas City Southern Railway Company," unpublished M.A. thesis, University of Missouri, 1936, pp. 9–14. See also Stilwell and Crowell, "I Had a Hunch," *passim.*

[7] "I Had a Hunch," Jan. 14, 1928, pp. 77–78, Jan. 28, p. 86; Stilwell, *Cannibals of Finance,* pp. 28, 39–41; Kansas City *Post,* July 20, 1907, sec. 2, p. 3.

that he did not receive special gifts of stock in return for his promoting activities, but one of his subordinates later declared that he made up for this by speculating in lands along the route of the railroad. He is said to have received $40,000 from a promoter of townsites in return for locating his railroad shops at Pittsburg, Kansas, and to have publicized a new town, Mena, Arkansas (named after Queen Wilhelmina of the Netherlands), so successfully that a syndicate made a profit of $150,000 from town lots within six months. Edward H. Harriman declared that Stilwell deliberately located his tracks several miles from existing towns in order to buy up the intervening land for speculation.[8]

Lacking experience in railroading and being eager to show quick profits to the waiting public, Stilwell often sacrificed thoroughness to speed. When later owners inspected the Kansas City, Pittsburg, and Gulf Railroad, they discovered many unnecessary curves and steep grades, light rails, temporary bridges, narrow cuts, and sections of unballasted roadbed, as well as inadequate shop facilities, sidings, and stations. It appears also that Stilwell gambled on finishing the railroad and earning profits before his various bond issues matured. Litigation over the Port Arthur Canal and a mild business depression delayed completion of the railroad, and after its inauguration washouts along the line and two epidemics of yellow fever in the Deep South cut into business. Stilwell also tried to build up lumber traffic in Arkansas by cutting rates, and this action embroiled him with connecting railroads, which for a time refused to accept his freight cars at junction points.[9]

By the end of 1898 Stilwell was once again in trouble, but this time his guardian spirits deserted him. George M. Pullman

[8] William R. Draper, "Kansas City Southern," *Railroad Magazine*, XLIV (Oct. 1947), 18, 21–22; George Kennan, *E. H. Harriman: A Biography* (Boston, 1922), I, 216–217.

[9] McMaster, "Kansas City Southern," pp. 33–35, 39–41; Stilwell and Crowell, "I Had a Hunch," Jan. 28, 1928, pp. 86–88; Draper, "Kansas City Southern," p. 27.

agreed to advance a new loan of $3,000,000, but to Stilwell's consternation Pullman died before signing the loan agreement. When he approached his Eastern and Dutch investors for money, they compelled him to appoint several new Eastern members to his board of directors. Soon a battle royal broke out between pro-Stilwell forces, mostly located in the Middle West, and anti-Stilwell forces, mostly Easterners, for control of the parent company, the Missouri, Kansas, and Texas Trust Company. Stilwell's principal enemies were Edward H. Harriman, who controlled such rival railroads as the Illinois Central and the Chicago and Alton; John W. ("Bet-a-Million") Gates, the flashy speculator who was later associated with William C. Greene; and Ernest Thalmann of the legal firm Ladenburg, Thalmann, and Company, the financial allies of Standard Oil.

Exploiting the Eastern fear that the railroad was being mismanaged, these three and others forced the company into receivership on March 30, 1899, and a year later Stilwell ceased to be president. Gates also forced him out of the parent trust company (now renamed the Guardian Trust Company), but eventually Stilwell disproved his accusations and was voted back into the presidency. But he never regained control of his Gulf railroad, which was now renamed the Kansas City Southern Railway. A local newspaper remarked sorrowfully that with a majority of Easterners on the board of directors it was no longer really a Kansas City line.[10]

For the rest of life Stilwell denounced the men who had raided his cherished railroad project, accusing them of forcing down stock quotations in order to "make a killing" and to prevent competition with other lines in which they were interested. In later years he lashed out at the whole "money trust" in a book, *Cannibals of Finance:*

[10] McMaster, "Kansas City Southern," pp. 36–45; Stilwell and Crowell, "I Had a Hunch," Jan. 28, 1928, pp. 89–90; Stilwell, *Forty Years of Business Life,* p. 11; Stilwell, *Cannibals of Finance,* chaps. vi–viii; Rippy, *Latin America and the Industrial Age,* p. 161.

Out West were two men [himself and Edward M. Dickinson, an associate] striving to help their nation, two men who had lived clean lives, men who did not know the first act in the game of corruption. . . . On the other side were unprincipled men, men connected with great banks, with their roots of influence reaching all over the land; with hundreds of thousands of dollars they had bought Senators and Congressmen.

Again, quoting Samuel Untermyer, he declared: "You cannot build a mile of railroad in the United States today without permission from the money god. . . . This is not a republic. It is a money oligarchy." [11]

There was something in what Stilwell said, for by 1900 monopolistic finance seemed like a Goliath over the land. It strains the imagination, however, to accept the picture which he painted of himself—David, clad in skins and armed only with a slingshot.

II

Stilwell rebounded from defeat with a resilience which amazed his friends. On February 10, 1900, about a month after his retirement from the presidency of the Guardian Trust Company, a group of admirers gathered at the Midland Hotel in Kansas City for a testimonial banquet in his honor, to demonstrate their faith in him with the time-honored symbol of a silver loving cup. Speaker after speaker heaped praise on him, and, not to be outdone, the irrepressible promoter declared that in his gratitude to Kansas City he had formed an even greater project. "My new proposition will do as much for Kansas City as the Nicaragua Canal," he predicted. "It will open up the Orient." Next day in the office of his friend, Dr. W. S. Woods, he explained what he had in mind. He intended to build a trunk-line railroad southwest from Kansas City across Kansas, Oklahoma, Texas, Chihuahua, and Sinaloa to a virtually unknown seaport of which he had heard, Topolobampo. Impressed by his optimism and arguments, Woods told him to go to Mexico and

[11] Stilwell, *Cannibals of Finance*, pp. 30–31, 35.

make the necessary arrangements, promising him $500,000 in subscriptions on his return.[12]

Like the Kansas City Southern project Stilwell's new idea was a combination of fantasy and shrewd insight. After the disappearance of the frontier line in the 1890's and the completion of the great American transcontinental railroads no new hinterland remained but the "Great American Desert" of the Southwest. At first the dryness of this area gave pause to railroad men, and the insolvency of the Atchison, Topeka, and Santa Fe Railroad in 1893 was blamed partly upon the losses suffered by its southwestern lines. By the turn of the century, however, public opinion was beginning to shift as Texas and Oklahoma grew in population and the Santa Fe and Southern Pacific Railroads earned profits in southern California. Might not the same be done in the Southwest? If so, the "Great American Desert" was desert no longer.[13]

Another factor in Stilwell's thinking was Kansas City's awakening interest in northern Mexico. In 1890, for example, a visiting delegation of merchants from Sonora brought about the establishment of an "International Bank" to compete with New York for Mexican exchange. During the late 1890's the gubernatorial administration of Miguel Ahumada in Chihuahua caused favorable comments in the United States for its efficiency and progress, and American-Mexican interests unintentionally broke ground for Stilwell by projecting two short-line railroads in Chihuahua. One of these, the Rio Grande, Sierra Madre, and Pacific Railroad, was developed by stockholders in a New York-owned ranching and mining company just south of the border for the purpose of carrying its products to El Paso. The other, the Chihuahua and Pacific Railroad, was the project of Alfred A.

[12] Kansas City *Star*, Feb. 11, 1900, pp. 1–2; Kansas City *Journal*, Feb. 11, 1900, p. 7. See also Stilwell's more colorful account in *Cannibals of Finance*, p. 97, and *Forty Years of Business Life*, pp. 16–17.

[13] John Moody, "The Kansas City, Mexico, and Orient Railway," *Moody's Magazine*, IX (Feb. 1910), 119–120.

Spendlove, general manager of the Chihuahua Mining Company, and Enrique C. Creel, one of the leading politicians of the state, manager of the Banco Minero of Chihuahua, and soon to be a leading *Científico* in Mexico City.[14]

Stilwell's trip to Mexico brought him his customary success. First of all he stopped at Chihuahua to explain his plan to Creel, who was delighted to hear of it and regaled his visitor with stories of great forests on the Sierra Madre and millions of tons of valuable ores on the dump heaps of old mines. He agreed to become vice-president of the railroad and turn over his own concession for the Chihuahua and Pacific, which included terminal rights at Topolobampo. Upon Stilwell's arrival in Mexico City he was received at the station by a relative of Díaz, who took him at once to the palace for an interview. According to Stilwell's account, when he spread out his maps before Díaz, the president told him that such a railroad had been his great ambition, and when Stilwell suggested a subsidy of $5,000 per mile, Díaz declared that by an amazing coincidence the Railroad Law of 1899 permitted a subsidy for a railroad along this route and that he would arrange for Federal and state governments to share the burden. Stilwell ended his account: "As he promised, the next day at eleven o'clock the concession arrived." [15]

The terms of the contract which Díaz and Stilwell drew up

[14] *Mexican Financier*, Oct. 18, 1890, pp. 87–88; Charles F. Lummis, "The Awakening of a Nation," *Harper's Magazine*, XCIV (Feb. 1897), 372–373; Powell, *Railroads of Mexico*, p. 157; United States, *Consular Reports*, no. 202 (July 1897), p. 352, no. 241 (Oct. 1900), pp. 117–118.

[15] An associate, W. A. Rule, had asked the governors of nine American states and the assistant secretary of state to send telegrams to Díaz endorsing Stilwell (Stilwell, *Forty Years of Business Life*, pp. 17–18). Díaz was correct in stating that the Railroad Law of 1899 authorized a subsidy for the proposed railroad, but Stilwell's account oversimplifies the granting of his concessions. What he received in April was only a preliminary decree. The Chihuahua and Pacific concession was formally transferred to his company by later actions on July 27 and Nov. 26 (México, Secretaría de comunicaciones y obras públicas, *Reseña histórica y estadística de los ferrocarriles de jurisdicción federal desde 1º de enero de 1900 hasta 31 de diciembre de 1903* [México, 1905], pp. 18, 36).

during 1900, modified somewhat in later years, have been described as among the most favorable to come from the Díaz government. They included a ninety-nine-year title to a right of way seventy meters wide from Presidio del Norte to Chihuahua and allowed free importation of construction materials for five years. Surveying was to start within two months, and the whole road was to be completed in four years. As usual, passenger and freight rates were fixed, and a deposit of 32,000 pesos was required as a bond. The exact subsidy promised seems to be open to question. Stilwell wrote later that it amounted to $5,000 a mile (apparently American money). A revised contract of July 15, 1902, specified subsidies of 12,000 pesos per kilometer and 7,000 pesos per kilometer on two parts of the line. A third contract of August 2, 1905, divided the railroad into five parts with subsidies ranging from 7,000 pesos to 15,000 pesos. One estimate of the total amount of the subsidy, appearing in 1910, set the figure at $3,000,000, gold.[16]

While he was in Mexico, Stilwell also came to terms with another promoter who had preceded him at Topolobampo—Albert K. Owen. At some previous time the two had apparently met and discussed the railroad project, and on April 21, 1900, they and Owen's wife signed a contract under which the Owens turned over to Stilwell certain lands and other rights which they possessed at Topolobampo. In return for Owen's help in developing the idea of a trans-Mexican railroad Stilwell promised a graduated scale of compensation, based on the amount of railroad actually built (up to 550 miles), and further payment for the lands at Topolobampo. He agreed to give Owen not cash but Mexican bonds and bonds of the Stilwell railroad company. Although Stilwell never carried out all his plans for

[16] México, *Reseña de los ferrocarriles*, pp. 36–38; *Diario oficial*, Aug. 10, 1900, as cited in Senior, "Kansas City, Mexico, and Orient Railroad," p. 60; *Diario oficial*, July 15, 1902, pp. 598–599, Aug. 2, 1905, pp. 457–458; Stilwell and Crowell, "I Had a Hunch," Feb. 4, 1928, p. 45; Landon Gates, "The Stilwell International Trans-continental Railroad," *Bankers' Magazine*, LXXX (April 1910), 615.

Topolobampo, he did use the land around the harbor, and when he failed to make the required payments to the Owens, Mrs. Owen sued him and was awarded $20,426.22 on August 19, 1913.[17]

When Stilwell returned from Mexico to Kansas City at the end of April 1900, he found that Woods, W. A. Rule, and other friends had carried out their promise to raise $500,000 for the new project. On April 30 the Kansas City, Mexico, and Orient Railway Company was incorporated in Kansas, with Stilwell as president and other officials and directors recruited from his closest associates in the old Gulf railroad company. A month later he organized two subsidiary companies, the Union Construction Company and the International Construction Company, to survey and lay the northern and southern sections of the railroad respectively. In July he allowed it to be announced that he planned to issue $35,000,000 of bonds, mostly through the Guardian Trust Company, and that he already had enough capital on hand to begin construction operations, since two or three million dollars had been subscribed and the Mexican government would eventually pay $3,500,000 in subsidies.[18]

But the Eastern financiers who had forced him out of the Gulf railroad company continued to dog his footsteps. Shortly after his return from Mexico the directors of the Guardian Trust Company reinstated him as president and raised his salary. Infuriated at news of this, Gates turned against the trust company and on November 30, 1900, secured a decree of receivership against it on the grounds that it owned a large amount of real estate in violation of its charter. Before the receivership was ended two years later, a considerable amount of the company's property had been sold off for a fraction of its real value,

[17] Senior, "Kansas City, Mexico, and Orient Railroad," pp. 55–58; St. Louis *Globe-Democrat*, Jan. 14, 1911, p. 4.

[18] Kansas City *Star*, April 27, 1900, p. 1, April 28, p. 1; Stilwell, *Forty Years of Business Life*, p. 18; *Moody's Manual*, 1903, pp. 643, 1516, and 1911, pp. 566–568; *Railroad Age*, XXX (July 6, 1900), 18.

and Stilwell's enemies in the Kansas City Southern management
further weakened the trust company by refusing to pay a debt
of $475,000 and by starting countersuits against it. These actions
made it impossible for the Guardian Trust Company to finance
the Kansas City, Mexico, and Orient Railway, but Stilwell
promptly organized a new financing company, the United States
and Mexican Trust Company, and transferred the Mexican concession to it.[19]

The identity of officials of the financing and construction
companies gives some idea of the breadth and effectiveness of
his appeal for funds. E. L. Martin, W. S. Woods, W. A. Rule,
and many other old friends of Missouri, Kansas, and Nebraska
made up the original nucleus of the Kansas City, Mexico, and
Orient Railway Company. Soon, however, new names appeared
in the list: Edward M. Dickinson, for thirteen years general
manager of the Union Pacific Railroad; J. T. Odell, who had
built the Bessemer and Lake Erie Railroad for Andrew Carnegie;
John F. Wallace, formerly general manager of the Illinois Central Railroad and chief engineer of the Panama Canal; George J.
Gould, son of Jay Gould and president of the Missouri Pacific
Railroad; Warren G. Purdy, ex-president of the Chicago, Rock
Island, and Pacific; and others. Vice-President Cecil Braithwaite
of London represented the many British investors whom Stilwell eventually attracted to his company. In accordance with
his promise Enrique C. Creel soon became a vice-president in
the company, and among several prominent Mexicans associated
with the project were two relatives of President Díaz, Lorenzo
Elizaga and Alonzo Fernández.[20]

The financing and construction companies formed only the

[19] Stilwell, *Cannibals of Finance*, chaps. xii–xiii, and *Forty Years of
Business Life*, pp. 19–20, 26–27. Stilwell quotes a letter from D. J. Haff
pronouncing his management of the Guardian Trust Company spotless.
Haff had been a director of the Kansas City, Mexico, and Orient Railway from its origin.
[20] Gates, "Stilwell International Railroad," p. 622.

foundation of an elaborate pyramid of corporations which Stilwell organized during the next decade to develop and speculate in resources along the route of his railroad. Stilwell had a hand in so many ventures that no one can be sure of drawing up a complete list. He set up the Western Tie and Lumber Company of Arkansas to sell lumber to the construction companies and to settlers. Much of the landed property was administered through the Kansas City, Mexico, and Orient Townsite Company, the Kansas City, Mexico, and Orient Land Syndicate, and numerous subsidiaries. Stilwell promoted mining properties in northern and northwestern Mexico through a great variety of companies. He was probably president of most of these, and he joined the boards of other companies, such as the Palmarejo Mining Company, one of the most famous British mining corporations of the late Díaz period.[21] Like Greene he had a taste for letterheads.

III

Stilwell's optimistic speech to his banqueting friends on the evening of February 10, 1900, was the opening gun of one of the most elaborate American-Mexican publicity campaigns of the later Díaz period. In setting forth the advantages of his railroad he used the same arguments, phrased sometimes in almost the same words, as those of Albert K. Owen twenty years earlier. This is hardly surprising, for his enterprise was almost identical

[21] In addition to companies named in the text Stilwell is known to have been associated with the Tri-State Development Company, the Chihuahua and Sinaloa Development Company, the Sierra Madre Development Company, the Fuerte Valley Mining Company, the Rio Grande Coal Fields Company, the Mexico-Orient Mining Syndicate, and the Urique Mining Company. There were undoubtedly others. See Senior, "Kansas City, Mexico, and Orient Railroad," p. 64; *Anglo-American and Mexican Mining Guide*, XIII (April 30, 1910), 57, Suppl., iv, XIII (Aug. 31, 1910), 117, XV (May 31, 1912), 70, XV (June 29, 1912), 83–84; United States, *Consular Reports*, no. 259 (April 1902), p. 483.

with Owen's railroad project, except that the American portion of it ran through the Southwest instead of the Deep South. He proposed to lay his tracks directly southwest from Kansas City, running diagonally through Kansas, Oklahoma, and western Texas to the Rio Grande at Presidio del Norte, about midway between El Paso and Laredo. From here the line would continue to Chihuahua, running partly over the tracks of the Chihuahua and Pacific Railroad, on to the southwest over the Sierra Madre, and down the valley of the Fuerte River to Topolobampo, near the mouth of the river (see Map 3).

The rail distance between Kansas City and Topolobampo was eventually fixed at 1,659 miles, and Stilwell called his road the shortest transcontinental line from any Midwestern center to the Pacific, fully four hundred miles shorter than any other railroad running west out of Kansas City. He expected it to funnel the products of the Pacific basin, especially the Far East, to his home city, for, as a journalist put it, "if Minneapolis can conduct a large trade with China, by rail and steamship, through Seattle, it would seem to be feasible for Kansas City to do the same thing through Topolobampo. The difference in distance [apparently by land and water combined] is insignificant. The Southern route would be open all the year round. No Montana snow blockades would detain train loads of tea." [22]

Similarly the railroad would form a great shortcut to the little-known resources and markets of western South America. Not long after Stilwell set his project in motion, the United States began to dig the Panama Canal, but if the prospect of competition alarmed Stilwell, he did not show it, for in 1910 John Moody reported that since Topolobampo lay on a direct line between Panama and the Orient the company expected increased trade after the completion of the canal. Such far-flung commercial ambitions required much more than a mere railroad line. Stilwell promised that his company would build a port as good as

[22] Gates, "Stilwell International Railroad," pp. 615–616; Kansas City *Star*, April 28, 1900, p. 1.

any on the Pacific coast and establish a line of steamers to the Far East, South America, New Zealand, and Australia.[23]

Stilwell and his publicists lavished their richest adjectives on the resources of the railroad's hinterland in the American Southwest and in Mexico. Landon Gates declared that "every mile of the Orient's line is capable of producing revenue," and a writer in the *Financial World* tumbled forth clichés and mixed metaphors to proclaim that the railroad

will throw open to the fortune hunter a new and vast domain. . . . Like all railroads, it will be a pathfinder. The advance courier for great manufacturing enterprises. All along its iron ribs prosperous cities and towns will blossom into existence. All these different sources will be like so many veins to carry freight and passenger business to the main artery, the railroad.[24]

In Kansas and Oklahoma the railroad could depend on the famous bumper crops which would draw settlers to the lands along the route and create new towns overnight, as in the days of the great "sooner" rush, and in Texas broomcorn, cattle, and cotton would furnish dependable traffic. Even cotton growers farther east in the Gulf states would find it profitable to ship their bales to the Orient along the new railroad.[25]

As for Mexico, Stilwell's writers added their superlatives to the waves of propaganda issued by railroads, land companies, and other more or less speculative ventures of the early twentieth century describing the west coast as a second Garden of Eden. Vice-President W. W. Sylvester of the Orient company, who accompanied Stilwell to Mexico in 1900, returned with a glowing account of the Fuerte Valley, although there is no evidence to indicate that his trip had taken him that far West: "Fuerte is Spanish for fertile. . . . The entire river valley is one of the

[23] Moody, "Kansas City, Mexico, and Orient Railway," p. 123; Stilwell, *Cannibals of Finance*, p. 126; *Building a Great Transcontinental Railroad* [New York, 1906], p. 16.

[24] *Building a Transcontinental Railroad*, pp. 7–8.

[25] Gates, "Stilwell International Railroad," pp. 619–620.

richest farming countries in the world. . . . Farmers there net $200 an acre." Stilwell himself told another writer that the valley, fertile as the Nile, would yield annually from five to eight cuttings of alfalfa and two crops of beans, corn, and potatoes, while farmers could pick grapes for three months each year, figs for four months, lemons for six months, oranges for nine months, and bananas and strawberries all year round. As for sugar cane, it matured in a year, and some fields were harvested for as many as twenty years without being replanted. "If the Hawaiian Islanders, numbering a bare 150,000 souls, are able to produce a crop of sugar worth $25,000,000 annually," asked the writer, "What may be expected of the Mexican west coast?" [26]

Between the last great American frontier and the paradise of Sinaloa the railroad ran through "the richest mineralized section of the world," for, according to Gates, the mines within thirty miles of its route had yielded fully one-third of all the existing coined silver in the world, even in a period when mules furnished the only transportation. Writing in 1910, he called attention to the Guggenheims' $5,000,000 smelter at Chihuahua, which was already too small after three years in operation. Sylvester called the Fuerte River "one vast gold placer mine" and declared that in Chihuahua the railroad would pass through "600,000 acres of semi-anthracite smokeless coal, in seams from two to eleven feet thick." Another writer termed the region between Urique and Choix "one of the richest copper districts of the world." As for timber resources, Sylvester reported that the railroad would pass through "extensive, untouched forests of long leaf pine, oak, mahogany and a species of tree that makes railroad ties that are almost indestructible." [27]

[26] Kansas City *Star*, April 28, 1900, p. 1; Courtenay De Kalb, "Topolobampo and the Fuerte Valley," *Nation*, LXXXII (May 31, 1906), 446–447; *Mexican Herald*, national ed., Sept. 16, 1909, p. 80.
[27] Gates, "Stilwell International Railroad," pp. 619–620; Kansas City *Star*, April 28, 1900, p. 1; *Railroad Age*, XXXIX (June 23, 1905), 1132.

It goes without saying that Stilwell's writings laid stress on his friendly relations with Díaz and the Mexican officials. The Mexican president professed himself much impressed by the long list of Stilwell's associates and by his great accomplishments "without the aid of Wall Street," and Stilwell, in his turn, pronounced Díaz "a second Solomon." In one speech at the Crystal Palace in London, Stilwell must have amazed the reticent English audience by declaring of Díaz:

If I were a painter, I would spend my days in carving [*sic*] his likeness out of solid granite; were I an historian, I would give my time to writing of the man as I know him; were I a poet, I would for ever sing his praises; but being neither a painter, sculptor, historian, nor poet, all I can do is to rest in the satisfaction that he is my friend and the friend of this railroad.[28]

In view of Stilwell's past financial difficulties and the activities of his Eastern enemies, his publicists took great pains to set forth the safe, solid financial condition of the new project. Other railroads could not compete for the heavy traffic of the Orient's hinterland, declared Gates, for none paralleled its route, and intersecting lines would cross it at right angles and would serve as feeders. Contributions from cities and towns in the area were taken as indications of future profits. For example, as early as October 1900 Sylvester reported that the people of Sweetwater and San Angelo, Texas, had given over $100,000 to the construction company, and other American communities and the Mexican states of Chihuahua and Sinaloa were to donate money also, to supplement the Mexican Federal subsidy. Gates praised the precise and generous terms of the Mexican concession, which "will be appreciated by us in the United States where we do not know from one year to another what heavy restrictions legislation will lay on our roads." [29]

[28] Stilwell, *Forty Years of Business Life*, p. 18; *Anglo-American and Mexican Mining Guide*, XI (July 29, 1908), 104.

[29] Gates, "Stilwell International Railroad," pp. 615–617; *Railroad Age*, XXX (Oct. 26, 1900), 337.

In one other respect the Kansas City, Mexico, and Orient Railway was expected to differ from other companies in the United States: "It will be a railroad that has not bled its stockholders; a railroad free from stock jugglery" in contrast to the "big fellows" who "play with railroads like a college boy . . . with his football." [30] Stilwell and others boasted of their low capitalization, for in 1910 the authorized bonded indebtedness was stated to be only $22,500 per mile, and John Moody estimated that the total amount of bonds and stocks issued would reach only $43,000 per mile in contrast to figures between $50,000 and $75,000 for other railroads. Gates admitted that the crucial test of the company's expectations would be its ability to meet fixed charges on bonds, but contrasting the Orient's estimate of $900 per mile for such annual charges with figures as high as $3,800 for other transcontinental railroads, he declared that "only a great calamity" could cause a receivership. In 1910 Moody reprinted an estimate that the Orient would eventually earn $5,000,000 a year, as against fixed annual charges of only $2,500,000, and concluded that Stilwell's securities "present exceptionally good opportunities for the investor who is willing to stake his money a little into the future." [31]

Not content with glowing adjectives, impressive statistics, and businesslike photographs in magazine articles and pamphlets, Stilwell presented himself to the investor as the very symbol of prosperity. Elegant in well-tailored suits, with his mustache neatly waxed, he granted interviews and spoke to civic meetings in bland, urbane sentences. Often he gave his hypnotic personality full play by inviting prospective investors to accompany him on tours of inspection, as railroad construction progressed.

[30] *Building a Transcontinental Railroad*, p. 3.

[31] The annual fixed charges of other American transcontinental railroads were listed as follows: Atchison, Topeka, and Santa Fe, $1,783; Northern Pacific, $1,778; Great Northern, $2,273; Southern Pacific, $2,281; Union Pacific, $2,534; and Western Pacific, about $3,800. See Gates, "Stilwell International Railroad," pp. 616–618; Moody, "Kansas City, Mexico, and Orient Railway," pp. 121–122, 124.

From all parts of the United States and England came businessmen and journalists, sometimes over a hundred at a time, to
travel for days at the expense of the company and see for
themselves what the Orient was doing. Stilwell wrote later:
"Never before have at least half of the stockholders in any
railroad seen the property they were helping build. They invested with their eyes open." [32]

Whether this was true or not, Stilwell certainly treated them
to a unique combination of high-pressure salesmanship and
sightseeing. Sometimes the groups went as far as Mexico City
over connecting lines, and on one occasion Creel gave a banquet for 130 tourists in Chihuahua, ordering food and waiters
sent in a special railroad car from the leading caterer in Mexico
City. The most influential visitors enjoyed the facilities of
Stilwell's luxurious private Pullman, lined with mahogany and
fitted out with bedroom, private bath, all kinds of dining
facilities, and even a reed organ which Stilwell, a Christian
Scientist, used for private religious services.[33] In a fanciful
picture of one such party Henry Baerlein describes Stilwell
expatiating "very glowingly" on his railroad to a group of
businessmen in his private car:

After this he gives them each a book of Christian Science hymns,
and with his secretary playing the harmonium he leads the voices;
and it is delicious when those corpulent old gentlemen take from
their mouths the fat cigars and warble. Sometimes one of them at
the conclusion of a hymn or even, prematurely, of a verse, will have
financial doubts as to the railways. He will ask a question and he will
be satisfactorily answered. Then the singing is resumed.[34]

Thus once again Religion served as the handmaiden of Business.

[32] Stilwell, *Forty Years of Business Life*, p. 30; *Anglo-American and
Mexican Mining Guide*, VIII (March 29, 1905), 36, XIII (April 30,
1910), 57.

[33] Kansas City *Star*, April 4, 1937, p. 30; Stilwell and Crowell, "I Had
a Hunch," Feb. 4, 1928, p. 46. Stilwell also composed hymns in his
spare time (Kansas City *Star*, May 5, 1906, p. 10).

[34] Henry Baerlein, *Mexico: The Land of Unrest* (London, 1913), p. 84,
note.

IV

Six months after the incorporation of the Kansas City, Mexico, and Orient Railway Company one of its vice-presidents, W. W. Sylvester, predicted that the whole line would be completed and in operation within two and a half years. Events were to prove him an extremely bad prophet. When the company was incorporated, a short stretch of track already existed, laid by the Chihuahua and Pacific Railroad Company east and west of Chihuahua. Stilwell's engineers decided to extend this section in both directions and begin construction on the Pacific coast and in Kansas at the same time. Perhaps fearing trouble from rival lines, they did not build out of Kansas City at first. Instead, on July 4, 1901, the first rail was laid and the first spike driven in the American section at Emporia, Kansas, after the traditional elaborate ceremonies. At about the same time work must have begun on the Pacific section, for by August 30 forty-five miles had been graded east of Port Stilwell, a newly named terminal on Topolobampo Bay, and on March 26, 1902, tracklaying began east of Chihuahua. One may form some idea of the extent to which Stilwell fell behind his own timetable from the fact that although he expected to complete this section to the Rio Grande by the end of 1903 only eighty-seven miles of track had been laid here fully four years after that.[35]

There is little reason to follow construction figures in any detail from this point. Just before its receivership in March 1912 Stilwell's railroad had placed in operation three unconnected segments of track: 642 miles, running from Wichita, Kansas, to Granada, Texas; 287 miles, running from Márquez, Chihuahua, through Chihuahua city, to Sánchez, just east of the mountains; and 73 miles, mostly in the Fuerte Valley, from Hornillos to Topolobampo Bay. The company did not yet have any track

[35] *Railroad Age*, XXX (Oct. 26, 1900), 337; XXXII (July 12, Aug. 30, 1901), 25, 193; XXXIII (April 4, 1902), 599; XLIV (Dec. 6, 1907), 802–803.

running into Kansas City but turned its freight cars over to the Santa Fe and other lines. However, an affiliated corporation, the Kansas City Outer Belt and Electric Railroad, had secured a valuable land grant running for six miles from the Missouri River around Kansas City, Kansas. By 1912 this stretch was graded and ready for tracklaying, and the company engineers planned to build a bridge across the Missouri River and extend the line to Wichita (see Map 3).

As the company inaugurated its few isolated strips of track, it purchased a little rolling stock here and there and began to haul local traffic. In succeeding years the company placed heavy orders, and by 1911 its rolling stock, both owned outright and held under car trusts, included 65 locomotives, 26 passenger cars, and 1,866 freight cars of various types.[36] During the company's first ten years of existence the predicted transcontinental cargo vessels had not yet put in an appearance at Topolobampo, but the Mexican and Orient Steamship Company, an affiliate of the railroad, operated small steamers and sailing vesssels on a regular schedule between Guaymas, Topolobampo, Mazatlán, and La Paz, Lower California, and the Pacific Coast Steamship Company supplied a monthly connection with San Francisco.[37]

The financial organization of Stilwell's operating and construction companies with their affiliates and subordinates was fully as complicated as that of his earlier projects. The Kansas

[36] Kansas City *Times*, March 9, 1912, p. 3. Moody listed trackage in operation on June 30, 1910, as follows: owned in fee (mostly in Mexico), 485.93 miles; operated through control of securities (in Texas), 237.43 miles; trackage rights, 17.13 miles; sidings, 93.08 miles (*Moody's Manual*, 1911, pp. 566–568).

[37] United States, *Consular Reports*, no. 306 (March 1906), p. 220; *Poor's Manual*, 1908, p. 552; *Bulletin of the Pan-American Union*, XXVI (May 1908), 1037–1038. The company applied for a concession to improve Topolobampo harbor, but it is not evident that any work was done (United States, *Consular Reports*, no. 329 [Feb. 1908], p. 103). It also contracted with the Hamburg-American Steamship Company for service between Topolobampo and the Far East after the completion of the railroad.

City, Mexico, and Orient Railway Company was incorporated
to operate most of the completed lines, but the laws of Texas
required a separate operating company, the Kansas City, Mexico,
and Orient Railway of Texas, for the five hundred miles of
track which the company expected to control in that state,
and another distinct company, the Kansas City, Outer Belt, and
Electric Railroad, was to possess the vital segment of track
leading into Kansas City and lease it to the principal operating
company.

For better or for worse, Stilwell followed the example of
many earlier American railroads and organized separate companies to grade the right of way and lay the track. His two
principal engineering outfits, the Union Construction Company
and the International Construction Company, were capitalized
at $10,000,000 and $31,000,000 respectively. He assigned them
sections of the route north and south of Lone Wolf, Oklahoma.
In return for constructing these sections, they were to receive
for each mile of track from $15,000 to $18,000 in bonds of the
railroad company, $16,000 in preferred stock, and from $12,000
to $12,500 in common stock. Since the International Construc-
tion Company had the longer and harder task of the two, it
was to receive $2,500,000 extra for construction in the Sierra
Madre and also the Mexican governmental subsidies, a two-
thirds interest in all new townsites, and stock in Stilwell's
various timber and mining companies.[38]

The Kansas City, Mexico, and Orient Railway, which was

[38] *Poor's Manual*, 1908, p. 554; Kansas City *Times*, March 8, 1912, p. 2;
Railroad Age, XXXV (March 20, 1903), 441–444. Eventually purchasers
of International Construction stock were promised the following on
dissolution: $17,225 of K.C.M. & O. 4 per cent bonds; $16,940 of its
preferred stock; and $12,600 of its common stock. In addition, each share
of International Construction stock carried with it 5.5 shares of stock in
Mexican Timber Field Company, 20 shares in Rio Grande Coal Fields
Company, 800 shares in Mexico and Orient Town Site Company, 10
shares in Chihuahua and Sinaloa Development Company, and 20 shares
in Sierra Madre Development Company (William Z. Ripley, *Railroads:
Finance and Organization* [New York, 1927], p. 17, note).

to operate most of the completed lines, did not issue any bonds at first but confined itself to cumulative and preferred stock at the rate of $20,000 of each per mile of track laid. Most of this went to the construction companies, but an undetermined amount was offered on the market. The railroad, in turn, was financed by a parent trust company, the United States and Mexican Trust Company, but since this was a new creation, it had to appeal to investors too. Thus when Stilwell set out on his promoting campaigns in the East and abroad after 1900, he carried a bulky portfolio of securities issued by the trust company, the railroad companies, the construction companies, and the various land, mining, and other affiliated companies. Doubtless he was prepared to sell some, at a considerable discount if necessary, and offer others as gifts or bonuses.

His first concern was to sell enough stock in the construction companies to start building. Determined to finance these companies and his whole far-flung project without appealing to the hated tycoons of Wall Street, Stilwell offered his securities directly to private investors, large and small. In this, as a later writer commented, he proved "quite extraordinarily skillful," and it has been estimated that over four thousand persons bought a total of $13,000,000 of stock in the construction companies. During the winter of 1901–1902 and again in 1903 he visited Europe and managed to attract a large amount of British capital with the aid of Baron Boxall, Sir Alfred Newton, Cecil Braithwaite, and other British financiers, some of whom soon appeared among the company directors. Stilwell also placed an undetermined number of securities in Belgium and the Netherlands.[39]

In 1906 the Kansas City, Mexico, and Orient Railway Company began to issue its first bonds, a series of first-mortgage gold 4 per cents, dated February 1, 1901, and designed for outright sale to the public, for purchase of equipment (at the

[39] *Railway Age Gazette*, LII (March 15, 1912), 461–462; Kansas City *Star*, Feb. 2, 1902, p. 2; *Railroad Age*, XXXVI (Dec. 25, 1903), 894.

rate of not over $1,000,000 per year) or for payment to the construction companies. By January 1907 only $370,000 of these bonds had been sold in Kansas City out of $1,500,000 offered. Stilwell announced a similar amount for sale in England, first to the shareholders of other companies with which he was associated and then to the general public. Sales appear to have been slow, and in February 1907 he offered a bonus of preferred and common stock. During 1908 and 1910 Stilwell visited Europe, and when he returned the second time, he reported that he had sold $5,000,000 of railroad bonds.[40]

According to *Moody's Manual of Railroad and Corporation Securities*, on June 30, 1910, the Kansas City, Mexico, and Orient Railway Company had issued $12,500,000 of cumulative pre-ferred stock, $12,264,135 of common stock, and $18,199,000 of first-mortgage bonds, in addition to £200,000 in 6 per cent five-year notes, due in 1913, and $1,618,885 of equipment trust notes. Only $6,000,000 of the bonds had been sold, however, while $3,489,000 of them remained in the treasury and the rest belonged to the construction companies. It is impossible to estimate how much the company actually received for these securities.[41]

Despite Stilwell's enthusiastic optimism, some persons had misgivings about his project from the beginning. In 1902, for example, the British minister to Mexico, George Greville, sent home a confidential dispatch about the Orient, full of suspicions of Stilwell's imprudence and wonder at the credulity of British investors: "I met [Mr. Stilwell] . . . with his English Court composed of Lord Monson, Mr. Chinnery and others who cer-tainly all seemed to be under the spell; indeed the Arabian nights could not present a more brilliant and dazzling picture

---

[40] *Moody's Manual*, 1911, pp. 566–568; *Railroad Age*, XLIII (Jan. 18, 1907), 100; *Anglo-American and Mexican Mining Guide*, IX (Sept. 29, 1906), 139, X (Feb. 27, 1907), 25, XI (June 27, 1908), 85, 93; *Moody's Magazine*, X (Aug. 1910), 87.

[41] *Moody's Manual*, 1911, pp. 566–568.

than [Stilwell's description of] the line of country between Chihuahua and the Pacific." [42]

Later in the decade, however, some of the "English Court" seem to have grown restive at the nonappearance of dividends and Stilwell's reluctance to "do what all reputable English Co.'s do"—issue annual reports and hold regular meetings of stockholders. A British periodical devoted to American and Mexican mines reported Stilwell's eulogies of Mexico un- enthusiastically and added: "This railway . . . is always doing wonderful things for everybody but the majority of the share and stockholders who have found the 'needful' and who are awaiting with what patience they may to see some return on their investment." [43] In the United States, although John Moody was publishing flattering articles about the Orient project in *Moody's Magazine*, his *Manual of Railroad and Corporation Securities* cautiously described the best securities as "good, but second-grade issues" and the others as highly speculative. In 1910 the editor of *Wall Street Journal* minced no words about the Orient's common stock, calling it "a gamble, and . . . hardly . . . in any respect an investment. It has possibilities but should only be bought for a long pull." [44]

Even before 1910 Stilwell's investors had good reason to feel uneasy, for such statistics as the railroad company published showed that it was losing money. It is true that during 1904, 1905, and 1907 the balance sheets indicated a slight operating surplus, never as high as $15,000, but in other years the lines "ran in the red," and by 1911 the annual deficit had risen to $145,118. [45] By November of that year unpleasant rumors about

[42] George Greville to Marquis of Lansdowne, Mexico City, Aug. 16, 1902, Commercial no. 14 (Confidential), Foreign Office, ser. 50, vol. 128, pp. 120–125, Great Britain, Public Records Office, London.

[43] *Anglo-American and Mexican Mining Guide*, XI (July 29, 1908), 108.

[44] *Moody's Manual*, 1910, p. 358; *Wall Street Journal*, March 4, 1910, as quoted in Senior, "Kansas City, Mexico, and Orient Railroad," p. 118.

[45] Complete figures are given in Senior, "Kansas City, Mexico, and Orient Railroad," p. 121, table.

the railroad had reached England, coupled with disconcerting reports about violence in Mexico, but supporters of the company breathed forth confidence and called its position "so unquestionably advantageous, we might say necessary, for the progress of Mexico that there is nothing to fear from any political changes in that country." If it could secure funds to extend its American line through Fort Stockton, Texas, to a junction with the Southern Pacific Railroad at Alpine, it could undoubtedly increase its through traffic to the north.[46]

If it could secure funds—there was the rub. Neither the published operating statistics nor the optimistic statements of company members gave any idea that by the beginning of 1912 Stilwell's company had come to the end of its capital and that his guardian spirits had shown him no new source from which to replenish it. The disconnected Mexican segments of the railroad could not earn their operating expenses, and the long American section of track ended in the middle of nowhere at a small west Texan village. Unable to produce an operating surplus, the company officials had borrowed money to meet the interest on its bond issues, creating a floating debt of $2,867,000. The company had failed to pay its employees during January and February 1912, and it owed a considerable amount of back taxes. Several persons in Kansas and Oklahoma were preparing to sue the railroad for alleged negligence of employees.[47]

Clearly the Orient needed new capital, but in 1911 when Stilwell had tried to float a new bond issue in Paris, he had run into legal difficulties and had had to withdraw it without any sales. During the first weeks of 1912 the prices of all his securities fell off, and very few were sold. At this point the stockholders of the construction companies took alarm, especially those of the International Construction Company, which was bound by its concession to maintain a minimum rate of construction in

[46] *Anglo-American and Mexican Guide*, XIV (Oct. 31, Nov. 29, 1911), 149, 173; Kansas City *Times*, Dec. 23, 1911, p. 1.
[47] Kansas City *Times*, March 8, 1912, p. 2

Mexico. If the railroad company collapsed entirely, it might cause the construction company to forfeit all rights and property in Mexico. Consequently, on March 7 representatives of the United States and Mexican Trust Company and of the construction companies applied for and secured a receivership for the Kansas City, Mexico, and Orient Railway Company. They said that they were acting on behalf of the British stockholders. The judge who granted the receivership appointed as receivers Edward M. Dickinson, who was Stilwell's general manager, M. L. Turner, and J. O. Davidson; and the finance committee under them was about evenly composed of British and American investors.[48]

Stilwell and the receivers tried to minimize the bad news and smooth it over with rationalizations: "No railroad has ever been placed on a paying basis until it [has] been through a receivership." Dickinson announced that he and the others had applied for the receivership principally in order that the finance committee might have time to raise $30,000,000 in New York and London, to pay debts and complete construction. Perhaps in order to stage a diversion but more likely because he could not restrain himself any longer, Stilwell now burst out against the "money trust" and their "Black Hand methods in Wall Street." On the day that the newspapers announced the Orient's receivership he appeared before a thousand people in Carnegie Hall and told them that the country was going to the dogs and that if the "money trust" wanted to do so it could completely ruin them in a week through its control of currency and finance. "The radicalism of the West," he declared, "is almost entirely caused by the exactions of the beef trust, the Standard Oil and the tobacco trust." [49]

[48] *Statist*, LXXXI (March 23, 1912), 619; Kansas City *Times*, March 8, 1912, pp. 1–2; Kansas City *Star*, March 8, 1912, p. 2-A; Kansas City *Post*, March 31, 1912, p. 2.
[49] Kansas City *Post*, March 9, 1912, p. 3, March 19, pp. 1, 9; Kansas City *Star*, March 8, 1912, p. 2-A; Kansas City *Times*, March 8, 1912, p. 2, March 9, p. 3.

There is some reason to believe that Stilwell, Dickinson, and their allies in the "friendly receivership" pinned their hopes on their British investors. If so, they were to be disappointed. London financial journals took a dim and haughty view of the receivership proceedings: these were only to be expected, in view of Mexican political disturbances and especially the company's "hot-air operations and high financing." One British writer remarked sourly: "Now that the horse is stolen the stable door is being locked." [50] As for the British investors, once they had secured a receivership and more control over the affairs of the railroad company, they were in no hurry to send good money after bad. They set up a bondholders' protective committee, deposited their bonds with it, and sat back to see what would happen.

Although Stilwell resigned as president after the receivership, his friends continued for a time to operate the railroad and the construction companies but without much success. They managed to raise $2,142,000 by issuing receivers' certificates and $475,000 on notes and built ninety-five miles of track to Alpine, Texas. In 1912, however, the Kansas and Oklahoma sections ran a deficit of over $33,000, and beginning in August the company could not meet interest payments on its first-mortgage bonds and its various notes. At that time some of the creditors requested a bill of foreclosure, but this was not granted for another year and a half. On July 6, 1914, the property of the railroad was sold for $6,001,000 at a foreclosure sale in Wichita, Kansas. Stilwell's Orient railroad project had slipped from his grasp forever.[51]

Having lost control of two railroad projects, he never attempted a third. In 1913 he was severely injured in an elevator

[50] *Statist*, LXXI (March 23, 1912), 619; *Economist*, LXXIV (March 23, 1912), 630; *Anglo-American and Mexican Guide*, XV (March 31, June 29, 1912), 37, 83.

[51] Kansas City *Post*, March 29, 1912, p. 1; Senior, "Kansas City, Mexico, and Orient Railroad," pp. 85–87, 121, table; W. Rodney Long, *Railways of Mexico* (U.S. Bureau of Foreign and Domestic Commerce, Trade Promotion Series, no. 16 [Washington, 1925]), pp. 135–138.

accident and remained an invalid for the rest of his life. Deprived of their natural outlet, his energies spent themselves in a series of books solving the world's problems through international co-operation in various forms and trying to convert mankind to "new thought" and "mental healing." It was said also that his "spirit voices" dictated novels, photoplays, and songs to him. The business world forgot him long before his death on September 26, 1928, and newspapers which published an obituary gave more space to his spiritualism than to his railroads.[52]

The dismal history of the Orient project after Stilwell's departure can be briefly told. In July 1914 several representatives of the bondholders, including William T. Kemper, a millionaire of Kansas City, incorporated the Kansas City, Mexico, and Orient Rail*road* to buy up the property of the bankrupt Orient Rail*way*. This action wiped out the interests of preferred and common stockholders in the old company. After long negotiation agents of the American and British bondholders drew up an agreement for reorganization in December 1915, but this was soon withdrawn. The new company scraped together only half of the purchase price of the line, and in 1917 the railroad went into receivership again, with Kemper as receiver. Between December 31, 1917, and March 1, 1921, the United States government operated the American sections, but after that time Kemper and his associates managed the line through various forms of organization.

During this whole period operating deficits for the American portion of the line continued to rise. Finally in 1928 the Atchison, Topeka, and Santa Fe Railroad purchased the American section of the Kansas City, Mexico, and Orient and absorbed the track into its great system. Shortly before this happened, the United States Circuit Court of Appeals praised Kemper for his diligence in trying to keep the railroad going, and the

[52] Stilwell and Crowell, "I Had a Hunch," Feb. 4, 1928, p. 46; Kansas City *Journal-Post*, Sept. 30, 1928, p. 6-B; Senior, "Kansas City, Mexico, and Orient Railroad," p. 21.

Kansas City *Star* declared that no one else could have kept the Orient from complete disintegration during the preceding years. The Kansas City *Times* pointed out after the sale that although the Santa Fe had paid $14,507,500 for the outstanding Orient securities the original investors did not receive as much of this sum as they deserved, for, about a month before the transfer was announced, Kemper persuaded most of them to sell their bonds for a fraction of their face value. When the final sale went through, he and his friends "cut a melon" of about $6,000,000.[53]

The Mexican sections of the Orient did not fare any better than the American section. During the chaos of the revolutionary decade regular service or maintenance was out of the question, and for some years after that many stretches of track remained partly destroyed or badly run-down. In 1928 the Santa Fe purchased the disjointed Mexican segments with the rest of the system but resold them immediately to B. F. Johnston, the owner of extensive sugar plantations in the Fuerte Valley. Johnston had elaborate plans to finish the railroad and use it to export winter vegetables into the United States. He went to work on the remaining gaps east of Chihuahua, and on November 2, 1930, inaugurated a bridge over the Rio Grande, linking American and Mexican sections as far as the Sierra Madre Occidental. But the Great Depression had already cut his traffic almost to nothing, and he soon began to negotiate with the Mexican government for the sale of his holdings. In 1940 the government bought up both stock and bonds in the Mexican line, incorporated it into the National Railways of Mexico, and set out to restore the line to something like first-class condition.

By this time the "express route to the Orient" had become a

[53] Senior, "Kansas City, Mexico, and Orient Railroad," pp. 87–100; Long, *Railroads of Mexico*, pp. 133–138; *Poor's Manual*, 1924, p. 320; Kansas City *Star*, March 5, 1928; Kansas City *Times*, Aug. 29, 1928, p. 1.

parody of its early publicity, for the weedy, ill-kept track, the decrepit, unpainted boxcars, and the wheezing locomotives were fit only for snail-like local service. The slow-moving natives, seeing Stilwell's symbol of progress remade in their image, nicknamed it "El Kansado" (from *cansado*, "the tired one").[54]

V

Jaunty and self-confident to the end, Stilwell never apologized for the failure of his Orient project. Instead he boasted of the benefits which he had conferred upon the West, estimated that his larger enterprises had earned profits totaling over $37,000,000, and declared: "No Company I ever formed ever failed to pay its debts; . . . no bank in the United States ever lost a dollar it loaned me or my companies."[55]

No amount of wishful thinking could undo the reorganization of the Orient railroad or Stilwell's expulsion from the company, but he had ready explanations for these misfortunes. Most of all he blamed a "whispering campaign" by the Wall Street "money trust," who, he declared, had deluged Díaz with warnings against him, urged investors not to buy Orient stock, and even resorted to wire tapping and private detectives.[56] These stories, taken together with Stilwell's "spirit messages," might suggest paranoia, were it not for two other considerations. In 1911 and 1912 progressives had convinced many Americans that a "money trust" dominated their economy, and he was a shrewd publicist.

Stilwell also blamed the failure of his Orient project on three years of poor crops in northern Mexico and on revolutionary disturbances during and after 1911. Ten more years of the Díaz government or another "equally strong and wise" would

[54] Senior, "Kansas City, Mexico, and Orient Railroad," pp. 101–116.

[55] Stilwell, *Forty Years of Business Life*, pp. 24–25, 28–30.

[56] *Ibid.*, pp. 21–23; Stilwell, *Cannibals of Finance*, pp. 130–135, 141–143, 165–167, *et passim*.

have worked wonders, he felt, but instead came the revolutions.[57] It was enough to make a peace-loving promoter long for American troops, and although Stilwell had not preached annexation hitherto, he joined the interventionists in 1915 and urged the American government to offer a protectorate to Mexico. After twenty years of American supervision he proposed to allow the Mexican people to end the protectorate by a majority vote, if they wished. "If the United States were willing to take in Mexico and make it a part of the most progressive nation in the world," he pontificated, "Mexico could legitimately have no other emotion than pride." [58] It may be noted that Stilwell did not make these suggestions at a time when he needed Mexican friends.

Despite the promoter's freehanded denunciation of these external conditions it is hard to accept them as the main reasons for his downfall. To what extent, for example, were revolutionary disturbances really responsible for his financial troubles? To be sure, according to Fred W. Powell, the Orient's track between Márquez and San Sóstenes in Chihuahua was "practically destroyed," but it is doubtful that Orozco and Villa started the Orient project on the road to ruin. The most serious destruction in northern Mexico occurred after Stilwell left the company in 1912, and even before Díaz' fall operating deficits suggested that the Orient was in distress.[59]

Stilwell's contemporaries had two other explanations for his failure: his own inadequacies and the inherent impracticability of his project. In the first place, they found continued evidence of his inordinate interest in speculation, both in lands along his

[57] Stilwell, *Forty Years of Business Life*, p. 3, and *Cannibals of Finance*, pp. 123–124; Arthur E. Stilwell, *To All the World (except Germany)* (London, 1915), pp. 233 ff. He was especially bitter about Villa, who, he said, had been a contractor on the railroad and had blown up one of Stilwell's silver mines out of personal malice (Stilwell and Crowell, "I Had a Hunch," Feb. 4, 1928, p. 46).

[58] Stilwell, *To All the World*, pp. 233–243.

[59] Powell, *Railroads of Mexico*, chaps. iii–iv, especially pp. 13–16; Senior, "Kansas City, Mexico, and Orient Railroad," pp. 76–80.

route and in securities of his companies. Professor William Z. Ripley, a railroad reformer during and after World War I, deplored the use of separate construction and operating companies and pointed, as a sure sign of weakness, to the basketful of securities given to purchasers of construction-company stock. As for the Orient bond issues, he declared that when Stilwell failed to sell a 4 per cent issue he simply substituted a 5 per cent issue with various stock bonuses. Ripley concluded: "No wonder . . . the 'Money Trust' is jealous." [60]

It is impossible to determine conclusively whether Stilwell was directly or indirectly guilty of fraud. When the receivers and the finance committee assigned experts to examine the books of his various companies in 1912, they found that he and his inner circle of friends had transferred funds freely from one company to another through dummy directors who held no stock, drew no salary, and only lent their names to the company letterhead. "There never was a meeting of all the stockholders," a journalist concluded. "Notices of meetings were sent out in the regular way and the stockholders sent in their proxies, leaving everything in the hands of the management." [61]

Probably such deviousness was necessary to preserve the hypnotic effect of Stilwell's publicity and to conceal from investors not only that his administration was speculative, but also that the project itself was a "long shot." The gloomy financial history of the nearly completed American section of the railroad suggests that if the Orient were to have any chance of success it must depend largely on through traffic between Kansas City and the Pacific coast. Thus the problem of Stilwell's failure returns to one of the basic themes of this book—the unexpected obstacles confronting promoters in Mexico.

Certainly the construction of the Orient's Mexican segments

[60] Senior, "Kansas City, Mexico, and Orient Railroad," pp. 82–83; *Anglo-American and Mexican Mining Guide*, X (Jan. 30, 1907), Suppl., ii; Draper, "Kansas City Southern," p. 22; Ripley, *Railroads: Finance and Organization*, pp. 16–17, 49–50, 155–156.
[61] Kansas City *Post*, April 6, 1912, pp. 1–2.

proved far more difficult than Stilwell or his engineers had expected. Some difficulties were self-imposed: for example, Stilwell should not have begun construction on the Pacific coast first, since all rails, ties, equipment, and American laborers used west of the mountains had to come by water and at considerable expense from San Francisco or Guaymas, Sonora. Other difficulties were no one's fault. When engineers began to operate locomotives near Topolobampo, they discovered such a heavy charge of minerals in the local water that rowboats had to bring in rainwater from islands in the bay. After sections of track had been laid, engineers discovered that torrential rains, tropical rot, and termites made maintenance work several times more difficult than in the United States.[62]

Worst of all, the Sierra Madre Occidental soon loomed up as a much more serious barrier than the first reports had given reason to expect. As early as 1903 the company admitted that it would need ten or fifteen tunnels and several bridges on this section, but seven years went by before even preliminary surveys were completed. After abandoning the idea of a forty-mile cog railway, engineers worked out several mountain routes requiring grades of only 2.5 per cent; decades later, however, when the Mexican government finally took over the disjointed segments, the best route had not yet been definitely chosen. As if this were not bad enough, a sandbar at the entrance of Topolobampo Bay admitted only vessels drawing less than twelve or fifteen feet, even at high tide. According to competent engineers, it would require unlimited expenditure to provide a practical deepwater port. No one can say whether Stilwell had any clear idea of this obstacle.[63]

[62] Senior, "Kansas City, Mexico, and Orient Railroad," pp. 70–72; *Railroad Age*, XXXV (March 20, 1903), 441–444; Powell, *Railroads of Mexico*, p. 13.

[63] *Railroad Age*, XXXV (March 20, 1903), 441–444; P. L. Bell and H. Bentley MacKenzie, *Mexican West Coast and Lower California* (U.S. Bureau of Foreign and Domestic Commerce, Special Agents Series, no. 220 [Washington, 1923]), p. 50; *Hoy*, Aug. 16, 1941, as cited in Senior,

In summary, it seems plain that he failed to complete his Kansas City, Mexico, and Orient project for many of the same reasons that explain his expulsion from the Kansas City Southern. The talents and interests which made him seem almost a miraculous salesman discouraged careful, methodical administration and pricked the envy of other financiers, both wealthier and with less scruples than he. What is more, he built his railroad across an international border into a foreign country with the same bland unconcern as if he were crossing another state line into Oklahoma or Texas. Then when he fell upon evil days, he blamed his failure upon scapegoats—the "money trust" and the Mexican rebels. Actually, if Harriman, Gates, and the rest of the "Black Hand of Wall Street" had let him alone, he would have come to grief sooner or later because of his loose administration or his speculative tendencies. Similarly, even if Orozco and Villa had spared Chihuahua from 1911 to 1916, Stilwell's hopes for the Kansas City, Mexico, and Orient Railway would have been derailed in a mountain pass or shipwrecked on the Topolobampo bar.

"Kansas City, Mexico, and Orient Railroad," p. 72; Osgood Hardy, "The Revolution and the Railroads of Mexico," *Pacific Historical Review*, III (Sept. 1934), 250–251.

IX

Mirage and Reality

ABOUT 1865 a traveler to Mexico was approaching the coast just before dawn after a dull trip across the Gulf. Standing on deck, he noticed far up in the sky something like a hard, white cloud, as the rays of the rising sun touched the peak of Orizaba—"sublime, without a base, a vision rather than a reality." Caught up for a moment in the world of fantasy, he was ill-prepared for the landing in Veracruz, a mean, forlorn little town, without a decent hotel or any object of the slightest interest save the ugly vultures hovering in its streets. Later, however, he realized that his introduction to Mexico had been somehow symbolic of the impressions which the country made on all its visitors: first a sense of "something poetical and beautiful, but transient, impalpable, and far off," followed by pity, disgust, and dismay at its squalor, and finally a "vague hope that Mexico is still to have another chance." [1]

The seven promoters of this study experienced these same sensations, but, being professional optimists, they suppressed any pity or dismay which they may have felt and sublimated their poetry into prospectuses. Indeed, they intended to give Mexico its "other chance." All agreed that Mexico needed help

[1] "Mexico" (pamphlet reprinted from *Saturday Review*, n.d.), pp. 5–6.

from the outside in the form of foreign capital and technology. All agreed that a significant number of Mexicans wanted such help, as long as it did not impair their sovereignty. All believed that they could furnish such help and at the same time earn substantial rewards for themselves. Yet somewhere they miscalculated, for only three of the seven ever saw their enterprises earn net profits, and none of these three found and kept the wealth he sought. One, William C. Greene, ended his life a bankrupt, and the other two, Edward Lee Plumb and Alexander R. Shepherd, might well have died richer if they had used their talents at home.

I

No one has ever prepared a general balance sheet for American capital employed in Mexico between 1867 and 1911 and probably no one ever will. On the basis of incomplete evidence, however, it seems clear that the fortunes of these seven promoters were fairly typical. A few individuals and companies in Mexico made far more money than these men, but in general American capital in Mexico showed roughly the same ratio of success to failure.

The most spectacular American "success story" in Mexico was that of Edward L. Doheny, the first to appreciate and capitalize the potentialities of Mexican oil. After an early career of prospecting somewhat like that of Greene, Doheny made his first "strike" in 1892 at Los Angeles and took a fortune out of the oil fields of southern California. In 1900 he transferred his attention to Mexico, organized an operating company, and "brought in" a small well near Tampico. The first years of his Mexican operations were unpromising indeed, but Doheny had enough confidence in his judgment to buy up about 40 per cent of the company's stock while it was still low. All in all, he and his partner, C. A. Canfield, spent about three million dollars between 1900 and 1904.

On Easter Sunday of 1904, when Doheny had practically reached the end of his resources, a newly drilled well yielded one thousand barrels, and from that time onward for more than a decade his luck held. In 1907 he founded the Huasteca Petroleum Company, and on September 11, 1910, a "gusher" in the new Huasteca field opened an era in Mexican economic history in which she soon became the third oil producer in the world. Meanwhile, beginning in 1908, Doheny's company paid regular annual dividends of 8 per cent, and by 1911 he was once again a millionaire. In 1916 he brought in his greatest gusher of all, Cerro Azul Number Four, and produced oil at the rate of a million dollars a week. Before 1925 the Doheny interests had produced 560,000,000 barrels and had replaced the railroads as the largest single American investment in Mexico.[2]

A second example of large-scale success in Mexican ventures was the great chain of mines and smelters controlled by the Guggenheim family. In 1890, shortly after the McKinley Tariff had placed a prohibitive duty on imported lead ores, Daniel Guggenheim secured a Mexican concession to build a silver-lead smelter in Monterrey. The smelter was an immediate success, and the Guggenheims built others at Aguascalientes, Velardeña, Chihuahua, and Matehuala, until their American Smelting and Refining Company (ASARCO) and its subsidiaries fairly blanketed northern Mexico. In order to obtain an assured supply of ore for these smelters, the Guggenheims sent John Hays Hammond and other skilled mining engineers into Mexico repeatedly in search of mines which might be bought up cheaply.

By 1911 they had fully earned their nickname of "smelters trust," for in many areas they could virtually dictate smelting charges to all but the largest mining companies. They controlled

[2] Fritz L. Hoffmann, "Edward L. Doheny and the Beginnings of Petroleum Development in Mexico," *Mid-America*, XXIV (n.s., XIII; April 1942), 94–108. Doheny's greatest rival for control of Mexican oil was Lord Cowdray (Sir Weetman Pearson), founder of the Mexican Eagle Company. A comparison of the position of these two rivals in 1910 may be found in H. S. Denny, "The Oil Excitement in Mexico," *Mining Journal*, LXXXIX (June 4, 1910), 711 ff. See also *Mexican Year Book*, 1912, pp. 162, 164.

a great variety of silver, lead, copper, and other mines, and one of these alone, the Esperanza mine in Michoacán, was yielding dividends of 160 per cent three years after its acquisition in 1903. Although it is impossible to divide the reported profits of the Guggenheims according to the countries in which they operated, there is no doubt that their Mexican interests contributed heavily to these profits during the Díaz period and for a short time after. Beginning in 1899, ASARCO paid regular annual dividends of 7 per cent on common stock, and in 1914 the company reported that it had paid out dividends totaling $104,322,169.67 since 1900.[3]

A few other American mining interests reported large, consistent profits during the Díaz period. Beginning in the 1890's, Robert S. Towne established ore-buying agencies in northern Mexico, acquired mines, erected smelters, and built the Mexican Northern Railway through the mining country south of El Paso. When he died in 1916, he left an estate of almost $2,500,000. In the same general area American and Mexican capital combined to found the Compañía Minera de Peñoles during the 1890's. This company declared enormous dividends on its small capital, eventually reaching 300 per cent in 1910, after which it increased the capital to 6,000,000 pesos. Similarly the Moctezuma Copper Company, a subsidiary of Phelps Dodge and Company operating in Sonora not far from Cananea, distributed $3,718,000 in dividends through 1910 on its outstanding capital of $2,600,000.[4]

In business, however, success often attracts more attention than failure, and it can never be calculated how many dozens of American companies quietly succumbed, in contrast to the few which issued large dividends. In addition, even if consistent,

[3] Bernstein, "Mexican Mining Industry," I, 389–401, 435–452; *Moody's Manual*, 1912, pp. 2875, 2877; American Smelting and Refining Company, Inc., *Sixteenth Annual Report* (1914), p. 8.

[4] Bernstein, "Mexican Mining Industry," I, 472–479, 485–494, 502–504, *et passim*; *Mexican Year Book*, 1912, pp. 165–166.

reliable statistics were available for every American mining
company operating in Mexico, it would still be difficult to determine exactly how many of its troubles were due to mismanagement, or even precisely how much its shareholders might
reasonably expect to receive from their investments. The *Engineering and Mining Journal* declared once that if a mining company had an active life of twenty years it ought to yield annual
profits of about 10 per cent.[5] Measured by such a yardstick, all
but a handful of large mining companies in Mexico would surely
fall short.

Few American mining, industrial, or agricultural companies
in Mexico returned such profits as Doheny or the Guggenheims,
but at least some of them lived up to their advertising. As for the
railroads, the largest block of American investment in Mexico
in 1911, not a single major line justified its advance publicity.
Not all of them sprawled across Mexico in disjointed segments
like the Kansas City, Mexico, and Orient or served purely local
interests like the Mexican Southern, but the completed lines
could show neither a flood of through traffic nor consistent
dividends over long periods of time.

The real test of railroad promoters' predictions lay in the
financial history of the great northern lines—the Mexican National and the Mexican International, successors to the Rosecrans and Plumb projects, and the Mexican Central and the
Southern Pacific of Mexico. The Mexican International Railroad, as has been shown, earned small, regular profits beginning
in the 1890's, but there is no indication in its annual reports that
it ever paid any stock dividends. As for the Mexican National

[5] *Engineering and Mining Journal*, LXXXIX (1910), 203. The *Journal*
writer calculated that investors were entitled to annual dividends of 7
per cent and that $30 must be set aside each year at 5 per cent interest
to amortize an original investment of $2,000. In the case of more specula-
tive mines, John Hays Hammond declared that annual dividends (as
distinguished from profits) ought to be as high as 15 per cent (*ibid.*, p.
10). See Appendix, Table 2, for a list of the most profitable American
companies in Mexico from 1900 to 1910.

and the Mexican Central, both railroads ran short of money in 1885 and 1886. The Mexican National underwent reorganization in 1886 and again in 1902, but the third management had better luck than its predecessors, and between 1906 and 1908 the company declared dividends totaling 4 per cent.[6] The Mexican Central Railroad remained under its original management, closely affiliated with the Atchison, Topeka, and Santa Fe Railroad, but its annual reports over a period of more than twenty years do not mention the word dividend.

Between 1903 and 1906 the Mexican government acquired a large interest in both lines, and in 1909 they were merged with the Mexican International and others into a new company, the National Railways of Mexico (Ferrocarriles Nacionales de México). During the first three years of operation the first preferred stock of this company earned dividends of about 2 to 4 per cent.[7] Meanwhile, between 1898 and 1909 the Southern Pacific Railroad had acquired control of a short line in Sonora and extended it down the Pacific coast as far as Tepic, calling the new line the Southern Pacific of Mexico.

Thus, when Díaz fell, two long northern railroad systems were at last prepared to reap all possible benefits from unified management and Mexican prosperity. Instead, the catastrophic civil wars of the next decade dispersed their traffic, destroyed or wore out their property, and all but put them out of business. The National Railways maintained a "very satisfactory" record until 1914; then the company began to operate at a loss, and by 1932 it had built up a deficit of nearly 400,000,000 pesos. The Southern Pacific of Mexico showed the effects of the upheaval as early as 1911, but it never sank so low as the National Railways, and in the 1920's its books sometimes showed a slight annual

[6] Powell, *Railroads of Mexico*, pp. 134–135; *Moody's Manual*, 1908, p. 512.

[7] John Moody called this a "low average net income on net capital" and found only a "very moderate" margin of safety for the total debt (*Moody's Analyses of Railroad Investments*, Third Annual Number, 1912 [New York, 1912], pp. 348–349).

surplus.[8] Nevertheless, the mother company did not regard it as a worth-while enterprise after 1911, and in 1951 the American directors were happy to turn their burden over to the Mexican government.

II

It would seem that for most American promoters the profits which they described so glowingly were a mirage, a fantasy of their overheated imaginations. Yet there was something very appealing in their prediction of a new American-Mexican economic order, and perhaps they did not exaggerate when they declared that their railroads were vital to American and Mexican industry alike.[9] What went wrong? If this importance was not imaginary, why was it not reflected in dividends?

Apparently the basic mistake of the promoters was that they oversimplified their problem and either minimized or completely ignored certain serious obstacles. For one thing, they consistently underestimated construction difficulties and costs, with the result that they were always appealing to the Mexican government to extend their time limits. Prudence should have led them to consult the history of the British-built Mexican Railway, between Veracruz and Mexico City. The first construction estimate for this line in 1833 was only 4,200,000 pesos, but before its completion forty years later the government alone was thought to have contributed well over 10 million pesos and private capital much more, because of inefficient operations, disturbed conditions during the civil wars, and unforeseen construction difficulties in the rugged mountains.[10] Owen and Stilwell planned to cross the western Sierra Madre, but there is no evidence that they knew or cared about the tribulations of the

[8] The accumulated deficit of the Southern Pacific of Mexico passed 64,000,000 pesos in 1924, but by 1932 this figure had been reduced to a little over 1,300,000 pesos (Hardy, "The Revolution and the Railroads of Mexico," pp. 254–255, 258–260).

[9] New York *Tribune*, Feb. 18, 1881, p. 4.

[10] Pletcher, "Building of the Mexican Railway," pp. 28, 56–57.

earlier company. Even in flat northern Mexico the Mexican National Railroad ran short of construction money in 1883 and had to stop laying track for three years.

Secondly, railroad engineers did not always locate their routes so as to tap the largest number of producing or market areas. None of the northern lines built enough spurs back into mining districts. On the other hand, the dry, sparsely populated north was oversupplied with parallel main lines, while the subtropical south and the southwest coast, producing raw materials of potentially great export value, had almost no railroads. Surely two efficient railroads in the north would have supplied the immediate needs of international trade as adequately as the four which appeared between 1880 and 1910. The duplication of northern railroads is explained in the writings of their promoters. They hoped to draw off Mexican trade from Europe to the United States and expected to populate the northern states with customers as railroads had done in the western United States. "Thousands of Americans will rush into Mexico as soon as railway facilities are furnished," predicted a Coloradoan. It developed that they preferred California and Arizona.[11]

Another will-o'-the-wisp which lured Owen and Stilwell into error was the hope of a great new trade between the United States and the Far East. The "Golden Orient" had long been a part of American mercantile folklore, and, like Mexico, it received much new publicity in the 1880's and 1890's as a market for "millions upon millions of dollars worth of American products," offering opportunities "such as were never presented to any other nation," and so forth.[12] But even after the opening of the Panama Canal, trade with the Orient fell short of expectations. In 1935, for example, the Far East claimed less than 20 per cent of American foreign trade and only about 6 per cent of

[11] Powell, *Railroads of Mexico*, pp. 191–192. The quotation is taken from an unidentified newspaper clipping in the Shepherd Collection.

[12] Charles S. Campbell, Jr., *Special Business Interests and the Open Door Policy* (New Haven, 1951), pp. 10–18 *et passim*.

our foreign investments. In spite of all that promoters and diplomats could do, American investments in the Far East lagged far behind those in Europe, Canada, and Latin America.[13]

Similarly sanguine hopes for American trade with Mexico, however, were not entirely disappointed. Joseph Nimmo estimated that American-Mexican trade increased about 123 per cent between 1876–1877 and 1882–1883, and he expected the trend to continue. In 1880 Matías Romero estimated Mexican exports at 35,000,000 pesos and predicted that the Mexican Southern and other railroads would raise this figure to 200,000,000 pesos, even without counting bullion shipments. Actually in 1910–1911 Mexican exports and imports totaled 293,752,150 pesos and 205,835,784 pesos respectively, and of these amounts the United States accounted for 76.43 per cent and 54.94 per cent.[14]

American-Mexican trade would have increased still further if the new railroads had attracted settlers from abroad, but immigration into Mexico remained a mere trickle in 1911, and the railroads were forced to depend more on the native Indian population for business than they had expected. Their promoters had publicized the low wages of Indian labor, only to find that they must somehow extract most of their passenger receipts from this same badly paid proletariat. In mineral areas and other regions where raw materials were produced for export, the railroads could count on rising freight receipts as the Mexican economy expanded, but even here they often prejudiced their long-run interests by charging high rates. In 1895 Bernard Moses described Indians carrying heavy clay jars from Toluca to market in Mexico City along a road parallel to the Mexican National Railway, and even after the fall of Díaz it was cheaper on the west coast to import German or Scandinavian paper via

[13] A. Whitney Griswold, *The Far Eastern Policy of the United States* (New York, 1938), pp. 468–469.

[14] Nimmo, *Trade between Mexico and the United States*, pp. 44–45; New York *Tribune*, Nov. 12, 1880, p. 5; *Mexican Year Book*, 1912, p. 11.

Cape Horn than to bring the tariff-protected Mexican product from Mexico City.[15]

The railroad companies could show reasons for their high rates. In 1907, for example, an experienced engineer estimated that it cost twice as much to run a locomotive in Mexico as in the United States. Mexican coal was poor, water scarce in many dry areas, and especially at first the lack of proper factories and skilled labor forced the railroads to import almost all machines and parts.[16] Except on the Mexican Railway, wooden bridges and light ballasting were the usual rule, so that roadbed and track deteriorated quickly, requiring frequent repairs and causing accidents and delays. Perhaps the most insidious enemy of the railroad companies was the rising rate of foreign exchange which resulted from the steady decline of silver and of the peso. Passenger and freight receipts were in silver, but most dividends and interest had to be paid in gold-based currencies, and each year the cost of securing these pounds sterling and dollars increased. In 1900 the Mexican National paid 2,021,262 pesos and the Mexican Central 2,901,371 pesos for exchange.[17]

In addition to mistakes of construction and operation, most railroad promoters and administrators failed to anticipate the increasing reluctance of the Mexican government to grant subsidies and its desire after 1900 for more control over existing railroads. When Limantour became minister of *hacienda*, he fixed his eye on the mass of unpaid subsidies, and in 1899 he put through Congress a law limiting future subsidies to a few major routes and prescribing strict maximum rates. Not satisfied with government regulation of railroads, he then pushed on toward outright management. Alarmed at the American trend

[15] Bernard Moses, *The Railway Revolution in Mexico* (San Francisco, 1895), p. 78; Díaz Dufoo, *México y los capitales extranjeros*, pp. 159–160.

[16] Doheny Foundation, *Mexico*, I, 193 ff.

[17] Gurza, *La política ferrocarrilera*, pp. 44–45. For an analysis of Mexican inflation during the Díaz period see David M. Pletcher, "The Fall of Silver in Mexico, 1870–1910, and Its Effect on American Investments," *Journal of Economic History*, XVIII (Spring 1958), 33–55.

toward consolidation and monopoly and determined to forestall a possible merger of the Mexican Central and the Mexican
National lines, he decided to beat the monopolists at their own
game. Between 1903 and 1909 he took advantage of the financial weakness of these two railroads to combine them and other
lines into the National Railways of Mexico, a private company
in which the government owned a little more than half of the
stock.[18]

In the latter year a bitter congressional debate over mining
legislation plainly foreshadowed a changing attitude toward
foreign capital in that field as well. At the suggestion of a congressional committee, the minister of *fomento* proposed a law
which would have forbidden foreigners to acquire mines in
border states without special permission and would have required all foreign mining companies to reorganize under Mexican laws. Americans and some Mexicans protested that this
last requirement would rob foreigners of all protection by their
own governments and frighten away foreign capital. For the
time being these arguments prevailed, and the objectionable
clauses were removed from the law.[19]

III

The organization of the National Railways and the quarrel
over the mining law of 1909 gave reason to suspect that the
"boom" days of American capital expansion into Mexico might
be ending, despite the phenomenal growth of the oil industry.
Americans did not propose to withdraw their capital, however,
for there seemed no reason why they could not continue to earn
profits, although at a slower rate. Alas, promoters and investors

[18] Powell, *Railroads of Mexico*, pp. 171–175; *Mexican Year Book*, 1908,
pp. 635–685; Gurza, *La política ferrocarrilera*, pp. 8–11, 62–86, 115 ff.,
et passim; González Roa, *El problema ferrocarrilero*, pp. 37, 123 ff., *et
passim.*
[19] Bernstein, "Mexican Mining Industry," I, 532–545.

had made one fatal miscalculation which crowned all their other wrong guesses. They assumed that Mexicans had broken the habit of revolutions and that peace and order were there to stay. Pascual Orozco, Emiliano Zapata, "Pancho" Villa, and a score of others soon disillusioned them.

American writers misjudged the Mexican situation in 1910 primarily because they misunderstood social conditions in Mexico. When they declared the Madero uprising a mere "family quarrel" or predicted that a few superficial changes would re-establish stability indefinitely, they failed to realize the depth and intensity of resentment among the landless peons and the other dispossessed of Mexico. In 1910 a revolt against Don Porfirio was like a trash fire in an ammunition dump.

The insensitivity of Americans toward Mexican discontent is not surprising, for over the years promoters and publicists had worked out a comfortable, calloused rationalization to "explain" low wages and poverty in Mexico. They blamed these as much on the peon himself as on his employer. Less productive than American labor, the Mexican was not entitled to comparable wages. Living in a mild climate, with few conscious physical needs, he did not want comparable wages. If he earned more than enough for the bare necessities of life, he would get drunk and stay away from work until the money was gone. Similarly many Americans approved of the feudal system of land tenure, although perhaps they would not have favored introducing it into the United States. How could the Indian be trusted to own land? He would only drink or gamble it away.[20]

It is only fair to recognize that Mexican aristocrats and intellectuals of the Díaz period usually encouraged Americans to

[20] For examples of this point of view see William E. Curtis and Trumbull White, *Free Silver in Mexico* ([Chicago], 1897), pp. 44–48; C. F. Lummis, "Awakening of a Nation," *Harper's Magazine*, XCIV (March 1897), 510.

accept this rationalization. Although the life of the poor was a favorite subject in Mexican literature, too many nineteenth-century authors regarded the dumb, unthinking peons as a natural part of the landscape: "It they love, it is from habit; if they get dead drunk, it is from need; if they quarrel, it is from moral instability; if they work, they do it out of fear." [21] Too many Creole intellectuals believed the Indian to be permanently and inherently inferior to the white man, an obstacle to progress, to be replaced wherever possible by foreign immigrants and trained *mestizo* farmers and artisans. Only in this manner could capitalism and science bring Mexico abreast to the United States and Europe—or so thought Limantour and his *Científicos*. They tried to forget that the Indians numbered over half of the nation's population. [22]

Ironically the capital and technology with which Limantour planned to modernize Mexico for the upper and middle classes also released the Indians and the lower-class *mestizos* from their medieval matrix of isolation and traditions. Railroads and mines, needing men, lured the peons away from the haciendas with higher wages and brought them into contact with American laborers and customs. Railroads and easy travel mixed the hitherto scattered people, helped to broaden their horizons, and showed them the plights and problems of others. The northern lines took Mexican Indians to the American border and brought back a variety of imported products to compete with *tortillas* and pulque for the Indian's few coppers and to awaken envy and ambition. Lastly, railroads and American immigrant labor introduced to the Mexican some of the radicalism of the Industrial Workers of the World (I.W.W.) and other labor movements with which to replace the tradition of obedience. An atavistic violence lay under the quiet surface of the Mexican Indian,

[21] Valadés, *El porfirismo: Crecimiento*, II, 252, 262–263.

[22] Frank Tannenbaum, *Peace by Revolution* (New York, 1933), pp. 31–33; Crosman, "Early Career of Limantour," pp. 119–122; Cosío Villegas, *Historia moderna de México*, III, 160–170, IV, 150–166.

and the "progressivism" of the *Científicos* and the American promoters helped to bring it out.[23]

Few American capitalists seem to have given much thought to the probable effects of unfreezing this great mass of Indians and *mestizos*. The fact that many Mexicans with whom they dealt encouraged them to belittle the lower classes does not excuse their failure to recognize the raw materials of a great social revolution. Racial and class frictions were no novelty to Americans, especially Southerners, and populism, anarchism, labor troubles, and other American social movements clearly showed the unsettling effects of economic expansion and development. No country had passed through the Industrial Revolution without social upheavals: even stable Britain had suffered her Luddite riots and her Peterloos. But American capitalists apparently expected Mexico, with her shallow republican institutions and enormous social imbalance, to modernize her economy along American lines in a few decades without revolution. If so, they were even more visionary than the "wild-eyed" socialists and populists whom they ridiculed.

Bringing modern improvements to undeveloped countries may benefit both parties, but the process imposes heavy responsibilities upon those who undertake it, and they should clearly understand these responsibilities at the outset. Nineteenth-century American investors usually felt that they had done enough when they had created railroads and mines, put them into operation, and extracted profit from them. Whether the native government divided the local benefits fairly was little or no concern of theirs. But when they sent their capital to Don Porfirio's Mexico, whether they realized it or not, they were strengthening a dictator who refused to spread the benefits of this capital evenly among his people and thereby made violent revolution inevitable. They might have argued that neither American promoters nor American diplomats of the period could have

[23] Max Handman, "The Mexican Revolution and the Standard of Living," *American Journal of Sociology*, XV (May 1921), 90–101.

brought about the liberalization of the Díaz government, even
if they had tried to do so. Thus the investor had only two
choices: invest his capital and strengthen Díaz or keep it out
of Mexico. Neither choice was ideal, and the one-sided publicity
of the promoters weighted the scale in favor of investment.

Today the problem of economic relations with undeveloped
countries is far more complex and the choices more numerous.
American investors and taxpayers pay more attention to internal
conditions in these countries than ever before. American capital
has also gone farther afield and encountered societies and problems even more intricate than those of Díaz' Mexico. In our day,
one should add, the American government co-ordinates, super-
vises, or even finances many of the modernization activities,
giving them unity and orientation which were denied to promoters fifty or sixty years ago. On the other hand, today we face
organized Communist rivalry, using techniques and weapons
which make the British and German salesmen and the Mexican
nationalists of the earlier times look like rank amateurs.

However complex the problem of bringing the twentieth
century to the Middle East, Indonesia, Latin America, and
Africa and however serious the modern Communist rivalry in
those areas, present-day modernization activities bear certain
fundamental similarities to those of American promoters in
Mexico. Like them we may actually facilitate social upheavals
and revolutions by bringing improved communications and
higher living standards for the common people. Like them too
we find ourselves obliged to reconcile economic progress with
political and social progress, so that, by strengthening a "stand-
pat" government, we may not simply widen the gap between
rich and poor. Today a Don Porfirio presents an easy target not
only to native reformers but to Communists as well.

In many undeveloped areas we have aligned ourselves with
aristocrats and conservatives. There may be good reasons for
this alignment, but these reasons should be explicitly stated and
periodically re-examined. Otherwise we may blunder again into

the impasse in which we found ourselves during the Mexican revolutions after 1911—tied to the country by heavy investments, yet cursed by the Mexicans, and in many cases eager only to cut our losses and withdraw as quickly as possible. In those days the watchword was all too often "Every man for himself" —investor, taxpayer, government official, and peon. It was not a good guide then, and it is not a good one now.

The abandonment of *laissez faire* in foreign investments and development activities does not mean that the American government must intervene to establish political and social democracy wherever American capital reconstructs a national economy. What it does mean is that the American people and their government can no longer allow private business interests to establish durable economic alliances with native autocrats merely for the sake of short-term security or profits. Instead, the American government and American business interests must work together to set up a flexible system of development which will permit social change in the developing country and identify American influence with the interests of its people. Logically, also, the American government itself should not make economic alliances with reactionary regimes merely for the sake of short-term military benefits, such as air bases and divisions in NATO or SEATO. If the United States does give economic aid to such regimes, the policy should be clearly recognized as temporary expediency and abandoned as soon as possible.

At all times we must remember what American promoters in nineteenth-century Mexico ignored: that, sooner or later, economic progress causes social progress and that social progress weakens or destroys reaction. If we build public works, eradicate disease, improve agriculture, and raise the general standard of living in the undeveloped parts of the world, we have doomed the local feudalism of land and class structure on which reactionary regimes usually rest. If, in the hope of security, we then ally ourselves with those regimes, we have defeated our own purpose.

Appendix

Table 1. Estimate of American investments in Mexico in 1911

Type of investment	Amount in millions of dollars	Per cent of total
Railroads	644.3	61.7
Mining	249.5	23.9
Government bonds	52.0	5.0
Banks	30.6	2.9
Oil	15.0	1.4
Rubber	15.0	1.4
Real estate	12.2	1.2
Manufacturing	11.4	1.1
Miscellaneous	14.6	1.4
Total	1,044.6	100.0

Source: Cleona Lewis, *America's Stake in International Investments* (Washington, 1928), p. 614. This estimate was originally prepared by William H. Seamon, an American mining engineer with long experience in Mexico. Seamon's report was first published in United States, *Daily Consular Trade Reports*, no. 155, p. 16 (66th Congress, 2d Session, Senate Report 645; Washington, 1920). Like most statistics pertaining to Mexico in this period these figures must be interpreted with caution.

Table 2. The most profitable American companies operating
in Mexico between 1900 and 1910

Company	Capital	Dividends (in per cent)	Years covered
Mexican Telegraph Co.	$3,589,400	355	1882–1910
Moctezuma Copper Co.	2,600,000	153	1902–1910
Greene Consolidated Copper Co.	8,640,000	71	1901–1907
International Lumber and Development Co.	6,000,000	59	1905–1910
Mines Co. of America	6,934,075	54	1903–1910
Mexican Telephone and Telegraph Co.	1,000,000	45	1906–1910
Guanajuato Power and Electric Co.	5,000,000	37.5	1902–1910
United States and Mexican Trust Co.	1,000,000	36.75	1906–1910
Mexican Northern Railway	3,000,000	33.5	1895–1906
Guanajuato Development Co.	4,000,000	30	1906–1910
Mexican Petroleum Co.	36,000,000	27	1907–1910
Intercontinental Rubber Co.	37,050,000 *	21	1907–1910
German-American Coffee Co.	3,270,250	10	1905

* Indicates authorized capital. Other figures indicate capital actually issued.
Sources: *Mexican Year Book*, 1912; *Moody's Manual*, 1912; *Poor's Manual*, 1902, 1907. This list is believed to contain nearly all American companies which paid large and regular dividends.

Index

315

Schofield, John M., 153
Scott, Thomas A., 63, 86, 91, 100
Seward, William H., 37, 153
Shelby, Charles F., 256
Shepherd, Alexander R., 155, 160, 297; benefits to Mexico, 183; early life and character, 184; member of District of Columbia government, 185-189; American opinion of, 186-189, 207, 210; on Mexican conditions, 191, 206, 215-218; organizes mining companies, 191-193, 195; relations with Díaz government, 194; description of his operations, 196-205; visits United States, 210; his achievements summarized, 211-212; criticized by stockholders, 212
    family: comes to Batopilas, 192-193; life in Batopilas, 207-209
Shepherd, Mrs. Alexander R., 192, 207-211
Shepherd, Grant, 203
Shepherd, W. E., 215
Sheridan, Phil, 153, 157, 159
Sierra Madre Land and Lumber Co., 231, 234, 256
Simmons, George W., 113-114, 115
Sinaloa Sugar Co., see Johnston, B. F.
Skilton, Julius A., 63, 82
Smith, James, 41
Sonora Railway, 67, 230
Southern Pacific Railway, 161, 230, 268, 301
Southern Pacific Railway of Mexico, 230, 300-302
Spendlove, Alfred A., 268-269
Stanton, Edwin M., 36
Stephenson, Edmund, 41, 51
Stevens, Horace J., 235, 255
Stevens, Lyndon H., 190, 191, 213-214
Stevens, Simon, 84
Stilwell, Arthur E., 201, 302-303; activities appraised, 260-262, 264-265, 292-295; early life, 262-263;

builds Kansas City Southern Railway, 263-264; loses control of Kansas City Southern Railway, 265-267; denounces Wall Street, 266-267, 287, 291; organizes Orient project, 267-268, 271; contract with Mexican government, 269-270; companies founded by, 271-273, 282-283; publicizes Orient project, 273-279; praises Díaz, 277; financial organization of his companies, 282-283; criticism of his publicity, 284-285, 288; loses control of Orient project, 285-288; urges American occupation of Mexico, 292
Stilwell, Hamblin, 262, 264
Stotesbury, E. T., 263
Sullivan, James, 89-90, 93
Sylvester, W. W., 275, 277, 280

Tarbert, Alfred A. T., 112
Terrazas family, 206
Texas, Topolobampo, and Pacific Railway, 113-114
Thalmann, Ernest, 266
Thompson, David E., 249, 251
Thomson, J. Edgar, 48, 77, 86
Topolobampo colonies, description of, 134-138; see also Owen, Albert K.
Torres, Luis, 245, 246, 248
Towne, Robert S., 299
Trescot, William H., 173
Truxton, William T., 108, 118

Ulloa, Jesús L., 205
Union Construction Co., 271, 282
Union Contract Co., 49, 56, 58, 63; see also Rosecrans, William S.
Union Liberal Humanidad, 239, 240
United States: trade with Mexico, 3, 25, 155, 304; visitors to Mexico, 27-28
    investments: in Mexico, 3, 5, 31-33; oil, 297-298; mining,

The Library of Congress has cataloged this book as follows:

PLETCHER, DAVID M

Rails, mines, and progress: seven American promoters in
Mexico, 1867–1911. Ithaca, N. Y., Published for the American Historical Association [by] Cornell University Press
[1958]

321 p. illus. 23 cm.

1. Railroads—Mexico—Hist. 2. Mining industry and finance—Mexico. 3. Investments, American—Mexico—Case studies. I. American
Historical Association. II. Title.

HE2818.P59   *385.1   58-59742 ‡

Library of Congress